W9-DEI-969

Sex, Priests, *and* Secret Codes

Sex, Priests, and Secret Codes

The Catholic Church's 2000-year Paper Trail of Sexual Abuse

Thomas P.
Doyle

A. W. Richard
Sipe

Patrick J.
Wall

Volt Press
Los Angeles

09 08 07 06   5 4 3 2

Library of Congress Cataloging-in-Publication Data

Doyle, Thomas P.
    Sex, priests, and secret codes : the Catholic Church's 2000-year paper trail of sexual abuse / Thomas P. Doyle, A.W. Richard Sipe, Patrick J. Wall.
        p. cm.
    Includes bibliographical references and index.
    ISBN 1-56625-265-2
    1. Child sexual abuse by clergy. 2. Catholic Church--Clergy--Sexual behavior. 3. Catholic Church--Discipline.
I. Sipe, A.W. Richard,
    1932- II. Wall, Patrick J. III. Title.
    BX1912.9.D69 2005
    261.8'3272'088282--dc22

2005018606

Volt Press
a division of Bonus Books, Inc.
9255 Sunset Blvd., #711
Los Angeles, CA 90069
www.volt-press.com

Printed in the United States of America

*To all the People of God
betrayed or abused
by those who should protect and comfort them
and to those who do remain faithful to Christ's example.*

Table of Contents

Preface

In some ways, this book is a sad book. It demonstrates without a shadow of a doubt that the sexual abuse of minors by priests is not a recent or a local phenomenon. Nor is the current crisis of clergy abuse just another pothole along the bumpy road in the history of the Catholic Church. Unfortunately this crime—and that is its proper name—has been an open wound on the Body of Christ for as far back as records are kept. History shows that in practically every century since the church began, the problem of clerical abuse of minors was not just lurking in the shadows but so open at times that extraordinary means had to be taken to quell it. If there is anything new about the sexual abuse of minors by members of the clergy, it is that over the past fifty years a conspiracy of silence has covered it. Rather than stifle the practice, this pall of secrecy has provided an atmosphere where abuse could fester as a systemic infection. In the process, the lives of children, priests, bishops—and indeed, the credibility of the Catholic Church itself—have been shattered.

Some people may attack this work as if it is a bad book. It is not. It lays bare the extent of clerical child abuse, the harm that betrayal and abuse inflicts on its victims, and the utter failure of the hierarchy to properly manage the priest perpetrators or provide succor to the children. But this book is not an assault on the Catholic Church. Its authors have devoted many years of their lives caring for and treating the victims of clerical sex abuse, counseling the hierarchy on their obligations with respect to clergy perpetrators, and defending the children, their families, and their rights. This book is written with anguish for the sufferings of the children abused and the harm that is being done to their church, not just by that modest proportion of priests who commit these crimes, but also by the bishops who failed in their fundamental duty to protect the faithful—by the abandonment of the most basic Christian values of honesty, fairness, and charity. Without bishops' cooperation in what's tantamount to a conspiracy—albeit not always deliberate—the secret system of dependency that enabled the abuse to occur could not have existed.

Nor is this book an attack on celibacy. The authors know celibacy, inside and out, and respect it as a well-worthwhile and sanctifying living style for those who choose to live it successfully without compromising their public stance with their private behavior. However, research indicates that a majority of Catholic clergymen do not live up to this ideal. Celibacy supports a lifestyle that could free a man to devote himself to church service in ways that marriage might not allow. That is not to say, however, that a celibate's service is any more dedicated or less selfish on that count alone. Indeed, the contrary is equally true: Marriage opens up all sorts of opportunities to provide service that celibacy effectively locks out. Although the authors do not take sides in the debate about mandatory celibacy—at least not in this book—they do demonstrate that the ongoing inability of the church to enforce the obligations of celibacy, coupled with the elitist and secret club mentality that it fosters, contributes to a climate that allows child abuse to happen.

This is, in fact, a glad book. It signals the end of an era. It reveals in a comprehensive way, and for the first time, the enormity of the crime of sexual abuse of children by priests and bishops and the failure of the hierarchy to handle it properly. But, most importantly, it describes the clerical network that enables the abuse to be perpetrated. When clergy sex abuse is sealed under wraps, it festers and breeds; when it is brought into the light of day, it withers. When victims of sex abuse hear about other victims confronting their abusers, they too find the courage to take a stand. During the year 2004, 1,092 new allegations against 756 Catholic priests were registered with church officials (Rachel Zoll, The Associated Press, February 18, 2005). Only after bishops were successfully sued for their complicity in the sexual abuse of minors for neglecting their civil and canonical duties did they sit up. When dioceses were confronted by financial losses in the hundreds of millions of dollars in court-awarded damages, they took action. The American bishops said that they had paid more than $800 million in settlements by 2005. At that time more than 750 cases of abuse waited to be settled in California alone. It's one thing to neglect to protect the faithful from sexual predators, it's quite another thing altogether to neglect to protect the church's assets from lawsuits. Action to protect church assets has never faltered or been neglected. Money speaks loudly.

There always will be people who sexually abuse children; research has not yet determined that abuse is more prevalent within the ranks of the clergy than in society as a whole. Of course, that's no excuse or consolation for the faithful. It's rightfully more scandalous when a priest, who is presumed to be celibate and held up as a model of all things holy, abuses a child.

In the future, some child abusers may squirrel themselves into the ranks of the clergy, but—with more discrete screening, more careful training of candidates, along with a hierarchy on alert, and an informed and challenging laity—it may be more difficult for them to do so. Abusers should not, and most likely will not find the sort of cover that the priesthood has afforded them up to now. When instances of sexual abuse are suspected or come to their attention, bishops must deal with the perpetrators according to the procedures laid down in canon law, and report them to the police as is required by civil law.

The information contained in this book has not been published before, although some parts of it have been culled from court documents that are public by nature. Some facts are repeated, but redundancy is kept to a minimum: The authors sometimes refer to different facets of the same situations to highlight different concerns.

It would be no more fair to question the loyalty of the authors of this book than it would be to question the loyalty of a Paul confronting Peter on circumcision, or an Aquinas defying the stodgy theologians of Paris in his day, or that of a Leonardo Boff or an Edward Schillebeeckx challenging the abuse of church authority in our day. The authors are dedicated to the church, defined by the Second Vatican Council as the People of God, *sancta simul et semper purificanda* (holy, but at the same time, always in need of being purified). As practitioners dedicated to healing and compassion—both for victims of sexual abuse and for the church that allows it to happen—the authors hope to see the day when this centuries-old open sore on the Body of Christ will be no more than a scar to remind the church of a disease that almost overwhelmed it, but was eventually healed.

Good Friday, March 25, 2005
A.W.R.S.
La Jolla, California

Part One

Sexual Abuse by Priests: History Speaks

There are few priests who fulfill all [their] obligations; whence I infer a most dreadful consequence: There are few priests who will be saved.

—Louis Tronson. Third Superior General of the Sulpicians, 1676–1700[1]

The idea that defect, shadow, or other misfortune could ever cause the church to stand in need of restoration or renewal is hereby condemned as obviously absurd.

—Pope Gregory XVI, 1832

Bishops should be diligent in fostering holiness among their clerics, religious, and laity ... .

—Second Vatican Council, 1965[1a]

Chapter 1

Clerical Sexual Abuse: The Paper Trail

One thousand years from now students of jurisprudence will look back at the laws passed at the beginning of the first century of the third millennium and find laws dealing with gun control, abortion, capital punishment, and prisoner abuse. They will rightly conclude that these issues must have been of great concern to us: Why would we have bothered to legislate for such issues if we were not having serious problems with them?

Then they will read official documents, newspaper accounts, and trial records and find that we held great debates about "life issues." They will discover that guns were a plague in our society, that abortion and the death penalty split the nation, and that we were sending prisoners to faraway places to be tortured. And then they will say: "See, even way back then, laws were not passed in a vacuum."

Laws are never passed in a vacuum. Legislators have enough to do dealing with real-life threats to society without wasting time on imaginary issues. Lawmakers, who return to the same issue over and over again, do it because the laws already on the books are not having their desired effect. Even the rare law that forestalls some hypothetical problem is passed because it anticipates a situation that poses a real threat in the present. There is always some reason for passing a law.

The same is true of Catholic Church laws. They, too, are not passed in a vacuum. Laws are passed, instructions are given, and decrees made in response to a perceived threat to the well-being of the faithful, the church as a body, or society at large. For instance, when Rome said birth control was immoral, it was not because of some hypothetical situation dreamed up in a moral theology textbook; it was because many Catholics believed birth control was morally acceptable and were already practicing it. And the more often Rome reinforces its stance on an issue, the more obvious it becomes that it is being disobeyed. Just like any other legislator, if Rome were to stop talking about an issue altogether it would be either because it had given up on it, or because it had gone away.

A review of the history of the churchs' legal system and case law demonstrates that there are some issues that never go away, no matter how hard Rome tries to legislate them out of existence. One of these topics is the consistent failure of clerics to observe their vows of chastity. From the early fourth to the early twenty-first century we find a constant flow of monastic rules and canons promulgated by individual bishops, gatherings of local bishops, councils of all the bishops, and papal decrees attempting to regulate the sex lives of the clergy. From the earliest days, when priests were allowed to marry, we find laws telling them to avoid sex; and when celibacy became mandatory for the clergy, we find laws against concubinage. We also find condemnations of homosexuality in the ranks of the clergy, the sexual abuse of minors by members of the clergy, and the solicitation of sex by priests in the confessional.

The sexual abuse of children by priests is found condemned over and over again in the unorganized decrees of local churches that were promulgated before the first comprehensive collection of laws and commentaries—the first code of canon law, the *Corpus Juris Canonici*—appeared in the middle of the twelfth century. It was repeatedly condemned in church councils, and when the papacy began to gain the kind of control it now has over the entire church, it was condemned by one Roman authority after another. In our own day, Rome has addressed the issue repeatedly, but in such secrecy that only some bishops were told about it. The extreme secrecy that was imposed on everybody dealing with the investigation of priests accused of soliciting sex from penitents was, in the last century, imposed on everybody involved in the investigation of clerical perpetrators of sexual abuse of children. Because of this secrecy, it has for all practical purposes become impossible for the church to deal with sexual abuse in an open and responsible manner and for the faithful to discover the extent of the current crisis and how it was covered up. However, by examining the evidence that is available, we can discover not just how prevalent the sexual abuse of children by priests was down through the ages, but also, particularly in our time, the failure of the bishops to manage it.

As we look at the legislation passed, the case histories, and the historical record, we can only conclude that, in the immortal words of the Bard, celibacy in the Catholic Church has been honored if not more, at least as much "in the breach as the observance."

Church authorities from the second century onward have repeatedly disparaged sex in all its human forms as dirty, sinful, unclean, and even unnatural. Many early Christian thinkers had a strong antipathy to marriage. The best assessment of marital sex was that it was a necessary evil, and the worst assessment was that it was a despicable act to be avoided. St. Ambrose (339–397 CE) considered sex part of a sinful world and a wound everyone must wear. Virginity was the goal of all believers in imitation of Christ who, Ambrose taught, had never been touched by physical desire. He linked women to sexual temptation that ultimately led to sin and death.[2]

The equally influential St. Jerome (342–420 CE) taught that the body must be controlled and Christians must avoid sexual attraction.[3] Even a husband who loves his wife too much, Jerome taught, is guilty of adultery.[4] Both Jerome and Ambrose held a consistently negative opinion of the human body and of sexuality. Though both are highly influential in the formation of Christian and Catholic theology, they are easily overshadowed by St. Augustine (354–430 CE) who, prior to his conversion to Christianity, had an active sex life and a relationship with a concubine who bore him a child. After embracing Christianity, Augustine also embraced the church fathers' skeptical view of human sexuality, but with some mitigation. Sex in marriage was permissible, even though he agreed with Jerome and Ambrose that chastity was preferable; the sexual organs and urges needed to be controlled and men needed to avoid sexual desire that was excited by women.[5]

This pessimistic and sometimes volatile attitude had to come from somewhere, but that "somewhere," according to many Christian scholars, was not the Gospels of Jesus Christ, the ultimate source of Catholic teaching. The Gospels make few references to sex and show none of the morbid fascination with sexuality that is found in the Christian literature of the first four centuries or the canonical formulations of the Medieval Period.[6]

The answer to the question of the source of traditional Catholic sexual teaching is complex. One of its roots can be traced back to the prevalence of Greek Stoic dualism, which regarded the flesh as evil and the spirit as good, and its influence on pre-Christian thought. Its leading spokesman was Seneca, a contemporary of Jesus and St. Paul. Under the influence of the Stoic tradition, Seneca held that the wise should avoid the corruption of bodily comforts and pleasures, especially those derived from sex.[7] Some early Christian writers, Augustine among them, subscribed to

Stoicism and even went beyond it in their vilification of sex. By the end of the Patristic Age (800 CE), two opposing views of human sexuality had emerged: Jerome and those who followed him stressed the dichotomy between body and soul and spirit and matter, and believed that sex was the primary expression of fleshly evil; whereas Augustine had tempered the earlier attitudes and held that sex was basically a useful and good force in human life but debased by sin and passion.[8]

These two attitudes toward human sexuality dominated Christian writing from the fifth century onward. Their approach to sex is based on two presumptions: the first, that sex is always bad and equals impurity; and the second, that sex is only justifiable for human reproduction and is evil when sought for other reasons, such as pleasure.

A third approach, which has roots in the Gospels, is that sex can be an act of love and is a crucial element in human relationships and an essential aspect of marriage. Although medieval writers did not accentuate this theme, its proponents were, oddly enough, primarily monks.[9] It is found in some of the medieval canonists but never gained the moral or legal high ground.[10] Nor was it conspicuous between the Middle Ages and the twentieth century. Finally, in 1939, Fr. Herbert Doms, a German priest and scholar, published *The Meaning of Marriage*, a work that espoused the idea that sex was not primarily for procreation but for expressing love. Furthermore, Fr. Doms said, people married for love and not primarily to procreate. This view was far from the church's official teaching and it got little notice until the Second Vatican Council (1962–65). After a bitter fight between a progressive group of council fathers (bishops and cardinals) and a minority group of conservative participants led by key members of the Vatican bureaucracy, the council voted to pass a revolutionary text in its pastoral constitution *The Church in the*

Modern World. The third opinion had finally been officially recognized and accepted as part of the official teaching
of the Catholic Church.[11]

However, medieval writers of the early period (tenth to
twelfth centuries) and theologians and canonists of the later
period (thirteenth to fifteenth centuries) were all influenced
by the earlier Stoic dualism. If sex was acceptable at all, it
was only when used for procreation.

What does Catholic teaching about sex have to do with
clergy sexual abuse and its many variations through the centuries? First, there is an obvious credibility gap of cosmic
proportions between the lofty ideals of clerical chastity, the
supremacy of virginity, and the narrow tolerance of marital
sexuality, and the way church authorities generally react to
the sexual activities of the clergy from priests right up to
popes. Second, the profound sense of shame that has grown
out of this pessimistic and negative dualistic understanding
of humanity, and sexuality in particular, helps explain the
church's obsession with secrecy. This secrecy surrounds clerical sex offenses and crimes. Church authorities demonstrate a reluctance to openly admit the existence of this
behavior to the unsuspecting public. Finally, the mystique
surrounding celibacy is necessary in order to sustain its
rationale and to attract men to initially embrace it in the
priesthood and religious life. The exaltation of the celibate
ideal has hinged upon selling the idea that celibacy and virginity (even re-invented) are far superior to the lay life or
the married state.

Celibacy is essential to the continuation of the power
and prominence of the clerical subculture, the home of the
elite minority who rule the Catholic Church. Despite the
documented history of celibacy violations through the centuries, Catholic leadership has strongly resisted any serious
consideration that there might be something wrong with
the concept itself. To abandon celibacy would be to risk the

demise of the fortified clerical world and the consequent loss of power and influence.

The Official Presumption: Catholic Clerics Are Practicing Celibates

Celibacy is the most prominent and controversial aspect of the Catholic priesthood. According to church law, all clerics are to live a celibate life. Although most people presume that all Catholic clerics practice celibacy, a significant number of clerics are allowed to marry. Priests and deacons of the Oriental or Eastern rites are not bound to celibacy unless they belong to religious orders. Within the Roman Catholic Church there is a class of clerics known as permanent deacons who are not obliged to celibacy if they are married when they are ordained deacons. There is also a group of former ministers from the Episcopal and Lutheran Churches who converted to Catholicism and were allowed to be re-ordained priests and retain their wives.

At issue, however, is the failure of significant numbers of Roman Catholic priests to observe the obligations of celibacy. The obligation is assumed when a man becomes a deacon, the final step before priesthood. Contrary to misinformation from some sources, the obligation of celibacy entails complete abstention from any and all forms of sexual and romantic contact between clerics and people of either gender of any age.[12] Celibacy also prohibits any form of autoeroticism, including what have traditionally been referred to as "impure thoughts." According to canon law, celibate clerics cannot enter into an ecclesiastically valid marriage.

All clerics in the Roman rite are obligated to celibacy, with the exception of those already noted. There are two main classifications of clerics: diocesan priests and religious priests. Diocesan priests are those who are attached to, or *incardinated* in a diocese and are under the authority of a bishop. Religious priests belong to a religious order or congregation and live a common life, at least in theory. Diocesan priests make a "promise" of celibacy and religious clerics take a "vow" of chastity.

The practical effects are the same for both. No form of sexual contact with men or women of any age is ever allowed. Celibacy and chastity not only preclude marriage, but dating, romantic or intimate relationships, casual sex, and any form of sexual activity be it heterosexual intercourse or any other variation.

The obligation of clerical celibacy has had a long and rocky history in the Catholic Church. From the fourth century onward, various popes and church councils mandated obligatory celibacy. Yet it was not until the Second Lateran Council (1139) that universal celibacy was decreed and marriages of clerics were declared invalid. This legislation was re-enacted at the Council of Trent (sixteenth century) and was included in the 1917 *Code of Canon Law*.[13] Although mandatory, celibacy was debated at the Second Vatican Council, and the decree "*Presbyterorum ordinis*" (Article 16), issued in 1965, reaffirmed the tradition. It leaned on the Gospel of St. Matthew as the foundation for the assertion that clerical celibacy is somehow willed by Jesus Christ.[14]

The Contemporary Dilemma

History records significant opposition to mandatory celibacy from clerics and laypeople alike in the period leading up to the finalization of legislation in the twelfth century. There was similar public dissent to it during the age of the Protestant Reformation. In our era there was little public questioning of the value of mandatory celibacy for Roman Catholic priests until the Second Vatican Council, during and after which, thousands of priests left the active ministry, mostly in order to marry. Mandatory celibacy was openly debated by clergy and laity with some bishops joining the ranks of the dissenters. Unofficial sources claim that approximately 125,000 priests—some 25,000 from the United States—have left their ministries between 1965, the year the council ended, and 1990. Verified numbers are not available.[15]

Despite the alarming number of departures, Catholic leadership has refused to seriously study the possibility of changing the legislation. Two years after the council reaffirmed celibacy, Pope Paul VI issued an encyclical letter specifically addressing priestly celibacy. It begins with the assertion that:

> Priestly celibacy has been guarded by the church for centuries as a brilliant jewel, and retains its value undiminished even in our time when mentality and structures have undergone such profound change.[16]

Beginning in 1979, Pope John Paul II spoke repeatedly of his total support for mandatory celibacy.[17] Until his death in 2005, he steadfastly refused to entertain any discussion on the subject and even prohibited Catholic bishops from engaging in any public debate about its value.

However, despite these prohibitions, the question of mandatory celibacy has been hotly debated by theologians, clergy groups, and laypeople. Most recently, several American priests' groups publicly asked their bishops to debate the issue.[18] And within the past few years, several ranking hierarchs have added their voices to those who support a change.[19]

Adding to the departures of priests and the growing willingness of the Catholic laity to accept a married clergy, is the specter of violations of the obligations of celibacy. Prior to the Second Vatican Council, the departures of priests from the ministry were shrouded in a blanket of religious and societal opprobrium and deep secrecy. Priests who left often became defectors or "non-persons" to their former colleagues, their former parishioners, and at times even to their families. Even more impenetrable was the wall of secrecy surrounding clerics who sexually abused young people.

In this day and age, within the Catholic Church, several significant forces are on a collision course with one another. First, there is the ideal upheld in the church's law, supported by pronouncements from popes and other church leaders; allied with these is the presumption that celibacy is indeed faithfully practiced by the vast majority of Catholic clerics and that it is essential to priestly ministry in the everyday life of the church. Approaching with increasing speed and vehemence are two other forces: Significant numbers of clerics have sexually abused young adolescents and frequently children. The public has a rapidly growing awareness that a surprisingly high number of clerics, supposedly celibate, are engaged in homosexual or heterosexual intimate relationships. On one side we have the ideal, vehemently defended by the pope, the Vatican bureaucracy, and many clergy and laypeople, and on the other, the undeniable reality that celibacy has not worked and does not work for what may well be a majority of clerics.

Hence the dilemma. Although church law and official teaching constantly proclaim to both civil and religious society that priestly celibacy is the norm and can be presumed of all clerics, the church's own legal tradition provides uncontested evidence of consistent violations of celibacy in a variety of ways, not just in our own era but reaching back through the centuries.

Violations of Celibacy and Early Church Law

The Catholic Church's legal tradition appeals to the New Testament scriptures as the basis for its often-changing code of sexual ethics. Later legislation against fornication, adultery, and homosexual behavior is attributed to the words of Jesus Christ as found in the Gospels or to the writings of the most prominent early church leader, St. Paul. In the post-Apostolic centuries (late first to early fourth) Christian writers began to elevate sexual misbehavior to a greater status than that found in the scriptural texts. The earliest mention of forbidden sexual behavior in the literature is from the *Didache,* a short manual of Christian morals and church practice that probably dates from the late first century.[20] The second chapter condemns various sexual practices and includes a prohibition against "corrupting youth."

The Catholic Church has had its own legal system from the earliest centuries. Although church law was not officially codified until 1917, traces of its formal legal tradition can be found as early as the fourth century. The earliest acknowledged legislation comes from the Council of Elvira (Spain, 309 CE). From the fourth century to the Middle Ages, most legislation was enacted by local synods, or councils of bishops spread across Christendom. In an attempt to keep the growing mass of legislation in order, laws or canons from the various synods and councils were eventually gathered into collections. From the fifth century to the twelfth, numerous unofficial collections appeared in the Eastern and Latin, or Western, churches. Although the papacy was in place from the earliest years of the church, it had not become the strong central power that we know today.

Human sexual behavior has long been a major focus of Catholic Church law. Half of the regulations, or canons, issued by the Council of Elvira dealt with sexual transgressions of various forms. The marriages of clergy posed special problems for the bishops at Elvira and for subsequent councils. Sexual transgressions of the clergy were treated far more severely than those of laypeople. The predominant pessimistic philosophy of human sexuality no doubt influenced the formulation of Elvira's most radical canon. This was the first legislative attempt at imposing the obligation of continence on the clergy, at least some of whom were married (Canon 33), and which, in the opinion of the prominent scholar of medieval history, James Brundage, unleashed a controversy that has nagged the church to the present day.[21]

Sexual sins ranked with homicide and idolatry as the most serious offenses in early church law. The three most serious were fornication, adultery, and sexual corruption of young boys.[22] The Council of Elvira passed four canons that confronted the sexual behaviour of clerics. The first of these (Canon 18) punished any bishop, priest, or deacon discovered to be a sexual offender with deprivation of Holy Communion even at the time of death. The second (Canon 27) forbade bishops or other clerics from having unrelated women living with them, and the third (Canon 33) ordered all married clerics to abstain completely from sex with their wives. The fourth canon (Canon 65) excommunicated clerics who knowingly neglected to denounce adulterous wives. Though it does not mention clergy specifically, an additional canon (Canon 71) condemned sex between adult men and young boys: "Men who sexually abuse boys shall not be given communion even at the end."[23]

The fact that reception of communion was prohibited even on the offender's deathbed is a clear indication of the extreme attitude of the early Christians toward what we now call ephebophila.

Attempts at imposing clerical celibacy in the early Medieval Period met with little consistent success. Popes and councils issued decrees that ranged from prohibitions of second marriages of widowed clerics (bishops and priests) to outright prohibition of marriage, and prohibitions of sexual activity between married clerics and their wives. Clerical concubinage was also the object of sanction by church authorities, but again apparently with minimal success. Brundage records that clerics who kept concubines were as common as those with wives and that penalties decreed for concubinage were rarely enforced.[24] The early canonical literature indicates that the more common sexual transgression of the clergy involved various forms of heterosexual activity, including fornication, concubinage, and even sex with one's spouse. There is also, however, a consistent stream of documents that clearly indicate that homosexual transgressions were common.

Homosexual Violations of Celibacy: The Penitential Books and Later Medieval Law

The Christian church came into being in the midst of the centuries-old Roman Empire. The lands and peoples of the Ancient Near East were under Roman occupation at the time of Christ. As the early Christian communities took shape and found their place in secular society, they came under the influence of and were shaped by Roman culture and the Roman legal system. The development of criminal penalties for same-sex relationships reflected the pre-Christian Roman attitude at one stage and the influence of the Christian emperors at the later, more important, periods. The single most important pre-Christian source is the *Lex Julia de Adulteriis* of Caesar Augustus, enacted about 17 BCE. The *Lex Julia* mentions a sexual offense known as *stuprum,* which originally was understood to mean a sexual offense against a virgin or widow, in contrast to adultery, which involved a married woman.[25] Though the *Lex Julia* remained the foundation for later Roman laws on sexual behavior, the meaning of *stuprum* appears to have been considerably expanded beyond that which was applied by the pre-Christian jurists.

The *Digest of Justinian*, a supplement that was added to the code of the Roman Emperor Justinian in 533 CE, contains an opinion of the Roman jurist, Julius Paulus, that expands *stuprum* to include same-sex relations with young boys:

> One who persuades a boy, abducted by himself or a corrupt attendant, into indecency … will, if the offense be complete, suffer capital punishment; if it not be fully effected, he is to be deported to an island. Corrupt attendants undergo the supreme penalty.[26]

The Institutes of Justinian, another supplement that was added to the *Code of Justinian*, shortly after the Digest, contains a similar opinion:

> Also, the *Lex Julia de Adulteriis* punishes with death not only those who are guilty of adultery, but those who give themselves up to works of lewdness with their own sex.[27]

Though the Digest and Institutes date from 533 CE or so, Julius Paulus wrote in the first decades of the third century, before the Constantinian era. This refutes the opinion that same-sex practices became criminalized only because of Christian influence. Christianity was legitimized by the Emperor Constantine the Great (d. 337 CE) after his victory at the Milvian Bridge in 312 CE. Christianity then emerged from the shadows, was officially tolerated and favored, and became an established religion. From then on, the most influential emperors were Christian, one of the most prominent being Justinian (483–565 CE).

In 342 CE, well before the publication of Justinian's works, the Emperor Constantius, the third son of Constantine, had promulgated a law that is found in the *Theodosian Code* condemning same-sex relationships and behavior.[28] Fifty years later, Emperor Valentinian II promulgated a statute that prescribed death by burning for sodomy:

> All persons who have the shameful custom of condemning a man's body, acting the part of a woman's to the suffrance of an alien sex (for they appear not to be different from women), shall expiate a crime of this kind in avenging flames in the sight of the people.[29]

There seems little doubt that the legislation of Justinian was strongly influenced by his Christian beliefs. In addition to the insertion of the opinion of Julius Paulus, the emperor enacted two new laws, known as *Novellae*, in 538 CE and 544 CE. Both laws are framed in Christian pietistic language and both connect same-sex relationships with the calamities that befall society as God's retribution. Thus it can be surmised that the motivation for the harsh punishments meted out to sodomists was state security.[30]

There is no direct evidence that the Christian emperors passed secular legislation specifically condemning sodomitic practices by Christian clergymen. However, before and parallel to the Justinian era there is evidence of Christian leaders passing laws against same-sex relations and in some instances specifically naming clerics.[31] Derrick Bailey refers to the cases of two bishops accused of sodomy as the only recorded examples of the enforcement of the *Novellae* of Justinian.[32] Though case documentation is sparse, that which exists seems to indicate that clerics accused of sodomy were not spared the harsh treatment of the secular laws.

The word "homosexual" did not exist until the nineteenth century and consequently is not found in any canonical or theological literature.[33] The notion of sexual identity is a late development in psychological literature and understanding. Sex between members of the same gender generally referred to sex acts between males and was known as sodomia, or "sodomy." Ecclesiastical writing also used the term *luxuria,* meaning "lust" or "lechery" and *peccatum contra naturam,* or "sin against nature."

Ecclesiastical and secular writing of the early Medieval Period did not commonly distinguish between sexual activity between adults of the same gender or adults and young boys. In fact, there is reason to believe that the presumptive form of homosexual behavior was what today we would call "ephebophilic," that is, between adults and young adolescents. This presumption is based on the fact that same-sex interplay in the ancient world was 90 percent adult-adolescent, or pederastic, as opposed to adult-infant, or pedophilic. This trend probably continued into the late Middle Ages and even beyond.[34] Consequently, when the literature refers to clerics committing *sodomia* it is probable that the reference is to sex with young boys but not to exclude sex with adults.

Along with the canonical legislation of the various church councils, the Penitential Books provide an excellent source of information about violations of clerical celibacy. The Penitentials originated as unofficial pastoral guidebooks for priests to be used when assessing penalties for sinners. Many Penitentials were authored by or at least attributed to prominent churchmen of the time. They originated in the Celtic churches of Ireland and England in the seventh century and remained popular until the thirteenth century. These books recorded the various offenses that came to the priests' attention. The assigned penalties indicate the gravity with which each offense was viewed by the early church.

Several of the more prominent books refer to sexual crimes committed by clerics and laymen against young boys and girls.[35] The *Penitential of Bede* (England, eighth century) advises that clerics who commit sodomy with children be given increasingly severe penances commensurate with their rank. While laymen who committed such crimes were excommunicated and made to fast for three years, deacons and priests were similarly excommunicated but made to fast for seven and ten years respectively. Bishops who sexually abused children were given twelve years of penance.[36]

The Penitential Books and the canonical collections regularly speak of the penalties levied against men guilty of sex with other males. The most severe penance imposed by the church was excommunication, or deprivation of communion, even at the moment of death. Lesser penalties included lengthy periods (years) of severe fasting. Clerics were not as protected as in more recent times. Early church penalties included excommunication for various periods of time, fasting, and degradation, which amounted to social death and the presumption of spiritual death as well.[37]

Sexual crimes "against nature" brought double liability for clerics. First, the crime itself was considered grave. The fact that the perpetrator was a cleric amounted to the added offense of "sacrilege" because the cleric's body was considered specially consecrated to God. The Third Lateran Council (1179), a medieval equivalent to our own Second Vatican Council, decreed that clerics who commit sins against nature be confined to a monastery for life or leave the church. After 1250, the penalties became much harsher because sodomy was often linked to heresy.[38] There is even some indication that in the popular view, sodomy was commonly identified with clerics.[39] Over time, the ecclesiastical offense was enshrined in secular law and offenders were then subjected to severe punishments, including fines, castration, exile, and even death. Accused clergy were first dealt with by church courts and then often handed over to the secular authorities for additional and sometimes much more severe punishment. The church added an additional penalty, "infamy of fact," which was tantamount to a civil death with complete ostracization and economic boycott. This penalty was imposed on clerics as well as laymen.[40]

At this juncture it is vital to understand the moral climate of the era. The official moral doctrine of the Catholic Church took a pessimistic and negative view of human sexual expression. This was not an age when lax moral behavior was approved of by what we now would call "liberal" theologians. The official teaching promoted a highly restrictive and gloomy approach to sex. The forceful legislation and extreme penances found in the Penitential Books and in other writings of the time reflect this attitude. Yet the church's "party line" was not successful in curbing clergy sexual excesses.

Blunt Talk: The Book of Gomorrah

The most dramatic and explicit outcry against forbidden clergy sexual activity is found in the *Book of Gomorrah*, written by St. Peter Damian about 1051. His work, the circumstances that prompted it, and the reaction of the reigning pope provide an ominous insight into the situation being played out in the modern Catholic Church.

Peter was an ordained Camaldolese monk who became a bishop and then a cardinal. Although he is considered to have been a stringent moralist and harsh critic of the clergy of his time, his work is nevertheless deemed credible by scholars.[41] He was an ardent church reformer. One of his strongest and most consistent themes was the sexual immorality of the contemporary clergy and the irresponsibility of lax superiors who neglected or refused to take strong measures against it. He condemned all forms of homosexual activity, yet sexual contact with young boys particularly angered and scandalized him.[42]

Peter's book and its contents are clear and to the point. He begins by singling out superiors who, prompted by excessive and misplaced piety, fail to exclude sodomites from their ranks (Chapter 2). He asserts that those given to "unclean acts" not be ordained or, if they are already ordained, be dismissed from holy orders (Chapter 3). He holds special contempt for priests who defile men or boys who come to them for confession (Chapter 6). Likewise, he condemns clerics who administer the sacrament of penance (confession) to their victims (Chapter 7). He refutes the canonical sources used by offending clerics to justify their proclivities (Chapters 11 and 12). And he assesses the damage done to the church by offending clerics (Chapters 19, 20 and 21). His final chapter is an appeal to the reigning pope, Leo IX, to take action.

Leo's response, included in the cited edition, is an example of inaction that appears to portend the responses of our own times. The pope praised Peter and verified the truth of his findings and recommendations. Yet he considerably softened the reformer's urging that decisive action be taken to root out offenders from the ranks of the clergy. The pope decided to exclude only those who had offended repeatedly and over a long period of time. Although Peter had paid significant attention to the impact of the offending clerics on their victims, the pope focused only on the sinfulness of the clerics and their need to repent.[43]

Leo IX died in 1054 and was followed by three popes with short reigns, none of whom are remembered for any action related to clergy sexual excesses.[44] Pope Alexander II was elected in 1061 and died in 1073. He was considered a strong supporter of the reform movement in the church and enacted various measures to stamp out corruption within the ranks of the clergy, including sexual immorality. Yet despite his official stance, Alexander tried to suppress the *Book of Gomorrah* by confiscating it. The outraged Peter responded forcefully with appeals to allies in the papal court as well as a series of thinly veiled threats about the pope's likely fate. His attempts appear to have been successful insofar as the *Book of Gomorrah* retained a prominent place in the writing of the time.[45]

Peter's blunt condemnation of both homosexual sex and clergy sexual excesses was not unique. It did, however, shed light on a problem that had become more visible in his lifetime. In his *Rule of the Monastery of Compludo*, Peter provides a vivid example of how sodomy with young boys was to be handled in one Italian monastery:

> A cleric or monk who seduces youths or young boys or is found kissing or in any other impure situations is to be publicly flogged and lose his tonsure. When his hair has been shorn, his face is to be foully besmeared with spit and he is to be bound in iron chains. For six months he will languish in prison-like confinement and on three days of each week shall fast on barley bread in the evening. After this he will spend another six months under the custodial care of a spiritual elder, remaining in a segregated cell, giving himself to manual work and prayer, subject to vigils and prayers. He may go for walks but always under the custodial care of two spiritual brethren, and he shall never again associate with youths in private conversation nor in counseling them.[46]

Peter Damian was an influential voice in what was later to be known as the "Gregorian Reform." This was a period of church renewal that began in the tenth century and became associated with its most influential voice, Pope Gregory VII, who reigned from 1073 to 1085. The control of rampant abuse of clerical celibacy was at the heart of the movement.[47] The efforts at enforcing celibacy or at least encouraging decent restraint consisted of a series of regulations, exhortations, and condemnations from various church leaders including bishops, abbots, and popes. The reform movement had its beginnings in the excessively corrupt society of the tenth century and culminated in the mid-thirteenth century. The cumulative effect of the prohibition of clerical marriage and concubinage was to remove any legitimate sexual outlet of any type for the clergy. Needless to say, the illegitimate forms of sexual release had been condemned anyway, but continued to occur despite the threat of spiritual death and temporal punishment. Now all forms of sexual outlet were both a sin and a canonical crime.

Church-imposed penalties were generally spiritual in nature, often consisting of periods of fasting and excommunication that varied from months to years to life. These penances were not private matters and the spiritual punishment was made significantly more painful by the social isolation that accompanied them. Physical punishment was imposed by secular authorities for more severe sexual crimes. Clerics were not always exempt if they were members of a monastic community.

The High Middle Ages

Often referred to as the "High Middle Ages," the twelfth to fourteenth centuries were periods of far-reaching change for church and society. This period saw the birth of the universities, the advent of scholasticism, and, in the church, the ascendancy of the papacy to a truly centralized power. This was also the era that saw the emergence of church law as a separate science with a powerful influence in ecclesiastical and secular life.

The single most valuable source of information for the entire early and later Medieval Period is the *Decree of Gratian,* which is the common name for the *Concordance of Discordant Canons.* Gratian, the author, was certainly a university professor and probably a monk. His background and personal life remain hidden, nonetheless his influence on canon law and church discipline has been far-reaching and profound. He worked at the University of Bologna and his work, completed in 1140, consists of a systematic study in dialectical form of a broad spectrum of legal/canonical sources extant at the time. It contains sources from Scripture, Roman law, canons from church councils, writings of the early church fathers, and liturgical, theological, and penitential texts.

Gratian included sections on a variety of violations of clerical celibacy. The format of his work consisted of a listing of the most important authoritative sources on a particular issue, followed by his own conclusions.[48] He strongly supported clerical celibacy and was opposed to all forms of violation, especially clergy marriages.[49] Although the Second Lateran Council (1139) had issued the definitive word on celibacy by declaring that marriages of clerics in holy orders were invalid, the law was not met with immediate universal acceptance, much less compliance. More important, however, was the issue of illicit violations both prior to and after the Lateran declaration. By illicit is meant both fornication and adultery. The canons and related documentation reflect the widespread and ongoing problem of clerics having sex with unmarried women and with the wives of other men. It appears that, in spite of the many attempts by church authorities to impose celibacy in the practical order, clerical concubinage persisted. An article in the journal, *The Jurist,* in 1972, described a situation that was far less than ideal:

From the repeated strictures against clerical incontinence by provincial synods of the twelfth and thirteenth centuries, one may surmise that celibacy remained a remote and only defectively realized ideal in the Latin West. In England, particularly in the north, concubinage continued to be customary; it was frequent in France, Spain and Norway.[50]

Clergy marriages and concubinage presume stability in the relationship. Casual sex by clerics was also condemned. Those convicted of such offenses could expect to lose any ecclesiastical office, and to be confined to a monastery for life, but not dismissed from holy orders.[51] Gratian also gave serious consideration to clerics who seduced and had sex with nuns. He demanded that punishment for sexual transgressions be more severe for clerics than for laymen.

Gratian also considered homosexuality, referred to in the *Decretum* by either *sodomia* or acts *contra naturam*. However, his treatment was far less extensive than that given to either marital sex or clerical celibacy. In general, Gratian considered homosexual sex to be far worse than either fornication or adultery.[52] He included a specific reference to sexual sins with young boys, which he called *stuprum pueri*.[53] *Stuprum*, in this context, refers to a sexual violation with the use of boys on the part of an adult male.

Gratian, known as the "Father of the Science of Canon Law," had a profound impact on the development of law and church policy for centuries to follow. The canon law scholars who followed Gratian, known as the *Decretists* because they based their studies on the *Decretum*, devoted significant amounts of ink to all manners of sexual behavior. The dominant concern regarding clerics was the violation of celibacy with women, be they the clerics' wives or not. In defiance of the ongoing efforts by various ecclesiastical authorities to enforce chastity, clerical celibacy was openly ignored. The *Decretists,* in their considerations of the official texts, sidestepped any debate on the value of the celibacy rule. Rather, they sought to concentrate their efforts on applying and enforcing the law as they knew it.[54] The commonly prescribed penance for celibacy violations was loss of office and income, but not necessarily degradation, or "defrocking" as it is commonly known.

The *Decree of Gratian* constitutes the first part of the most extensive and authoritative source for the history of Catholic Church law and policy, namely the *Corpus Iuris Canonici,* first published in 1500.[55] The second volume contains various collections of papal decrees and documents, several of which deal with clerical celibacy.

Despite the presumed "definitive" regulation issued by the Third Lateran Council (1179), clerical marriage, concubinage, and casual fornication continued to be widespread and public. As time went by and it became obvious that celibacy was not working, some bishops and even popes took a more pragmatic approach. According to Brundage:

> In practice, both Popes and lawyers knew that strict enforcement of the celibacy policy was not working and was perhaps not workable. Enforcement procedures were gradually modified to take account of the realities. Although the law continued to prescribe stern punishment for concubinary priests, some decretals of the late 12th and early 13th century tolerated clerical fornication so long as it was discreet, directing prelates to take action only against notorious offenders. ... If clerical marriage remained a problem despite generations of

campaigns against it, clerical concubinage was an even greater one.[56]

Faced with evidence of unofficial tolerance of celibacy violations, the Fourth Lateran Council (1215), meeting just thirty-six years after the Third Lateran Council, reiterated the previous council's condemnation of celibacy violations, particularly those that were homosexual in nature. This condemnation was to be expected since celibacy was theoretically the "law of the land." What was far-reaching about this council's stand, however, was the fact that it also condemned prelates (e.g., bishops, archbishops, and abbots) who sheltered or supported clerics guilty of sexual violations:

> Prelates who dare support such in their iniquities, especially in view of money or other temporal advantages, shall be subject to a like punishment.[57]

Clerical sodomy continued to be a problem, though it was not as intensely debated as were clerical relationships with women. The Third Lateran Council had already included a canon that specifically prohibited homosexual sex in general and decreed that clerics guilty of this crime were to be dismissed from the clerical state or confined to a monastery for life. The former amounted to social exile and shunning, the latter to imprisonment.[58]

It is essential to distinguish between celibacy violations of the secular or diocesan clergy and the violations found in the monasteries. In the first place, clerical marriages only applied to the secular clergy since monastic life, by its very nature, had always presumed the vow of chastity, which precludes marriage and any form of sexual activity. The monks were generally isolated in their monasteries with no personal income or property and little or no contact with women, at least in theory. The primary historical sources and the scholarly studies of these texts indicate that celibacy violations with women were far more common among the secular clergy but not unknown among the monks. On the other hand, the monks became known for the frequency of homosexual activity, especially with young boys.[59]

Elizabeth Abbot, in her *History of Celibacy* (1999), documents how decadence in the monasteries of the West in the Middle Ages sank so low that monks had concubines, openly consorted with unmarried women, and in some cases even married. Homosexuality was also rampant and had been a more deeply entrenched problem, as is evidenced by regulations in the Rule of St. Benedict (c. 480-547 CE), considered to be the Father of Western Monasticism. The preponderance of *sodomia* among the monks makes sense when one considers that they lived a common life and were theoretically isolated from women and ordinary social life.

In his rule, Benedict commanded that no two monks were to sleep in the same bed. Nightlights were to be kept burning and the monks were to sleep clothed. Many monasteries enacted their own rules forbidding various kinds of sexual behavior and added punishments that were often more severe than those meted out to the secular clerics.[60]

The recurrence of church regulations against celibacy violations indicates that these violations were both widespread and publicly known. Michael Goodich claims that the number of thirteenth-century references to homosexuality suggests that it was commonly regarded as a clerical vice. The frequent mentions of the suppression of sodomy among the clergy in ecclesiastical legislation support this theory.[61] While it may not be safe to presume a consistent attitude of tolerance by church officials, one can certainly say that there was a double standard that prevailed throughout the Christian world. It is also noteworthy that the legislation and related theological literature says little about the wisdom of celibacy but much about regulating it in the face of consistent evidence that it was hardly working.

It is not known how many secular and religious priests there were in Europe at the end of the Medieval Period (early fifteenth century), nor is it known how many actual cases of celibacy violations were heard in all European church courts combined. Evidence from tribunal records that have been studied shows that sex offenses were the most numerous on the docket and clerical sex offenses, especially concubinage, continued to pose significant problems.[62]

Although most celibacy violations remained subject to church law, statutes against sodomy for laypeople as well as for clerics were introduced into secular law in the twelfth century.

Summarizing the Medieval Period, it is clear that the bishops were not as preoccupied with secrecy as they are today. Clergy sexual abuse of all kinds was apparently well-known by the public, the clergy, and secular law enforcement authorities. There was a constant stream of disciplinary legislation from the church but none of it was successful in changing clergy behavior. Despite a millennia of failure, the popes and bishops never gave serious thought to the viability of mandatory celibacy. The variety of spiritual punishments was joined, in the later period, with severe corporal penalties inflicted by secular authorities. Finally—and most importantly—from time to time, church authorities recognized that the fundamental problem lay not just with dysfunctional clerics, but irresponsible leadership.

Enforcement and Punishment

The Catholic Church was clearly the dominant social force throughout most of Western history. By the Late Middle Ages (fourteenth century), church authorities were collaborating with secular powers in the enforcement of certain church laws. Separation of church and state did not exist at that time, so our contemporary reaction to the intermingling of ecclesiastical and civil issues, offices, and powers must be tempered with an understanding of the age.

The church relied on the threat of physical and spiritual punishments to enforce its laws. These included periods of fasting that sometimes extended for years. Excommunication for specified periods of time was also common as was banishment to a monastery. The same punishments were imposed on errant clerics with the addition of suspension from church office, removal of income source (benefice), and even degradation or defrocking.

The canonical sources give an indication of the extent that church authorities collaborated with civil powers to enforce its own laws. Violations of clerical celibacy were considered a grave public scandal and a matter of public interest. Homosexual relations were also considered horrific and severely detrimental to the community's social and moral health and were punished regularly by civil authorities from the late twelfth century on. At the beginning of the Gregorian Reform (eleventh century), the church reformers cast aside the more humane due-process procedures prescribed by the early church fathers in favor of the more brutal means of interrogation and punishment brought in by the invading Germanic peoples. Thus, according to Richard Fraher, writing in 1989:

> By the 11th century even the Gregorian reformers, self-proclaimed restorers of the virtues of pristine Christianity, seized upon procedures by ordeal when they began their campaign to purify the church by stamping out simony and clerical concubinage.[63]

The practice of remanding to secular authorities clergy convicted of celibacy violations (especially if they involved homosexual relations) continued into the sixteenth century. Since clerical concubinage and clerical sodomy were considered so horrific, the concealment of occult crimes was generally rejected in favor of prosecution. This approach was motivated by the search for deterrence and the recognition of public interest. In short, there is evidence that the lay public, especially the nobility, did not readily tolerate the sexual sins of the clerics.[64]

The juridical procedure usually involved a trial by a church court followed by transfer of the convicted cleric to the secular authorities where the secular judge would hear evidence, mandate the torturous interrogation of the prisoner, and finally, if the original conviction was upheld, order the punishment to be carried out. These punishments included the death penalty, even for clerics.[65]

The enforcement and punishment of crime in the Middle Ages was vicious and inhumane not only by modern standards but by ancient Christian moral standards. Though the majority of church authorities in the Medieval Period opted for the harsh and violent approach, there were those who taught that the path followed exceeded the bounds of reason and law. Their voices would not dominate until the modern period.[66]

Collaboration with secular powers to enforce church law, especially against heresy, clerical sexual violations, and a variety of other sexual offenses, continued and has been highlighted for posterity by the saga of the Inquisition. The word itself describes the office instituted by the church in the mid-thirteenth century to stamp out heresy. The notorious Spanish Inquisition (late fifteenth century) was somewhat different in that it was more closely bound up with the secular powers. In addition to prosecuting and punishing heretics, the Spanish Inquisition, which was abolished only in 1834, also dealt with a variety of other crimes including clerical sexual offenses.[67] Chief among these was the infamous crime of *sollicitatio,* or solicitation of sex in the course of sacramental confession.

The Catholic Church permeated every aspect of life and was the dominant social, economic, intellectual, and political force in Western civilization until the late sixteenth century. The Protestant Reformation, brought on by the church's own myriad excesses, forever changed the role of the Catholic Church in society. The Reformation also brought significant changes in the manner in which the church handled clergy sexual deviance.

The Protestant Reformation and the Council of Trent

The Black Death hit Europe in the mid-fourteenth century (1348) and recurred several times until the mid-fifteenth century when, historians agree, the worst period of the plague had passed. There was little change in the canon law of sex and marriage from the end of the thirteenth to the sixteenth century. There is, however, significant evidence of an increased concern about "unnatural sex," particularly between males, based on the increased volume of local legislation dealing with homosexual behavior. Clerical *sodomia* was included in this concern.

Although there were no papal or conciliar decrees issued between the Fourth Lateran Council (1215) and the Council of Basle (1431–1449), there was considerable legislative and enforcement activity on the local level. Analyses of the ecclesiastical and civil records of several cities and dioceses at the time are revealing. In Florence, for instance, a special civil magistrate, the Official of the Curfew and the Convents, was mandated to deal with male homosexuality. The very title of the office reveals a popular contemporary view of homosexuality, namely that it was predominant among young students and the Catholic clergy.[68] Documented evidence from ecclesiastical court records as well as papal interventions in individual cases give the impression that clerical sexual activity with males and females was an open scandal.[69]

There had always been dissenting and critical voices of Catholic theology, law, customs, and practices, so the Protestant Reformation was not an unprecedented phenomenon. The difference was that the reformers, who were not necessarily united, caught the attention of the general public and of the political and ruling class.

Martin Luther and the other major reformers, such as Ulrich Zwingli and John Calvin, all rejected mandatory celibacy.[70] The rejection was motivated in great part by what the reformers saw as widespread everyday evidence that clerics of all ranks commonly violated their vows with women, men, and young boys. In reference to life in the monasteries on the eve of the sixteenth-century Protestant Reformation, Abbott says that the monks' "lapses" with women, handsome boys, and each other "became so commonplace that they could not be considered lapses but ways of life for entire communities."[71] Up to this time, the church's leaders continued to advocate the long-standing remedies of legislation, spiritual penalties, physical penalties, and warnings, none of which worked.

The sixteenth century reforming wave differed from those of past centuries because it was not initiated at the top by popes and bishops; it was, rather, fueled by popular discontent and led by local clergy. This reformation spread rapidly and, unlike previous reforms, was not a unified movement but a collection of diverse individuals and groups with different, and at times opposing, agendas. These agendas often began with criticism of church discipline, then moved into doctrinal matters, but they were also practical and political.[72]

In rejecting celibacy, the reformers attacked the theological basis of the discipline, arguing that it had no foundation in Scripture or ancient tradition. The major force, however, was moral outrage. Living in the midst of a clerical world of non-celibate behavior, the reformers believed that it caused moral corruption. Indeed, according to Brundage:

> The sexual habits of the Roman Catholic clergy, according to reformers, were a sewer of iniquity, a scandal to the laity, and a threat of damnation to the clergy themselves.[73]

The Catholic Church reacted to the reforming attempts with the Council of Trent (1545–1563). Secular princes had urged a reforming council, but the popes resisted until 1545 when Pope Paul II summoned the bishops to the Italian city of Trento.[74] The council met in twenty-five sessions and, after several periods of adjournment, closed in 1563, when most of the major reforms were enacted.

The reaffirmation of clerical celibacy did not pass without strong opposition from a significant number of bishops. Many argued that mandatory celibacy was simply not working and accomplished no more than denying priests' "wives" and children a share in their estates.[75] A canon was proposed that would have permitted marriage for clergy, but it was rejected and mandatory celibacy was enforced once again. The canon upholding celibacy was followed by one that extolled it as superior to marriage:

> If anyone says that the married state excels the state of virginity or celibacy, and that it is better and happier to be united in matrimony than to remain in virginity or celibacy, let him be anathema.[76]

In its final session, the council also dealt with concubinous clerics. The detailed canon describing the procedures to be followed by bishops and the penalties prescribed for guilty clerics demonstrate that the definitive legislation of the Fourth Lateran Council was indeed not that definitive in practice. The council mentioned not only priests but guilty bishops also.[77]

The conciliar legislation was hardly original in any way. It provided no reason to presume that it would be any more successful in getting clerics to accept celibacy than had prior laws. This council, however, was able to bring about a far greater observance of celibacy than any other, at least for a time. The reason was not in the canons themselves but in another conciliar innovation, namely the establishment of seminary education for prospective priests. Prior to the Protestant Reformation, the education of candidates for the priesthood was uneven and random. Parish priests had little more education than the people they served. The learned among the clergy were generally not diocesan, but those who belonged to the monastic and mendicant orders.[78] Henceforth all candidates for the clerical state and for the priesthood were obliged to attend special schools meant to provide intellectual, cultural, and moral formation. Reverence for celibacy was to hold top priority.[79] The Council of Trent dictated that every diocese was to establish its own seminary. Many of these schools remained inadequate and provided only substandard preparation. In 1641 a French priest, Fr. Jean Jacques Olier, founded a seminary and attracted diocesan priests to devote themselves to educating men for the priesthood. Their congregation became known as the Society of Saint-Sulpice and they established their first seminary in the United States in Baltimore, Maryland in 1791.

While the seminaries were responsible for a reduction in the widespread violations of clerical celibacy, they also had a long-lasting downside of a profound though not so obvious nature: They isolated prospective clerics from an early age to the time of ordination in an all-male environment. Formation in celibacy involved convincing the young men that life without sex of any kind was highly preferable to marriage. The spiritual benefits were openly promoted while the practical consequences remained mysteriously unspoken yet ever present and operative. Celibacy presented a path to spiritual superiority, which in turn supported the mystique that the clerics were somehow made of much stronger moral fiber to be able to withstand the urges of the flesh and devote themselves so totally to God. This mystique further isolated clerics and fortified the clerical caste as a social and religious elite. All positions of power were filled by celibate clerics. Promotion to the episcopate hinged not only on freedom from obvious celibacy violations but on the degree to which a man had espoused himself to the other-worldly ideal as a person set apart.

The seminaries were far from successful in bringing about a deep internal metamorphosis in all priestly candidates. Celibacy violations with women, men, and young boys continued, but for a time were much less visible. By 1566, in the first year of his pontificate, Pope Pius V (d. 1572) recognized a need to publicly denounce clerical sodomy. The constitution *Romani Pontifices* promulgated legislation against a variety of actions and practices, including the "crime against nature." This short canon condemned all who committed this crime and prescribed that they be handed over to secular authorities for punishment. Clerics, however, were to be first degraded, presumably by an ecclesiastical court, and then bound over to secular authorities.[80]

Two years later the same pope apparently found it necessary to fire another salvo at clerical sodomy. The constitution *Horrendum* specifically addressed clerics who committed "the sin against nature which incurred God's wrath" (*"quae contra naturam est, propter quam ira Dei venit in filios diffidentiae"*) and stipulated that they be punished with deprivation of income, suspension from all offices and dignities, and, in some cases, degradation.[81]

Solicitation of Sex in the Confessional

The sacrament of penance is one of the seven basic rituals of the Catholic Church. It is the means whereby church members are reconciled to the community after sinning. Most important, however, is the belief that this sacrament is the means by which Catholics are absolved of their sins and reinstated in God's favor. Indeed, the Council of Trent had stated that penance is essential for eternal salvation for those who fall into serious sin:

> For those who fall into sin after baptism the sacrament of penance is as necessary to salvation as is baptism for those who have not already been baptized.[82]

In the earliest centuries the sacrament was received in public and generally only once in a person's lifetime. The person was expected to confess or admit his or her sins before the assembly and then was admitted to the "order of penitents" and subjected to a lengthy period of severe fasting, prayer, and almsgiving. After the penance was completed, the penitent was absolved of his or her sins by the bishop and reconciled to the community and to God.

By the sixth century, the public administration of this sacrament had given way to a new form that was private and individual. The practice began in the Irish monasteries and was probably based on the custom of having a personal spiritual director, a tradition that encouraged the confession of one's faults with the imposition of a penance. This form quickly spread throughout the Christian world. The Fourth

Lateran Council (1215) mandated that every Catholic must confess his or her sins to a priest at least once a year.[83]

The essential elements of the sacrament are: the confession of sins by the penitent to the priest coupled with an expression of a firm intention not to repeat the same sins; the imposition by the priest of a penance such as prayers or fasting; and the recitation by the priest of the formula of absolution. Catholics believe that when the absolution is pronounced their sins are forgiven by God and their guilt absolved. To receive absolution validly the penitent was taught to confess his or her sins in kind and number, and profess sorrow and a purpose of amendment. Only a priest or bishop can administer the sacrament of penance and grant the absolution. He is considered a judge insofar as he weighs the gravity of the sin confessed, determines whether the penitent is truly sorry and worthy of receiving absolution, and imposes a sentence. The church's foremost theologians have taught that the priest's absolution was absolutely essential since the grace, or special divine favor, was conveyed not because of the penitent's spiritual state or sense of contrition but by the priest's action. The medieval theologian Duns Scotus taught that the essence of the sacrament was the pronouncement of the words of absolution without which there was no remission of sins.[84]

The sacrament of penance, or "confession" as it was popularly known, usually took place in a church, although the early legal literature provides no clear guidance in this regard. Confessions were most often heard face to face with nothing separating the penitent and the priest. In the sixteenth century the confessional, which was inaugurated in Milan by St. Charles Borromeo, was mandated by the Council of Trent (1545–63).[85]

Confessionals had various shapes and sizes but generally were constructed so that they provided a physical barrier between the priest and the penitent as well as a screen to preserve anonymity. Since the Council of Trent, confessionals are now found in most churches.

Despite the general rule that confessions should take place in a confessional, the practice of face-to-face confession continued and confessions were sometimes heard in priests' private homes and even in their private quarters.

To fully appreciate the power of the sacrament of penance one must understand the Catholic tradition of sin according to which a sin is an offense against God, usually by committing or omitting some external human act. As the doctrine of sin developed over the centuries, thoughts and inclinations, depending on their content, began to be included as potential sins. By the Medieval Period the scholastic tradition had developed some significant distinctions of sin, namely that there were two grades: mortal sin and venial sin. The church taught that those who died in the state of mortal sin were consigned to hell for eternity; venial sin was a lesser evil that did not result in eternal damnation.

The church also taught that its leaders, especially the popes, were empowered by God to determine what was and was not a sin. Consequently, as time passed, finite church leaders declared a broad spectrum of human acts to be sinful and therefore frowned upon by the infinite Creator of the Universe.

Sexual sins are the category that has traditionally caused Catholics the most stress and worry. The pessimistic view of sex that has prevailed throughout church history was at its worst in the Middle Ages and post-Reformation period. Some believed that any form of sexual enjoyment was sinful, even that which occurred between spouses.

The guilt, shame, and fear that welled up as a consequence of mortal sin could be quickly disposed of with the priest's absolution, but this came only after the sins were duly confessed.

The act of sacramental confession became the occasion for the most heinous form of clergy sexual abuse, namely the solicitation by the priest-confessor of sex with the penitent. The court records reveal that the actual sexual acts solicited included intercourse, oral and manual sex, verbal sex, and sadomasochistic sex. The documentation reveals that most victims were women (including young girls), although there is ample evidence to show that homosexual solicitation took place with great regularity.[86]

In canon law there are really two separate crimes involved. The first is the act of solicitation itself, which amounts to the manifestation of a desire to have some form of a sexual encounter. Generally this occurred verbally in the form of a request or urging. Then there was the matter of the sexual encounter itself. A careful reading of the cases on this crime indicates that the moralists and ecclesiastical judges considered the priest liable for at least two separate crimes or sins and the seduced penitent possibly liable for one, namely the sexual act.

Solicitation is especially odious because the victim who seeks forgiveness and comfort is at his or her most vulnerable. The priest's power to grant or withhold absolution, to assign and control penances, and his superior education and exalted social status makes the relationship inherently unequal. Added to this is the mysterious secrecy that surrounds the sacrament. The priest is under a most serious obligation never to reveal anything he hears in confession, even the fact that someone received the sacrament from him. The penitent is not covered by a similar obligation, yet is caught in a kind of canonical "Catch-22." Some penitent Catholics were so intimidated and convinced of the absolute necessity of absolution for their salvation that they succumbed to the solicitation because they feared the refusal of absolution. Also, if the penitent later decided to denounce the soliciting priest, he or she ran the risk of being accused of false denunciation and excommunication.

False denunciation became a crime even more odious than solicitation itself. The imbalance is indicative of the clericalism that has endured through the centuries. Traditionally, the penalties for solicitation have been far less severe than those assessed for false denunciation of a confessor. The present *Code of Canon Law* is an accurate reflection of that tradition. The section on the sacrament of penance contains a canon stipulating that if someone confesses to a priest that he or she has falsely denounced another priest, the penitent is not to be absolved of the sin until a retraction has been made and damages repaired.[87] The code makes no similar provision for a priest guilty of solicitation. Moreover, both the 1917 and 1983 codes stipulate that one who falsely accuses a priest of solicitation incurs an automatic interdict, a penalty similar in many ways to excommunication. On the other hand, there is no automatic penalty for a priest who solicits sex. Rather, the codes stated that the penalty of suspension was to be imposed along with other deprivations from ecclesiastical offices and, in more serious cases, dismissal or "defrocking" is recommended.[88] The canons reflect a serious imbalance because solicitation is only part of the criminal act by the priest; the actual sexual act is the other.

Solicitation for sex by confessors was first recorded by Peter Damian in his *Book of Gomorrah.*[89] He heaps great scorn and condemnation on "spiritual fathers" or confessors who engage in sex with female or male penitents and equates such actions with incest. We can presume that this problem was not isolated or unique but somewhat common. It represents a grave violation of the trust placed in the priest by the so-called spiritual child. The very concept of a "spiritual father" implies a power imbalance and a significant degree of control wielded by the priest over the layperson. It is not difficult to imagine the scenario because it is remarkably similar to those encountered in the civil courts in our own age when priests have taken sexual advantage of boys, girls, men, and women who have entrusted their spiritual destiny to them.

Following Peter's eleventh-century broadside there were other references to "spiritual incest." Gratian condemned priests who engaged in sex with their spiritual daughters and cited three decisions from two confirming authorities, Pope Symmachus (d. 514 CE) and Pope Celestine I (d. 432 CE). In each case the pope rightly condemned a priest who engaged in sex with a "spiritual daughter." Both were to be punished, indicating a presumption of some degree of consent on the part of the woman. However her penance was less severe than that assigned to the offending priest. It is not readily clear if "spiritual daughter" implied a woman whom the priest had baptized or one with whom he was involved in a counseling relationship. It matters not, however, because the popes recognized the evil that ensued as well as the misuse of ecclesiastical power.[90]

St. Thomas Aquinas was the best-known and most influential theologian in the history of the Catholic Church. He wrote that although a spiritual relationship, as a legal entity, did not arise between a woman and her priest confessor, the fact that she had received the sacrament of penance from him created a spiritual bond that was similar to it.[91] Consequently he says, "if he ha[s] carnal intercourse with her, he sins as grievously as if she were his spiritual daughter. The reason is that the relations between priest and penitent are most intimate."[92] Consequently, the sexual violation of a penitent by a priest is the moral equivalent of spiritual incest. It is described as such in the official theology and law of the church, a fact that points to the gravity of the harm done by the intrusion of some form of sex into such a sacred relationship.

The popes had issued decisions in individual cases condemning priests who seduced their "spiritual daughters." The canonists and theologians railed against this odious form of abuse, but by the end of the High Medieval Period (fourteenth century) there still were no official laws condemning the practice. One possible reason is the fact that the practice was considered so evil and the penances imposed so severe, that these proscriptions alone were deemed sufficient to prevent widespread abuse. Another possible reason is the fact that individual, auricular confession as the common and prescribed way of administering the sacrament of penance was not commonplace in those days.

In the opinion of the most trustworthy scholars of church law, the earliest diocesan legislation governing solicitation in the confessional came from Spain in the early sixteenth century. However, the Council of Treves (1227) decreed that confessors who were guilty of solicitation should lose their office and be excommunicated. Pope Pius IV (d. 1565) issued the constitution *Cum Sicut Nuper*, the first papal legislation condemning solicitation. It was directed at the Catholic Church in Spain and it would be another sixty years (1622) before his successor, Pope Gregory XV (1622–1623), would extend that same constitution to the whole church, making it the first universal legislation condemning solicitation. In his condemnation, Pope Gregory included under the rubric of "sex" both the request for some form of physical contact and sexually explicit conversation. In practice, female penitents frequently objected to being subjected to detailed questioning about their sex lives.

The legislation included penalties to be imposed on convicted clerics. It delegated competence or jurisdiction to prosecute cases to all local bishops and members of the Office of the Inquisition. The law was specific and straightforward. It was not published secretly but made known to all. Unfortunately, the local dioceses in several European countries (especially Spain, France, and Germany) paid little attention to the papal decree and continued to ignore accusations of solicitation and to treat accused priests with undue mildness.[93]

Canonists sent numerous requests for interpretations and clarifications to the pope. They wanted to know what types of questions constituted solicitation, what exactly constituted confession, whether solicitation occurred if it happened outside of the place for confessions, whether religious-order priests were subject to the law, and what amount and kind of corroborative proofs were needed.[94]

The next major legislation was the papal constitution *Sacramentum Poenitentiae*, issued June 1, 1741, by Pope Benedict XIV (1740–58).[95] This strong restatement of the law was prompted by the impact of the casuists who had succeeded in watering down the essence of the 1622 decree to the point where it was ineffectual in the life of the church. The pope decreed that all attempts to lead penitents astray were to be condemned.

This document is especially important for the following reasons: It condemned the practice of priests granting absolution to the very persons with whom they engaged in solicitation. This crime is mentioned in both codes of canon law and is considered especially odious.[96] It cast aside the canonical equivalent of a statute of limitations stating that it mattered not when the solicitation occurred. The priest accused was to be prosecuted and punished no matter how much time had elapsed. The overall tone of Benedict's decree revealed a significant sensitivity to the spiritual damage done to solicited penitents. Superiors (bishops and their equivalent) were ordered to take special care of those led astray by confessors. People who confessed they had been solicited were to be strongly urged to denounce the one soliciting. The standards of proof were relaxed to allow for one corroborative witness, and the document itself was to be widely publicized.

The 1741 document was deemed so important that direct reference was made to it in the 1917 *Code of Canon Law* (Canon 904)—the church's first official codification of laws—and the entire text is included as an appendix.

Little more could be added to the detail and force of Pope Benedict's decree. Yet the problem continued. A major impediment to prosecuting sexually abusive confessors was the reluctance of victims to come forward and press charges. Pope Gregory's and Pope Benedict's decrees contain statements urging solicited penitents to turn in their perpetrators. Since this obviously was not successful, the church authorities turned to more stringent measures. It introduced legislation imposing severe punishments, including excommunication, on people who failed to denounce priests who had solicited them in the confessional.[97] The 1917 code retained this excommunication in Canon 2368.2, which stipulated that the person solicited not be absolved until he or she had either denounced the offending cleric or seriously promised to do so in the near future.

Charles Henry Lea, in *A History of the Inquisition in Spain*, a monumental study of solicitation cases from the Spanish Inquisition, points to the obvious impact of clericalism in undermining the church's own legislation. In spite of the harsh measures promulgated by the popes, local courts continued to discriminate in favor of the confessors. Local judges appealed to the dignity of the priesthood and scandal to the church as excuses for adding unrealistic burdens of proof on accusers.[98]

Although most of the solicitation cases involved women, Lea references at least one Spanish priest who was tried and exiled for having victimized a young boy.[99] Stephen Haliczer, in his *Sexuality in the Confessional: A Sacrament*

Profaned also refers to homosexual solicitation, as well as solicitation of young victims:

The growth of monastic colleges, the increasing role of the priesthood in providing primary education for boys to which girls had no access, and the establishment of seminaries also provided homosexual priests with many opportunities.[100]

The cases studied by Lea and Haliczer reveal youthful victims to be in the minority, however this is not sufficient to draw any conclusions about the actual age ratio of victims. Haliczer adds a further observation that some priests resorted to the confessional to seduce young girls, but many who preferred young boys were able to seduce their students outside the confessional.[101] In practice, only a small number of offenders were denounced and, of these, only a fraction were brought to trial. Those who were tried, however, were nearly always convicted.[102]

The investigation and prosecution of accused priests was a public matter. The amount of legislation and the recurring attempts by the papacy to enforce its legislation and eliminate favoritism toward accused priests clearly indicates that the problem was considered to be especially destructive to the clerical establishment, the laity, and secular society. The consistency and amount of legislation from the sixteenth to the nineteenth centuries led to a strong presumption that such errant sexual behavior by some priests was not only widespread but predictable. Lax interpretation of papal statutes and favoritism toward accused priests appears to have been the norm rather than the exception. Despite this laxity, the number of completed trials—said to be a small minority of actual cases—leads to the staggering view that the crime of solicitation was a predictable way of life in the church.

The Spanish and Mexican Inquisitions have been the subject of most studies of confessional solicitation. This means only that court records were better preserved and more readily available, and not that solicitation rarely occurred in other countries.

Haliczer studied 223 cases from 1530 to 1819.[103] Lea, in his survey of tribunal registers, found 3,775 completed cases between 1723 and 1820. He also noted that a large proportion of the accused occupied prominent positions.[104]

Numerous canonical inquiries regarding solicitation were submitted to the Vatican between 1741 and the promulgation of the first code of canon law in 1917. All were concerned with some aspect of the application of the law and none of the responses in any way minimized the evil of the crime itself. Finally, in 1917, a code was promulgated containing specific canons condemning solicitation, false denunciation, and the failure to denounce.

The Vatican Secret Directive

The Vatican issued legislation in 1922 about solicitation and other forms of clergy sexual crime and again in 1962 when Pope John XXIII (d. 1963) approved the publication of *De Modo Procedendi in Causis Solicitationis*, a special procedural law for processing cases of solicitation. Unlike all previous papal legislation on this subject, these documents were buried in the deepest secrecy. Although the 1962 document was promulgated in the ordinary manner and then printed and distributed by the Vatican Press, it was never publicized in the official Vatican legal bulletin, the *Acta Apostolicae Sedis*.[105] The document was sent to every bishop and major religious superior in the world. The dispositive section of the document is preceded by an order whereby the document is to be kept in the diocesan secret archives and not published nor commented upon by anyone. No explicit reason was given for this unusual secrecy, nor was any justification given for the document or some of the innovations contained in it.

The 1922 document bears the same title as that of 1962. However, it is still buried in secrecy; it has never been located and has not been made available even to canon lawyers.[105a] There is a 1959 letter of Bishop Francis Leipzig from Baker, Washington, that makes specific reference to the document when he appointed a notary in a case "*De Crimine Pessimo*, which is now pending before our tribunal." The other sources of confirmation of the existence and nature of the document are footnotes in scholarly articles. They identify the content when they comment that the sexual abuse of a minor by any cleric has consistently been reserved to the Congregation for the Doctrine of the Faith (CDF) and any questions involving the application of penalties at that time for past incidents could still only be resolved by that congregation.[105b]

The 1962 document is a procedural law text providing detailed steps for the process to be followed when prosecuting accusations of solicitation. Heretofore, the bishops were to follow the general law of the code in processing cases. The new document introduced several significant elements, including an exceptional degree of confidentiality imposed on the document itself and the people involved in processing cases.

Until 1962, the official policy had been publicly known. The 1917 code provided a relatively open process for dealing with sexual abuse by clerics. Confidentiality was required to protect reputations, yet the entire issue was not enshrouded in this highest level of secrecy.

The 1962 legislation, a reflection of the church's policy on clergy sexual crimes, introduced the following innovations:

- Local ordinaries (bishops and heads of religious orders) were given the right to process cases covered in this document; however, they retain the option of sending them to the Vatican's Congregation of the Holy Office for prosecution.

- Tribunal and other church personnel who were involved in processing cases were bound by the church's highest degree of confidentiality—the Secret of the Holy Office—to maintain total and perpetual secrecy; those who violated this secrecy were automatically excommunicated and the absolution, or lifting, of this excommunication was reserved to the pope himself.

- Even the accuser and witnesses were obliged to take the oath of secrecy. Although the penalty of automatic excommunication was not attached to the violation of their oath, the official conducting the prosecution could, in individual cases, threaten accusers and witnesses with automatic excommunication for breaking the secret.

- Anonymous accusations were not automatically ruled out, though they were generally rejected; they were to be considered and acted upon if circumstances required and if there appeared to be some semblance of veracity to the accusation.

- Title V of the document specifically included homosexual acts between clerics and members of their own sex (Par. 70), bestiality, and sexual acts of any kind with children (Par. 73). The document used the Latin word "*impubes*" (lit. beardless) taken to mean "before the age of reason," which is defined in Canon 88 as seven or under. The code also contains a canon prohibiting sex with minors, which is defined in canon law as a person sixteen or under. A careful reading of the relevant paragraphs of the 1962 document (Par. 71–73) leads to some confusion as to whom the crimes apply. It is clear that sex with children and with males of any age, as well as sex with animals, is included; is unclear if sex with young girls is.

The other sex crimes included under Title V are not crimes connected with solicitation but the actual sexual abuse itself. These are to be processed in the same manner as crimes of solicitation. Thus the three classes of clergy sexual abuse were cloaked for the first time in the highest degree of secrecy.

Little was known about the 1962 document until reference to it was included in a letter sent by the CDF to every bishop in 2001. Titled *Sacramentorum Sanctitatis Tutela,* that letter dealt with grave crimes reserved for consideration to that same Vatican office.[106] The 1962 document had been issued prior to the promulgation of the revised *Code of Canon Law* in 1983, and therefore would, under ordinary circumstances, have lost its legal force by then. *Sacramentorum Sanctitatis Tutela,* however, clearly indicates that the 1962 document had been in force until May 2001.

When the existence of the 1962 document was publicly revealed—in March 2003—it surprised many bishops and canon lawyers who claimed they had not known of its existence. Furthermore, there is little if any evidence that the document was ever referred to in any of the hundreds of civil cases brought against dioceses and religious communities over the last fifteen years of the twentieth century.

The 1962 document is significant because it reflects the church's insistence on maintaining the highest degree of secrecy regarding the worst sexual crimes perpetrated by clerics. The document does not say why it was issued, nor is any reason given for the imposition of extreme secrecy and the inclusion of other crimes in Title V. One can only presume that cases or concerns that had been brought to the attention of the Vatican authorities had prompted the decree.

Because the archives of the Holy Office, now known as the CDF, are closed to outside scrutiny, it is impossible to determine the number of cases referred to it between 1962 and the present. Moreover, local dioceses are prohibited from ever revealing the very existence of cases, much less the relevant facts.

The public exposure of clergy sexual abuse of youth that began in the mid-1980s was mistakenly believed by many to be a new phenomenon, which of course it was not. Yet, despite a series of high-profile cases from around the world, the Vatican issued no disciplinary documents until 2001. The pope had made several statements about clerical sexual abuse, but this was the first attempt by the Vatican to take concrete steps to contain the problem. This document, which is a set of special procedural norms, is not exclusively about sex abuse, although that is the predominant theme. It is about the processing of certain crimes considered by the Vatican authorities to be so serious that their prosecution is reserved to the Vatican itself.

The 2001 document reflects much that is found in the 1962 procedural norms. There are significant developments however:

- The bishop or other superior of an alleged perpetrator of sexual abuse was obliged to send the results of his preliminary investigation to the Vatican, and officials there would decide if the case would be processed in the Vatican or returned to the local diocese for prosecution.
- The canonical age of a minor was raised from 16 to 18.
- The statute of limitations was extended to ten years and, in the case of sexual abuse of a minor, this time would begin to run from the victim's eighteenth birthday.

- All officials involved in processing cases were required to be priests.
- Files of cases completed on the local levels were to be sent to the Vatican for retention.
- The Pontifical Secret, formerly known as the Secret of the Holy Office, was imposed on all officials connected to any cases, but no mention was made of imposing the secret on accusers or witnesses.

This 2001 document reflects the same attitude of exclusivity and secrecy that has marked the church's attitude toward clergy sex crimes from the early twentieth century to the present.[107] Although some of these sex crimes are also criminal acts in secular society there is no requirement or recommendation to report accused clerics to civil authorities in any Vatican documents from the eighteenth century to the present. Indeed, private statements by high-ranking and influential church officials reveal a highly defensive and obstructionist attitude. Fr. Gianfranco Ghirlanda S.J., former rector of the Gregorian University and dean of its canon law department, has stated that church leaders should attempt to solve abuse cases themselves without referring them to civil authorities in order to avoid future civil implications.[108] A *Baltimore Sun* article dated May 22, 2002 cites Archbishop (now a cardinal and president of the Pontifical Council for the Interpretation of Legislative Texts) Julian Herranz as saying that bishops should not be required to turn files on abusive priests over to civil authorities. Other news sources cite church officials who blame the U.S. secular media for escalating the sex abuse issue and even of persecuting the Catholic Church.[109]

The defensive reaction of high-ranking churchmen and influential Catholic media reflects a long-standing attitude at the highest level of church authority: denial and blame-shifting. Church leadership now, as in the past, has strongly resisted any attempts to study its own role in the unsuccessful handling of abuse cases. It is even more resistant to any consideration of the viability of mandatory celibacy itself.

Clergy Sexual Abuse in the Modern Era

Sexual abuse of minors and adults by Catholic clergy has continued without interruption from the post-Apostolic era to the present. Despite claims from church leaders that the current outbreak of abuse accusations is new, there is sufficient evidence to conclude that the only new aspect is the aggressive exposé by the secular press. The most telling evidence in our own era, as in the past, is found in the records of the institutional church.

When, on January 6, 2002, the *Boston Globe* published its first story about sexually abusive priests in the archdiocese, the investigative team speculated that perhaps ten or twelve similar cases might unravel. The *Globe* got the courts to order the release of sealed church documents and by the time its reporters had completed their investigation, more that 150 priest-abuse cases had been identified and 1,200 stories had been written. The secret system of concealment by church officials and psychiatrists was breached. The patterns of abuse, the conspiracy to cover up abuse, and the neglect to inform and protect others from abuse were laid bare. Quickly it became apparent that the pattern and practice of clergy sexual abuse was not limited to Boston. But Boston exposed a template to which the entire American Catholic Church conformed.

Several grand jury investigations have concluded that some dioceses have been complicit in the abuse of minors and are not capable of managing the problem (e.g., Rockville Center, New York; Boston, Massachusetts; Phoenix, Arizona;

and New Hampshire). More than a dozen more grand juries have yet to report the findings in their jurisdictions.

Father Gerald Fitzgerald, who founded the Servants of the Paraclete in 1947, wrote in 1952 that he had already treated a handful of priests who abused minors. He found them "lacking in appreciation of the seriousness of their offence and situation" and he favored laicization for any priest who "tampered with the virtue of the young." He stated in a letter to Bishop Robert Dwyer of Reno, Nevada, that "in practice, real conversions will be found to be extremely rare. Many bishops believe men are never free from the approximate danger once they have begun."

Especially damning evidence turned up in files produced in the civil trials of sexually abusive priests. For instance in 1957, Fr. Fitzgerald, who treated the priests, wrote to Archbishop Edwin Byrne of Santa Fe, New Mexico, that he thought it unwise to "offer hospitality to men who have seduced or attempted to seduce little boys or girls." He then wrote the following words, all the more ominous in light of today's crisis:

> If I were a bishop I would tremble when I failed to report them to Rome for involuntary laicization. Experience has taught us these men are too dangerous to the children of the parish and the neighborhood for us to be justified in receiving them here. ... They should *ipso facto* be reduced to lay men when they act thus.[110]

By 1963 the Paracletes were treating so many sexually abusive priests that they had developed a shorthand to describe the offence—"Code 3." In the same year, Fr. Fitzgerald wrote to the bishop of Norwich, Connecticut, reminding him of the "gravity of this offence (sex abuse of a minor) which has strong civil and even stronger divine retributive sanctions."

Despite Fr. Fitzgerald's serious reservations and dire prognosis, the Paraclete facility, which had been treating problem clergy since its foundation in 1947, began specializing in the treatment of pedophile priests in 1966.

The dearth of publicized accusations and civilian prosecutions prior to 1985 point to the success of the church's secretive strategies for handling abusive clerics. The number of civil cases of proven clergy sexual abuse from the 1980s was sizeable enough to conclude that the problem was present but well hidden. Writer, psychotherapist, and researcher A. W. Richard Sipe has studied clerical celibacy for decades. Reflecting on the state of affairs in the middle of the twentieth century, he stated in a recent affidavit:

> When I entered the priesthood (1959) the sexual activities of supposedly celibate priests and religious were kept from the public by a closed system which I have referred to as the "celibate/sexual system." ... In the late 1950s and early 1960s, when knowledge left the closed system it entered into the psychiatric system. ... For the next ten years the sexual problems of the Catholic clergy were subsumed under the umbrella of other psychiatric problems, especially alcoholism.[111]

Sipe refers to several early efforts by some clergy to confront clergy sexual abuse. The first of these was at a meeting sponsored by the National Association for Pastoral Renewal held at Notre Dame University in 1967. In 1968, the National Conference of Catholic Bishops commissioned a series of investigations into the U.S. priesthood, which were published in 1972. These included psychological investigations conducted by Eugene Kennedy and Victor Heckler.[112]

The American bishops publicly acknowledged their concern in the mid-eighties, and one bishop admitted in a 1995 deposition that the problem was being discussed by them as early as 1971.[113]

A significant factor in the cover-up has been the power of clericalism and religious duress felt by individuals and imposed on secular institutions. Victims have been emotionally unable to disclose their abuse at the hands of clerics simply because of the church-instilled fear of divine retribution against them for saying anything negative about a priest. The same fear has prevented parents from even believing the tales their children have told them or, if they did believe, from going public.[114]

Church leaders have used their positions of power to persuade civic leaders to cooperate in facilitating and supporting their methods of handling claims of clergy sexual abuse. Police captains saw to it that priests caught in compromising situations were secretly returned to their bishops, and judges took care that charges were never filed. Influence with the publishers and editors of the secular news media assured that no stories ever appeared.

Most candidates for the priesthood or religious life have not been adequately prepared to lead a life devoid of intimacy or sexual expression. Formation took place in an all-male environment where women were considered a serious threat to celibacy and chastity. Church authorities commonly warned against heterosexual relationships and "solitary sins." In a section dealing with priests resigning their ministry, a 1961 Vatican instruction on the training of candidates for the priesthood stated the following:

> Sometimes these religious priests affirm that it is now impossible for them to observe chastity, first because of bad habits contracted in youth, which were sometimes correct-

ed but still never completely eradicated, and secondly because of sexual tendencies of a pathological nature, which they feel cannot be brought under control either by ordinary or extraordinary means, even those of a spiritual order, in such a way that they frequently fall into solitary sin.[115]

Dire warnings were issued against the many dangers that could cause clerics to stray. This same document quotes Pope Pius XII who said in a 1950 statement:

But they are likewise to be warned of the dangers into which they can fall on this account. Consequently, candidates for Sacred Orders are to be exhorted to protect themselves from dangers from their earliest years.[116]

This 1961 instruction sets standards for prospective priests. It cites Canon 1371 (1917 Code) and mandates that candidates who have "sinned gravely" against the Sixth Commandment with a person of the same or the other sex is to be immediately dismissed.[117] The same section makes explicit reference to homosexual activity:

Advancement to religious vows and ordination should be barred to those who are afflicted with evil tendencies to homosexuality or pederasty, since for them the common life and the priestly ministry would constitute serious dangers.[118]

There have been significant warnings to church leaders about the impending exposure of celibacy violations. Dr. Conrad Baars and Dr. Anna Terruwe presented a scholarly paper to the 1971 Synod of Bishops at the Vatican and shortly after to the U.S. Conference of

Catholic bishops. Citing forty years of combined psychiatric practice treating about 1,500 priests, they concluded that 20–25 percent of North American priests had serious psychiatric difficulties and 60–70 percent suffered from emotional immaturity. They concluded that the psychosexual immaturity manifested itself in heterosexual and homosexual activity.[119]

The following year, Kennedy and Heckler's study was published and their findings concurred with those of Baars and Terruwe, concluding that just 7 percent of American priests were psychologically and emotionally developed; 18 percent were psychologically and emotionally developing; 66 percent were underdeveloped; and 8 percent were maldeveloped.[120]

Kennedy and Heckler stated that the underdeveloped and maldeveloped priests (74 percent) had unresolved psychosexual problems and issues that are usually worked through in adolescence, adding:

> Sexuality is, in other words, non-integrated into the lives of underdeveloped priests and many of them function at a pre-adolescent or adolescent level of psychosexual growth.[121]

Eighteen years later (1990) Sipe, with twenty-five years experience of counseling priests to his credit, published the results of an extensive study on the lived reality of mandatory celibacy.[122] His data was based on interviews with 1,500 priests or their sexual partners between 1960 and 1985. He concluded that 6 percent of priests were sexually involved with minors, 20–25 percent with adult women, and 15 percent with adult men. Sipe published a revised edition of his 1990 book in 2003. Titled *Celibacy in Crisis: A Secret World Revisited*, this work opens a window into the secret world of celibacy as it is lived well into the contemporary crisis. In a private communication Sipe stated that his original estimates remain valid.[123]

The large number of priests who have left the active ministry since the Vatican Council is another indicator of the fragility of celibacy, which the institutional church refuses to acknowledge. Although an estimated 125,000 priests[124] departed the ministry between 1965 and 1990, the Vatican continues to exalt the clerical state, insisting that celibacy is liveable and essential to priesthood and refusing to entertain any discussion to the contrary.[125]

The Baars and Kennedy studies were motivated in part by the numbers of priests departing the ministry in the years following Vatican II. Both studies clearly predicted impending disasters, especially related to the sexual behavior of clerics. The American bishops listened to neither study and consigned both to the shelves as irrelevant, but in reality, much too challenging for the bishops to digest and accept. Sipe's prophetic 1990 book suffered a similar fate. His work has been largely ignored and the bishops have yet to call on his expertise.

Throughout the centuries, the hierarchy has not been prophetic or proactive in relation to the never-ending violations of celibacy. Clandestine marriages and stable but nonmarital relationships are the least offensive and problematic category since they reflect a normal sexual development. Sexual abuse of vulnerable adults is true abuse but has been tolerated and is often dismissed by church authorities with the myth that it was somehow caused by the victim.

The most deplorable version of sexual activity is the sexual abuse of children and young people. The official *Catechism of the Catholic Church*, in a remarkable passage, accurately describes what has been happening to thousands at the hands of the church's own ordained representatives:

> Connected to incest is any sexual abuse perpetrated by adults on children or adolescents entrusted to their care. The offense is com-

pounded by the scandalous harm done to the physical and moral integrity of the young, who will remain scarred by it all their lives; and the violation of responsibility for their upbringing.[126]

The catalyst for the current chapter in the celibacy debacle was a known and treated pedophile priest in Lafayette, Louisiana, who in 1984 finally pled guilty to having raped thirty-nine of his many victims. This case led to the creation in 1985 of the 100-page book, *The Problem of Sexual Molestation by Roman Catholic Clergy: Meeting the Problem in a Comprehensive and Responsible Manner* (Cf. Part II, Ch. 4).[127] This handbook, commonly called the *Manual,* was prepared solely on the initiative of the three authors with the moral support and input of a number of influential bishops. The U.S. Conference of Catholic Bishops, though aware of the manual, dismissed it as unnecessary claiming that they possessed all the data contained in it and already had policies and procedures in place.[128]

The most dramatic indicator of the predictability of clerical abuse and the institutional church's failure to act responsibly is the number of sexually abusive clerics identified in the United States alone over the past two decades. Reliable but unofficial figures point to 2,600 verified names of accused priests, deacons, and religious brothers. The John Jay College Survey, commissioned by the bishops, found 4,450 accused clerics from 1950 to the present. A review in 2005 recorded an additional roster of 1,000 complaints bringing the number of abusive priests to over 5,000. This is twice the number expected by survivor's groups, which means the final total will be far more than had been expected.[129] Included in this number presumably are the sixteen U.S. bishops who have been publicly named as sexual abusers.[130]

Unofficial Vatican sources and other ranking prelates have attributed the contemporary phenomenon to media exaggeration,[131] weakness of faith, and secular materialistic morality, among other reasons. The most prestigious source, the pope, has attributed the problem to personal sin on the part of clergy abusers as well as to external forces such as an overly sexually charged American culture, but has adamantly insisted that mandatory celibacy is not connected to it:

> These scandals, and a sociological rather than theological concept of the Church, sometimes lead to calls for a change in the discipline of celibacy. However, we cannot overlook the fact that the Church recognizes God's will through the interior guidance of the Holy Spirit and that the Church's living tradition constitutes a clear affirmation of the consonance of celibacy, for profound theological and anthropological reasons, with the sacramental character of the priesthood. The difficulties involved in preserving chastity are not sufficient reason for overturning the law of celibacy.[132]

Conclusions

The Catholic Church has attempted to impose celibacy on its clerics since the fourth century. The church's own legal documents and authoritative pronouncements from then until the present clearly reveal a consistent pattern of non-celibate behavior by significant numbers of priests. The church's canonical crusades targeted both legal and illegal sexual behavior. The legal behavior consisted of various attempts to prevent married priests from having sex with

their wives. The illegal behavior included widespread concubinage, homosexual activities, and sex with minors.

The Protestant Reformation and the Council of Trent
were pivotal points in church history. The church's role and
place in society were fundamentally transformed after this
period and this change influenced the way clergy sexual mis-
deeds were handled. Prior to the Reformation, the Catholic
Church was the largest organized Christian body in the
Western world. It was intimately intertwined with most
aspects of secular society, including the governmental and
judicial arms. The church was the most powerful element of
society and also the most influential. This role was so dominant that the church's power was secure, not depending in
any way on public affirmation or monetary donations.
Thus, the Catholic Church was not concerned about adverse
publicity generated by the illegal or immoral conduct of its
clergy in the same way it is today.

The Reformation shook the Catholic Church to its political and religious roots. Secular leaders chose sides, and their
alignments with the reformers or the institutional church
determined the religious affiliation of their people. For the
first time in its history, the institutional church found its
power and monolithic control threatened. From that point
on, one sees a pattern of secrecy emerging with the church's
response to clerical sexual issues.

Although the canonical legislation contained specific
canons that criminalized the sexual abuse of minors, there is
no evidence that violations of this crime were ever prosecuted according to the church's own norms.[133] The 1962 document issued by the Holy Office was in effect until 2001. Yet
no documentary evidence produced by dioceses in civil suits
between 1985 and the present contained any reference to
this document or any indication that the prescribed norms
were ever followed.

Throughout the centuries, clerical celibacy developed along two parallel lines: the doctrinal and disciplinary statements establishing and extolling celibacy, and the consistent but futile attempts at enforcing the legislation. There have been certain moments in this chronological development when the challenge to celibacy was especially dramatic—such as the eleventh century, which resulted in Peter Damian's *Book of Gomorrah* and the Gregorian Reform, the Protestant Reformation followed by the Council of Trent, and the current drama.

The church's leadership has been consistent in two areas: the adamant defense of the celibacy ideal[134] and inability to enforce it. There have been other consistent patterns in the official church response to clerical sexual activities:

- Victims have never been accorded compassionate pastoral treatment commensurate with the grievous emotional and spiritual damage done to them by sexually abusive clerics and the church's leaders.
- Church leaders have known about and expected a variety of violations of clerical celibacy, especially sexual abuse of vulnerable people.
- Church leaders have used their influence in the community to protect secrecy and prevent clergy offenders from becoming publicly known.
- The penalties imposed on clerics for violation of celibacy laws have generally been lenient. In the contemporary period, penalties were imposed only when the church leadership was forced to act, but usually the accused clerics were simply moved to another location. No canonical penal investigations were initiated until the period after 2002.

The ideal of mandatory celibacy has not been realized for a significant number of Catholic clerics throughout history. The institutional church has lived with the realization of consistent violations, many of them criminal in nature, yet it has denied the possibility that the policy of mandatory celibacy might be fundamentally flawed. The refusal to even study the viability of mandatory celibacy, as well as the self-serving manner with which the church has handled violations of the canons, have resulted in grave harm to thousands of victims of clerical sexual abuse.

Clergy sexual abuse of minors and vulnerable adults has occurred from the earliest centuries. It has been known to church authorities and is a predictable but highly unfortunate feature of clerical life. It has been denied and hidden by bishops and popes who have consistently acted in a conspiratorial manner to prevent instances of abuse from becoming publicly known, especially to law-enforcement authorities.

Such patterns of behavior shock Catholics and non-Catholics alike. People are perplexed as to how the Catholic Church, with its tradition of strict and unbending sexual morality, can at the same time not only tolerate but enable thousands of sexually dysfunctional clerics with little or no honest regard for the physical, emotional, and spiritual devastation of their countless victims. Yet this sad state of affairs is predictable—but certainly not acceptable—within the much broader context of the institutional church's traditional image of itself.

The church teaches that its hierarchical governmental structure is of divine origin. Ultimately all real power rests in individual office holders and not in collective bodies. The pope is the embodiment of all judicial, legislative, and executive power for the entire church (Canons 331, 333) and each diocesan bishop possesses similar fullness of power in his own diocese (Canon 381). Since there is no separation of powers there are no effective checks and balances. In effect, the hierarchical structure takes on many of the characteristics of monarchical government. For centuries, the Catholic Church has claimed to be a "perfect society," a juridical term denoting its independence and self-sufficiency. That claim made way for the introduction of juridical and sociological categories into ecclesiological thought[135] and was adopted at a time when papal authority was being centralized, lay control was being weakened, and the church's legal structure was evolving. Consequently, the church's governing structure and the clerical sub-class that held all positions of power within it took on an absolute value. The concept "good of the church" meant, in effect, the good of the church's governing structure and its power holders.

The Second Vatican Council resurrected the ancient definition of the church as the "People of God," with emphasis on the dignity and rights of all its members. The revised *Code of Canon Law*, however, preserved the monarchical nature of the main church offices of pope and bishop as well as the privileged nature of the clerical state.[136] Critics of the present state of affairs have studied the reign of Pope John Paul II since its inception in 1978 and have concluded that he has turned the church back from the visionary days of Vatican II to the monarchical state of Vatican I (1870). Theologian Anthony Padovano, in an address to the national conference of the reform movement, Call to Action, November 7–8, 2003, said:

> This papacy has destroyed the effectiveness of the International Synod of Bishops, the most impressive collegial structure set up by Vatican II. It has taken direct aim at freedom of speech and inquiry with its mandatum of episcopal approval for Catholic theologians and threatened them thereby with dismissal and loss of livelihood if they are not compliant. ... This is not a papacy that people turn to for healing; indeed it has left in its wake countless wounded Catholics, the collateral damage it inflicted

as it imposed on the Church an abusive system of authority and control.[137]

The monarchical concept of church has existed for centuries. This political structure has sustained and nurtured the clerical subculture that governs it and controls not only the temporal aspects but the spiritual as well. The church teaches that the sacraments are the indispensable means for eternal salvation for Catholics. The clergy and hierarchy control access to the sacraments. This profound source of power protects and enables the clerical culture, the monarchical government, and the deep and mysterious influence that the institutional church wields over individual Catholics and secular powers as well.

The apparent complicity of church leadership in the tragedy of clergy sexual abuse throughout the centuries is explained in great part by the tenacity of the "perfect society" model. The collision course then is not simply between the "celibacy for the kingdom" ideal and the perennial leniency toward clergy who violate its obligations. It goes far deeper: The clash is between the defense and protection of the church as Kingdom and the life and vitality of the church as Christian Community and People of God.

Chapter 2
Sex, Sin, and Psychiatry

Up until the 1950s, clerics in positions of responsibility within the American Catholic Church were aware of sexual activity by priests, including sexual activity with minors, because as bishops, religious superiors, or vicars, they were aware of rumors, suspicions, reports, and complaints of abuse. They dealt with problems as they arose. Although that knowledge was kept from the general public, it was known within what's called the "celibate/sexual system." In the late 1950s and early 1960s, that knowledge left the system and entered into the psychiatric system. Psychiatry and psychology were used to treat offending clerics, contain scandal, and placate the civil legal system if the cleric ran afoul of the law of the land. Victims and their families were usually reassured by church authorities with the mantra "Father is our problem and we will take care of the problem." Most of the time, however, the problem was subsequently ignored.

For close to a decade after psychiatry began to be used as a treatment resource, the sexual problems of the clergy were subsumed under the umbrella of other psychiatric problems, especially alcoholism, the first condition to be differentiated as a specific disorder afflicting clergy. A 20 percent lifetime incidence of alcohol problems among Catholic clergy was projected in the 1960s. Instances of sexual acting out were often causally related to a history of excessive drinking.

Over time, psychosexual disorders were differentiated from alcoholism, depression, schizophrenia, characterological disorders, and sin. Although the terms "pedophilia" (sex with a pre-pubescent child) and even more so, the term "ephebophilia" (sex with an adolescent) were not in common usage, there is no doubt that by 1976, the problem of Catholic clergy sexually acting out with minors was recognized as a serious mental health concern.

The first public discussion of priest sexual abuse of minors took place at a meeting sponsored by the National Association for Pastoral Renewal held on the campus of Notre Dame University in 1967. All American Catholic bishops were invited to attend.

Then, in 1968, the newly formed National Conference of Catholic Bishops authorized a series of investigations of the priesthood in the United States and these were published in 1972. The reports contained detailed and extensive historical, sociological, and psychological investigations. The investigations found that two-thirds of Catholic priests in the United States were underdeveloped emotionally and only one-tenth were developed. These findings reflected observations already made by professional psychotherapists treating priests at various centers throughout the United States.

The Kennedy–Heckler study, already noted, found that 57 percent of Catholic priests were underdeveloped, 29 percent were developing, 8 percent were maldeveloped, and only 6 percent were developed emotionally. These figures were scientific verifications of what was experimentally known by bishops and religious superiors.

The Advent of Reporting Laws

The institutional secrecy surrounding sexual activities with minors on the part of Catholic priests and religious began to crumble in 1962 when states first began to pass legislation requiring people who know about sexual abuse of children to report it to the appropriate civil authorities. These laws highlighted the growing awareness, based on professional research, of the severe harm that sexual abuse engendered in child victims. By 1968, virtually all states had reporting laws, and in 1974 federal legislation mandating the provision of reporting laws in each state was passed. However, Catholic Church authorities were still not mandated to report knowledge of the sexual abuse of minors in every state, and even where they were obliged, they did not necessarily comply with the law.

Statutes criminalizing sexually acting out with minors had been passed in the 1930s and 1940s, but these laws were rarely enforced until many years after the passage of statutes mandating the reporting of such misbehavior. However, the 1974 federal legislation put pressure on psychiatry and psychology because it was the first outside intrusion into the confidentiality of the relationship between therapist and patient. In 1976, prompted by the duty to report suspected sexual activity with children, Dr. Leo Bartemeier, a psychiatrist who had been consulting with church authorities since the 1930s, and Richard Sipe, a psychotherapist with extensive experience of clerical abusers, estimated that 6 percent of all Catholic clergy and religious acted out sexually with minors.

The Opening of Catholic Treatment Centers

Already in 1924 priest-psychiatrist Thomas Verner Moore was treating priest and nun patients at Mount Hope Retreat (later named Seton Institute) in Baltimore, Maryland. In the same year he proposed to build a hospital on the grounds of the Catholic University in Washington, D.C. to care for the mental health needs of troubled priests. In 1936 he wrote two landmark articles in *The Ecclesiastical Review:* "The Rate of Insanity in Priests and Religious," and its companion piece, "The Detection of Presychotics Who Apply for Admission to the Priesthood or Religious Communities"[137a] constituted the first recorded psychological guide for the screening and selection of candidates to the priesthood. It took another two decades before psychological testing gained acceptance in the screening of clerical candidates.

In the early 1950s, Fr. William Bier, a Jesuit from Fordham University, advocated psychological testing of candidates for the priesthood to eliminate problem priests, including those who acted out sexually. Fr. Bier's writings and advocacy of the use of screening tests reflected a growing awareness within the Catholic Church that sexual activity by men professing celibacy constituted not just a predictable sin, but contained psychological components as well. Previously, a priest who had sex or fell in love was regarded as someone afflicted with ordinary and expectable moral/spiritual problems.

The growing recognition of the psychological dimension of such problems coincided with the opening of Catholic treatment centers devoted seriously to the treatment of priests and religious. The U.S. Jesuits trained nine priest-psychiatrists, and programs that took into account the psychological dimension of moral/spiritual problems were conducted for novice masters and spiritual directors in the early 1950s.

Fr. Jerome Hayden, a Benedictine priest and psychiatrist, founded a psychiatric center primarily for children with psychological problems—The Marselan Institute—in Massachusetts in the 1950s. The Marselan Institute was the predecessor to St. Luke Institute, which Fr. Michael Peterson founded in 1981 when Fr. Hayden died. St. Luke's moved to rural Maryland and evolved into the most prominent treatment center in the United States for priests with behavioral problems. Between 1986 and 2001 over three hundred priests with sexual problems were treated there.

In 1954, Dr. Francis Braceland, a devout Catholic who attended daily mass, became medical director of The Hartford Retreat in Connecticut. This venerable institution—it had opened as The Asylum in 1822—has since been renamed the Institute of Living. Dr. Braceland was vitally interested in the interface of religion with psychiatry. He edited a book on the subject, *Faith, Reason and Modern Psychiatry*, (P.J. Kennedy and Sons, New York: 1955) that included essays by some of the leading scholars of the time: Dr. Gregory Zilboorg; Dominican psychologist, Fr. Noel Mailloux; Dr. Rudolph Allers; Dr. Karl Stern; and Jesuit priest, Fr. John La Farge. Dr. Braceland consulted widely with bishops and religious superiors about the psychiatric problems of priests and encouraged the referral of problem priests to his institute.

As stated earlier, in 1947, the Servants of the Paraclete, in the person of Fr. Gerald Fitzgerald, opened their first spiritual retreat center to care for troubled priests in Jemez Springs, New Mexico, and, in 1959, they opened a renewal center in Nevis, Minnesota. These were spiritual renewal centers providing a monastic spiritual retreat that originally did not incorporate psychiatric and psychological elements into their programs. However, by the 1990s they had treated over 1,200 priests with sexual problems. In 1957, specialized treatment centers for priests with alcohol problems had been set up as "Guest Houses" in Rochester, Minnesota, and Lake Orion, Michigan.

From 1953 until 1978 St. John's University Institute for Mental Health, Collegeville, Minnesota, conducted groundbreaking summer workshops that brought psychiatrists and clergymen together to discuss the behavioral problems occurring at the interface of religion and psychiatry. Over 2,400 clergy participated in these programs.

In the late 1960s and early 1970s, coinciding with a growing awareness among Catholic bishops and religious superiors that sexual and moral/spiritual problems had psychological dimensions, a number of Catholic treatment centers specifically for priests and religious were opened. Southdown was opened close to Toronto, Canada, in 1966, and the House of Affirmation was opened in Wittensville, Massachusetts, in the early 1970s, Others were opened in Montero, California, Webster Groves, Missouri, and Birmingham, England. All of these institutions incorporated psychology and psychiatry into their spiritual treatment programs.

With the opening of these facilities, referrals of priests with sexual addictions increased. This increase did not occur because sexual behaviors by priests were new problems, or because the facilities were opened for the express purpose of treating sexual disorders; rather, the psychological treatment of problematic priests highlighted the frequency of psychosexual disorders in the clergy. Cases of recurrent, troublesome, and undeniable sexual abuse compelled Catholic bishops and religious superiors to increase referrals to these new facilities.

Awareness of the Problem Spreads

Awareness of the dimensions of the problems presented by sexual addictions expanded as psychology and psychiatry broke through the barriers of secrecy and victims and perpetrators became willing to talk more openly about their experiences.

The Servants of the Paraclete began to incorporate psychiatric elements into their treatment of priests, treatments that were specifically attuned to problems of a sexual nature. Psychiatric awareness blossomed from a realization of the need to address a priest-patient population suffering from compulsive sexual disorders stemming from an arrested psychological development that could not be treated by spiritual direction alone. Paraclete priests undertook training in psychology and sexuality at the Institute for the Advanced Study of Sexuality in San Francisco in the early 1970s in order to prepare for the opening in 1976 of treatment programs focused directly on psychosexual disorders.

Priests with psychosexual problems were not a new phenomenon in the mid-1970s, but the awareness and acceptability of psychiatric modes of addressing these problems was relatively new. The establishment of treatment centers afforded bishops and religious superiors an additional way to handle problems they had been dealing with all along within a more exclusive and secret atmosphere. The existence of Catholic treatment centers and the types of treatment modalities available were widely known within the Catholic hierarchy and were used by bishops and religious superiors to refer priests for psychological treatment. These treatment centers certainly included therapeutic regimes for psychosexual disorders involving minors. Promotional literature advertising these centers was sent out periodically to each bishop by many of the centers. The Paraclete treatment programs were well advertised, known, and respected.

In 1976 the Servants of the Paraclete opened what was perhaps the first program in the world with a regime designed to treat psychosexual disorders in priests including disorders involving the sexual abuse of minors. The ability of the Catholic community to design and implement such an innovative program is both a reflection of the need for a program and the degree of knowledge of the scope of the problem of sexual misconduct with children by Catholic priests and religious. The fact that preparations for the opening of this program were years in the making demonstrates widespread knowledge of existing sexual misconduct with minors by Catholic clergy in the 1950s and definitively by the late 1960s and early 1970s.

The Paraclete programs treat only Catholic priests and religious sent to them by bishops or religious superiors, who are responsible for all treatment costs and are provided with periodic progress reports on these priests or religious brothers. It is reliably estimated that, to date, 2,100 priests and religious have been treated for psychosexual disorders, including sex with minors, at a cost of over $80 million.

The Bishops Conference contributed money in the 1970s to the Paracletes to support the development of their program. Since the goals and purposes of the treatment program were well known within the Catholic hierarchy, the goals and purposes would have been known to the Bishops Conference as well. The conference also issued directives regarding the retention or destruction of the treatment reports provided to the bishops, and the Paracletes and its staff followed these directives.

It is obvious, therefore, that in the 1960s and certainly, by the 1970s, the bishops of the United States, individually and collectively, were well aware of certain psychological problems of priests, including sexual involvement with minors, and were also aware of modes of addressing psychosexual problems other than spiritual renewal and geographic transfers.

The Bishops' Response

Prior to 1966, the National Catholic Welfare Conference (the organization that preceded the National Conference of Catholic Bishops, the United States Catholic Conference, and the current United States Conference of Catholic

Bishops) had a Family Life Bureau whose purpose was to study family life issues, which included adult-child sexual contact and the resultant trauma.

By the late 1970s Catholic treatment centers were using cutting-edge psychological and psychiatric modalities to treat priests and religious who had abused minors. So, the question naturally arises: What care was given to child victims of sexual abuse by priests? What steps were taken to protect Catholic children and their families from the known risk of abuse by clerics?

There is much evidence to show that victims who complained were consistently seen as traitors and disloyal to their church. Many victims have reported feeling that they were viewed as seducers, seductresses, sinners, or, in some cases, opportunists, and treated largely without sympathy. One archbishop said—as recently as the early 1990s—that priests who got involved with minors were the "naive victims of streetwise youngsters."

Although only a small percentage of parents or victims of sexual abuse complained directly to bishops and religious superiors, their numbers were high enough to provide the authorities with sufficient data to be aware of the victims, their pain, and the harm done to them. Complaints were discouraged by the reception they received. Victims and their families were deceived, confused, ignored, not given credence, or discouraged. These families were inhibited by false, incomplete, and misleading information designed to serve the interests of the church hierarchy rather than those of the child victim. This pattern was consistent in dioceses and archdioceses across the United States.

A victim is mistreated if, after he or she registers a complaint or allegation of abuse, the church authorities refer them to agencies or people who will not respond to their complaints or problems objectively, or fail to act in the victim's best interests. There are many examples of such treatment on record in civil and criminal cases of sexual abuse by priests. Victims are mistreated if church authorities enter into lengthy negotiations that go nowhere and result in the victims and their families becoming discouraged or if church officials fail to act in a timely fashion to promote a victim's welfare. Victims and their families are mistreated if church officials make false promises, impart false or incomplete information, or hold out false hope of reconciliation or appropriate action. Even in 2005, there is ample evidence that these methods are not entirely discarded by bishops or their lawyers. In fact, church lawyers time and again are "ruthless" in their treatment of victims and their families in depositions and in court proceedings. Bishops wash their hands of their lawyers' behavior, even when they know allegations of abuse are credible, by asserting that they cannot interfere with the legal process.

Secrecy Is Breached: Public Exposure

In 1984, in the diocese of Lafayette, Louisiana, evidence that a bishop had prior knowledge of sexual impropriety by a priest escaped the secret system and entered the public domain. Prior to 1985, there had been criminal prosecutions and lawsuits alleging sexual misconduct with minors by priests and religious, but evidence of prior knowledge by their superiors did not leave the secret system. This case also laid bare for the first time how the hierarchy handled instances of sexual abuse.

The National Conference of Catholic Bishops appreciated the significance of this breach of traditional secrecy. The conference's general secretary and its general counsel, along with a canonist from the Apostolic Delegate's Office in Washington became concerned and involved. They regarded the entry of this knowledge into the public arena as a serious threat to the secrecy of the system they had instituted for dealing with sexual abuse.

The media, unaccustomed to investigating religion in general, were particularly reluctant to defy the hierarchy with any exposure of clergy malfeasance. As a general rule, Catholic bishops had been able to control the media and, sometimes, even the civil courts. They lost some of that control in the Lafayette case. Even then, only a small part of the total amount of clergy misconduct was ever made public; detailed knowledge by the public of the scope of the actual abuse was not widespread. An independent Catholic newspaper, *The National Catholic Reporter*, revealed in print some details of the Lafayette case.

In 1992, a particularly egregious case of priestly sexual misconduct involving children was widely reported in both the print and visual media. A Catholic priest, James Porter, by his own admission, abused nearly two hundred victims. This case brought to light the fact that numerous priests and bishops of five dioceses had known about the abuse, but chose to conceal it, transferring Fr. Porter without adequate supervision, notice, or warning to potential victims in other areas of assignment. Frank Fitzpatrick, a victim of Fr. Porter's abuse, pushed the Boston media and law-enforcement authorities in Massachusetts and Minnesota to pursue him. Then for the first time, other victims of abuse by priests, realizing they were not alone, came forward to discuss publicly their own experiences. Fr. Porter was finally prosecuted and received an eighteen-year prison sentence and died in prison in 2005.

Between 1985 and 1992, there was a growing sensitivity to the realization that Catholic bishops and religious superiors could be concealing knowledge of criminal activities by Catholic priests and religious. A growing number of people who had been violated began to share their experiences with psychologists, psychiatrists, spouses, parents, friends, press, and attorneys. The exposure of evidence of ongoing concealment of Fr. Porter's activities by numerous Catholic bishops led to the realization by some victims and their families that they too had been deceived by religious authorities.

When in January 2002, the investigative team of the *Boston Globe* began to report the cases of abuse by Fr. John Goeghan, a new phase in the exposure of clergy sexual abuse took center stage. Within a year the pope summoned all the American cardinals to Rome, the American bishops assembled in Dallas to pound out a new charter to deal with offenders and to protect children, and Cardinal Law of Boston was effectively forced to resign his office. Subsequently Fr. Goeghan, who was the alleged abuser of 150 minors during his ministerial career, was convicted of one incident of indecent touching and sent to prison. There he was murdered in 2004 by a fellow inmate who claimed he had been abused as a boy.

The Boston saga continued in 2005 when Fr. Paul Shanley, notorious for his tolerance of the North American Man/Boy Love Association (NAMBLA), was convicted of child abuse and sentenced to twelve to fifteen years in prison. All these acts in the drama of abuse unveiled the sometimes unholy alliance that had been forged between religion and psychiatry over the past half-century to conceal the abusive behavior of individual priests and the devious means some bishops had used to keep abuse secret.

The effects of what played out on the Boston stage has reverberated worldwide. Sexual abuse by Catholic priests is no longer the dirty little secret whispered about in bowling alleys and pubs, and denied with mock shock in chancery halls. Abuse of minors by bishops and priests is a fact with no place to hide.

Harm to Victims: The Open Wound

The sexual abuse of a child by a priest frequently develops gradually and follows set patterns:

1. The sexual contact arises from a relationship involving immense trust on the part of the minor;
2. The child is extraordinarily vulnerable in that the priest is seen as an agent of God;
3. An affectionate relationship often precedes the sexual contact so that the child feels that he (usually) or she has a very special relationship with the priest;
4. There is an incredible helplessness on the part of the abused child—most abused minors either feel responsible for the abuse occurring, or so powerless that they feel they cannot disclose the abuse to their parents or, often, anyone else;
5. Such secrecy surrounds the abuse that disclosure is inhibited—sometimes reinforced by threats—allowing the abuse to continue; and
6. If the abuse is revealed, bishops rarely treated the child victim in a responsible, pastoral manner. Moreover, the parents' trust in their bishop permits manipulation, intimidation, and, in some cases, active deceit, with additional negative consequences to the welfare of the child.

The effects of abuse can sometimes be seen immediately by parents, but only confirmed by trained professionals in the form of depression, moodiness, withdrawal, or acting out. But the origins of this distress can be difficult to discern without competent professional assistance. Many times, the effects are quite subtle and become clear only in retrospect. The impact of the betrayal can be so grave that it is often buried in memory and only retrieved after symptoms such as anxiety, depression, and alcoholism are dealt with many years later.

In 1984 and 1985, Fr. Michael Peterson of St. Luke Institute, Fr. Thomas Doyle, a canonist at the Papal Nunciature, and Mr. Ray Mouton, a civil attorney representing Fr. Gilbert Gauthé, the priest in the Lafayette case, prepared an extensive report on the civil, canonical, and psychological aspects of the sexual involvement of priests with children (Cf. Chapter 4). This report included well-documented statements regarding the long-term harmful effects on a child victim of sexual abuse. In September 1993, the Ad Hoc Committee on Sexual Abuse of the NCCB admitted that their report, "*Restoring Trust*," identified virtually the same issues that had previously been analyzed in 1985 for the bishops.

In 1985 David Finkelhor, Ph.D., and Angela Brown, Ph.D., digested what was known from previous research and found that there could be no doubt about the potential for long-term harm to child sex-abuse victims. They found that the interplay of four dynamics constituted the active ingredients of the sexual abuse of children by priests and religious. They described these dynamics as: traumatic sexualization, stigmatization, betrayal, and powerlessness. The atmosphere of secrecy surrounding the response of bishops, superiors, vicars, or priests to the notice of abuse accentuated the dynamic of victimization.

A Conspiracy of Silence

Certainly, the vast majority of Catholic priests (90 to 95 percent) do not sexually abuse minors. But, because the consequences of the abuse of a child by a person holding spiritual power are so dire and long-lasting, even a small proportion of perpetrators within the ministry is a matter of extreme public interest and urgency. Moreover, the fact that such abuse occurs in other parts of society does not lessen the need for responsible action by U.S. Catholic bishops in regard to their own priests, bishops, and lay members of their church.

By *de facto* tolerating such abuse while at the same time proclaiming the sexual safety of its members, a situation is created that restricts the ability of the authorities to properly supervise and investigate priests who abuse children and discipline them when they are found guilty. Bishops are not alone in hiding abusive bishops and priests; priests do not expose brother priests they know to be abusing minors; this is part of the secret system that can also involve lay Catholics who feel it would be disloyal to speak up.

Exposure of one part of the system—abusive priests—threatens to expose a whole system that tolerates more widespread, but possibly not as abusive, violations of celibacy within the priesthood. In the words of one prosecutor (Dallas), there has been what has been tantamount to a conspiracy on the part of the bishops to avoid scandal, despite a known risk of harm to the welfare of the children. Secrecy in the face of knowledge of the risk of harm to children is not only reprehensible, it is potentially illegal.

Duties Abandoned

At a national conference, the U.S. bishops have established binding guidelines for seminary training, and for evaluating seminary faculties and students. They have researched issues that concern Catholic life in the United States and published national policies for dealing with them. They also operate the largest Catholic news service in the world and communicate with the laity through numerous pastoral plans and pastoral letters.

However, with reference to the sexual abuse of minors by priests, the bishops have failed in the past and continue to fail the church in many respects:

1. They still fail to acknowledge fully and warn Catholics sufficiently of the propensity of some priests and religious to act out sexually with others and not simply minors.

2. The bishops have promulgated national standards for priestly training and formation. They still fail to address and implement sufficiently the need to identify seminarians who—because of their own psycho-sexual immaturity—are at risk for non-celibate behavior and so are not suitable for a public ministry involving minors; this is because they have not addressed the members of seminary faculties who themselves are insufficiently mature and not celibately developed.

However, since their Dallas meeting in June 2002, the bishops have established and implemented a national policy that includes an informed and supervisory laity to present a plan to prevent sexual activity with minors by Catholic priests and religious. That effort spearheaded by the National Review Board and the Office of Child Protection at the USCCB holds some promise of improved supervision of priests and bishops.

Conclusion

The long-term effect of sexual abuse on children can be pervasive and debilitating. These pervasive and debilitating effects are well known and have been discussed in case histories and studies presented in psychiatric, psychological, and popular literature for many years. Bishops and religious superiors and their advisors in the field of psychology and psychiatry knew and could appreciate long ago the harm resulting to a child victim of abuse by a trusted priest or religious. A number of experts say that consequences of abuse by a Catholic priest are more dire than the results of incest. Yet a number of bishops and their lawyers, even in 2005, minimize the effects of clergy abuse and denigrate victims and their symptoms.

The bishops of the NCCB and the USCC employed a system of secrecy to conceal widespread evidence of sexual misconduct with minors by Catholic priests and religious. This behavior was known to the hierarchy and concealed from the laity. This concealment included the making of ambiguous, false, and misleading statements concerning the behavior of priests and religious when it was known that a significant number were sexually abusing minors. This conduct was so widespread and well known that it resulted in the establishment of a number of Catholic therapeutic centers devoted to the treatment of Catholic priests and religious. Because the recommendation of a bishop or superior was required for evaluation, treatment, or hospitalization in these centers, it is reasonable to conclude that they knew of the existence of the abuse in advance. Already in 1924, priests with these problems were being referred to Catholic hospitals. The Servants of the Paraclete opened the first treatment center in the world in 1976 with a program to treat this disorder. Yet this material information was not conveyed to the Catholic public for the safety of Catholic children. Only pressure from the press, victims, lawyers, and public indignation moved the hierarchy to action. Even many good initiatives have been reactionary and lacking moral leadership to the extent that the church has been harmed, in some ways irreparably.

Part Two

The Church on Notice

A bishop, God's steward, must be blameless; he
must not be arrogant or quick tempered or
addicted to wine or violent or greedy for gain;
but he must be hospitable, a lover of goodness,
prudent, upright, devout, and self-controlled. He
must have a firm grasp of the word
that is trustworthy.

—TITUS. 1:7–9

Chapter 3

Canon Law, Civil Law, and Psychiatry Speak Out

The document that follows, *The Problem of Sexual Molestation by Roman Catholic Clergy: Meeting the Problem in a Comprehensive and Responsible Manner,* (Chapter 4) is the product of the cooperation of three people: Fr. Thomas Doyle, O.P., J.C.D., a secretary-canonist at the Apostolic Delegation, now called the Apostolic Nunciature in Washington, D.C.; the late Fr. Michael Peterson, M.D., a psychiatrist and founder and director of St. Luke Institute, Suitland, Maryland, (now located in Hyattsville); and Mr. F. Ray Mouton, J.D., civil attorney from Lafayette, Louisiana. It was written in 1985 in the wake of the publicity surrounding the sexual abuse of minors by Catholic priests in Louisiana, and a copy was given to every American bishop at that time.

The report, or "Manual" as it came to be called, was intended to be kept confidential, but within a short period of time it was being copied and disseminated around the United States and abroad. Sometimes referred to as the "Doyle-Mouton Report" or the "Mouton-Doyle-Peterson Report," it is being published in print form here for the very first time.

In its original form, the report consisted of about one hundred pages of text dealing with various aspects of the civil and canon law, and the medical, insurance, and pastoral concerns of the sexual abuse of children by the clergy. Fr.

Peterson attached copies of several clinical articles about the nature, treatment, and curability of pedophilia. The manual was not commissioned by anyone in any position, official or otherwise, in the Catholic Church. It was an entirely private undertaking, written by Mr. Mouton and Frs. Doyle and Peterson in response to a situation they believed was quickly developing into a very serious problem for the church. The authors never received any compensation for their work or work product and paid for the production costs out of their own pockets. As one reads that report today, the authors' presumption of the goodwill of bishops and near bias in favor of bishops' concerns for image, money, and control are apparent. That inclination to favor bishops' concerns is all the more striking in light of their denial, resistance, and intransigence to adopt measures dealing with abuse in the subsequent twenty years.

In late fall 1984, Fr. Gilbert Gauthé of Lafayette, Louisiana, was facing serious criminal charges and the diocese hired Mr. Mouton to defend him. A civil suit had already been initiated by Glen and Faye Gastal, whose son had been abused by Fr. Gauthé.

In January 1985, Mr. Mouton went to Washington D.C., and met Fr. Peterson to explore with him the possibility of sending Fr. Gauthé to St. Luke Institute for treatment, and Fr. Doyle, the papal nuntiature's canon lawyer who was charged with monitoring the correspondence regarding Fr. Gauthé. It was then that the idea of formulating some sort of policy or advisory statement to help bishops deal with the problem of priestly pedophilia came into being.

At that meeting, Mr. Mouton indicated that there were several other priests in Lafayette who had been involved in the sexual abuse of children and that the diocese was covering them up and thus hurting his chances of a successful defense of Fr. Gauthé. He had hoped to reach a plea bargain for Fr. Gauthé, which would have enabled him to be hospitalized or otherwise confined to a secure facility where he would be treated. The discovery that other priests were engaged in pedophilia would weaken Mr. Mouton's plan insofar as the district attorney, Nathan Stansbury, would not be able to treat Fr. Gauthé lightly. Fr. Peterson indicated that he knew from confidential sources that there were many other priests around the country who had sexually abused children.

Fr. Doyle told Archbishop Pio Laghi, the Papal Nuntio, of the gravity of the situation and Fr. Peterson spoke with him a few days later. The nuntio then called Archbishop Philip Hannan of New Orleans and invited him to a meeting in Washington with Bishop Gerard Frey of Lafayette, Louisiana, along with their lawyers, and Frs. Doyle and Peterson. The purpose of the meeting was to clarify the issues, especially those of the other priests.

After that meeting, Fr. Doyle suggested to Archbishop Laghi that a bishop be delegated to go to Lafayette to help manage what had become a crisis. Because of his legal background, Bishop A.J. Quinn, auxiliary bishop of Cleveland, was chosen.

At that time also, the Gastals were instituting a civil suit against the diocese of Lafayette for failing to take proper precautions when they had been warned about Fr. Gauthé's abuse. Fr. Gauthé had in fact been reported to the bishop several times since 1972. Before long, it was discovered that he had abused scores of young children. All, with one exception, were young boys. In the end, he pleaded guilty to thirty-nine counts and was sentenced to twenty years in prison.

Frs. Doyle and Peterson and Mr. Mouton, believing that cases of child abuse by priests were increasing, decided on their own to write a report for the bishops to assist them in dealing with the problem. Bishop Quinn suggested that the report respond to a set of questions covering as many different angles and aspects of the issue as could be conceived of.

The three men also proposed that the NCCB establish a committee (or project) to supervise detailed research into the canon, civil, and criminal law implications, and the insurance, medical, and pastoral aspects of the problem of clergy abuse of minors. The research would be made available to the bishops to help them make enlightened decisions about the problem. They also proposed a Crisis Intervention Team consisting of people with legal, medical, canonical, and pastoral expertise to help bishops with specific cases.

A key aspect of the proposal included the creation of a uniform method of case management, or at least, case following. Within a few months after the Fr. Gauthé case, by the middle of 1985, there were several civil court actions involving priests and dioceses. Over the years since then, there have been more than two thousand.

However, there had been no uniform case management or following by any church agency. Consequently, there had been no way of determining the development of civil law jurisprudence, of tracking the nature and amount of settlements, or of studying legal strategies. The absence of case following gave rise to rumor and innuendo about the monies spent, judgments of courts, numbers of perpetrators, and the names of dioceses involved. Even the National Review Board and the John Jay study initiated by the bishops in 2002 have not completely answered all the concerns surrounding abuse, its occurrence, and costs.

The proposal was presented to Archbishop Laghi, who had been receiving daily briefings on the overall situation from Fr. Doyle, and a number of other cardinals and bishops were told about the project informally. Fr. Doyle received support from everybody he spoke to. His conversations with bishops indicated that they had been aware of and worried about the problem.

In May 1985, Fr. Peterson presented a draft of the canonical section of the report to Cardinal John Krol of

Philadelphia who praised it and promised to support the entire project. He said he would talk about it to Cardinal Bernard Law of Boston and Bishop Quinn. Cardinal Law said he would get the project into the NCCB by creating a special ad hoc committee of his own Committee on Research and Pastoral Practices.

The final draft was completed on May 15, 1985. That same month, Frs. Doyle and Peterson and Mr. Mouton met with Archbishop William Levada, the secretary of Cardinal Law's committee and now Cardinal Ratzinger's successor as head of the Congregation for the Doctrine of the Faith, and he reacted positively to the progress being made. A short time later, however, Archbishop Levada phoned Fr. Doyle to say the project had been shut down because another committee of the NCCB was going to deal with the problem of sexual abuse by priests and a duplication of efforts would not make the other committee look good. Although Fr. Doyle was told that the NCCB Committee on Priestly Life would be looking into the issue, that committee did nothing.

Frs. Doyle and Peterson and Mr. Mouton proceeded on their own and contacted Bishop Quinn (who was then an ally) to ask him to take copies of the manual to the NCCB June meeting in Collegeville, Minnesota, which he did. The president of the NCCB announced after an executive session at which the problem of pedophile priests was discussed that a committee to work on the issue had been formed, headed by the late Bishop Michael Murphy of Erie, Pennsylvania.

Three presentations had been made in the executive session: one each by NCCB attorney Mr. Wilfred Caron (on civil law), Bishop Kenneth Angell of Providence, Rhode Island (on canon law), and Dr. Richard Issel (on psychology). Bishops said later the psychologist was excellent and the lawyers mediocre at best. This sentiment was stated in a letter from Cardinal Krol to Fr. Doyle.

Fr. Doyle learned in June from Bishop Anthony Bevilacqua of Pittsburgh (later Cardinal of Philadelphia) that there was actually no committee and no action was planned. The announcement was merely a public relations ploy. Fr. Doyle later learned that the Committee on Priestly Life was *supposed* to consider the issue. If it actually did, there is no trace of it.

When the announcement was made, Bishop James Malone of Youngstown, Ohio, specifically stated that such a committee existed. Yet, in a deposition, Sister Sharon Euart, an assistant general secretary of the NCCB/USCC, stated that the first committee ever established to study priestly pedophilia was that which was created in 1993 and headed by Bishop John Kinney of Bismarck, North Dakota (now St. Cloud, Minnesota).

Nothing was ever said to Frs. Doyle, Peterson, or Mr. Mouton about the manual. They were never told what happened to it within the NCCB. Reliable sources say that, although the existence of the manual was well known, it was disregarded because it was never properly submitted for consideration.

In later years, after the manual had been widely circulated and had become well known to attorneys and others involved in the issue of clergy abuse, people, especially reporters, would often ask bishops or officials at the NCCB whether they knew about it or possessed it, and if so, why had no action had been taken either at the time or since. These questions elicited a variety of answers. Not one response accurately reflected the facts.

The general response from the NCCB, almost always through the office of its general counsel, Mark Chopko, was that the NCCB already knew everything that was in the manual. The NCCB had already taken appropriate action and that the idea of a special committee and an ad hoc team of experts was not deemed appropriate. Mr. Chopko added that the NCCB could not bind individual bishops and that Frs. Doyle and Peterson and Mr. Mouton were "only interested in selling their services to bishops and mak[ing] money off of the problem." Mr. Chopko also stated that there were "problems" with the content of the manual. The motivation for composing and submitting it to the bishops was either grossly misunderstood or understood but intentionally misconstrued by the officials at the NCCB. It has occasionally crossed the minds of Fr. Doyle and Mr. Mouton that the officials at the NCCB/USCC who have consistently made derogatory comments about the project are trying to shift the onus of responsibility for dealing with the problem from themselves to someone else, or conjure up some sort of excuse for failing to act in the face of explicit warnings about sex abuse, its extent, and probable consequences. Nobody in the NCCB ever contacted Frs. Doyle or Peterson or Mr. Mouton.

In December 1985, a copy of the manual was sent to each bishop in the United States through the St. Luke Institute. There was no response from anyone to this gesture. Some individual bishops, when asked by the press, indicated that they had found it helpful. The NCCB, however, never acknowledged its existence, nor has it ever contacted its authors in relation to any of the meetings they have held concerning the issue of clergy abuse since that time.

In 1992, Fr. Doyle received a letter from the NCCB president Archbishop Daniel Pilarcyzk in response to a letter he had sent after the first VOCAL (later changed to the LinkUp) conference of victims of clerical sexual abuse held in Chicago in October 1992 (Cf. Letters).

The bishops' conference has discussed the issue in plenary sessions at least five or six times. Once it videotaped its discussion for public viewing. The conference has also issued at least five statements on the subject and sent several memos from its general counsel to all diocesan bishops.

The early suggestions for a research committee as well as a Crisis Intervention Team were never implemented. It was not until October 1993 that the NCCB appointed a committee of bishops, headed by Bishop John Kinney, to study the issue. This committee did meet and issued two reports, "Restoring Trust," Volume I in 1994 and Volume II in 1995. These efforts were plagued by lack of cooperation, as Chairman Kinney noted. The bishops did not show enough interest or moral resolve to effect any impact on the public confidence. Quite the opposite: The public registered growing impatience and even disdain for bishops' public relations maneuvers.

In 1988, the once supportive Bishop Quinn wrote to Archbishop Laghi, complaining about comments Fr. Doyle made to the press saying, "The truth is, Doyle and Mouton want the Church in the United States to purchase [Doyle's and Mouton's] expensive and controvertible leadership in matters relating to pedophilia."

The contention that the authors of the manual sought monetary gain probably originated with the general secretariate of the NCCB/USCC. When asked about the manual by reporters, the conference general counsel responded with essentially the same line as Bishop Quinn.

In 1989, Monsignor Daniel Hoye, then General Secretary of the NCCB, was deposed by plaintiff counsel in a civil suit stemming from the abuse of a woman by a priest, Fr. Vance Thorne. In his deposition and in a related affidavit, Monsignor Hoye made the following statements:

> The report was neither requested by nor presented to the NCCB/USCC. ... The report gave short shrift to the on-going diocesan and NCCB/USCC efforts at prevention of sexual abuse. ... A key aspect of the Mouton-Doyle-Peterson report was the proposal that a national 'team' at least supplement, but more

often displace, diocesan officials in responding to complaints of sexual abuse on a local
level. ... The authors of the report were rather
pointed in their dire predictions of the fiscal
disaster for the church unless such a team
were hired. ... One of the authors intended to
be part of that expert team retained at considerable expense by the NCCB/USCC.

The manual was a threat to the cloak of secrecy under
which church authority operated. Bishop Quinn and
Monsignor Hoye misrepresented the purpose of the report,
the aim of the action proposals, and the intentions of its
authors. The report was, if anything, overly deferential to
bishops. It made no mention, either critical or otherwise, of
the efforts of the NCCB/USCC or individual dioceses, nor
did any of the authors ever mention those efforts in public or
private statements. They were, in fact, unaware of any such
efforts and no bishop ever mentioned them. But speaking up
at all about clergy sexual activity was impolite at best and
defiant and disloyal at worst. In private conversations, several bishops admitted that the conference had nothing to offer
and needed direction in dealing with sexual abuse issues.

Critics of the report used many excuses to disregard it.
Some have falsely characterized the proposed Crisis
Intervention Team as a "Swat Team." There was never any
intent that a team would displace diocesan officials. The
team was intended to be available for bishops at their
request and visit a diocese only as a resource for the bishop
and diocesan officials. On two occasions this approach was
used at the request of bishops and the results were highly
successful. Although the team had no authority from the
conference or any other source, it never suggested it would
make decisions or set policy. Resistance was a harbinger of
the bishops' concerns that they lost control of the problems

of abusing priests and bishops. The secret system simply could not brook such a voluntary intrusion.

In drawing up the proposal for the Crisis Intervention Team the authors did propose a budget—$3 million for a period of three years. This figure included the retention of a full-time coordinator for the team, an office, and travel expenses, as well as expenses for the expert members. Mr. Mouton did offer to apply for this position. He, like the other two authors, was deeply committed to solving the problems of abuse. Mouton's appointment would have involved a significant personal and financial sacrifice on his part.

The budgetary aspect of the proposal was met with initial approval by individual bishops with whom the authors discussed the idea. It was not a bone of contention until the general secretariat began using it as an excuse to defend its actions (or inactions) and to discredit the manual and its authors. Neither Fr. Doyle nor Fr. Peterson ever envisioned themselves as ongoing participants in the project. Mr. Mouton's commitment to the work was not related to obtaining the position of coordinator. He offered himself to the project because of his experience, but held no ambition to be its coordinator.

Spokespersons for the conference had referred to policies, procedures, and "ongoing" efforts prior to 1993, but Sister Euart stated later, under oath, that the conference had no committee on sex abuse until 1993. The conference had basically done nothing about the problem apart from those actions evidenced by documents and statements that are on record. Between 1985 and 1988, spokespersons for the conference stated many times it could not establish a committee of any kind because it had no authority to impose any kinds of obligations on individual dioceses. Nevertheless, an ad hoc committee was established in 1993.

Bishop Quinn's letter and Msgr. Hoye's deposition indicate that the proposal to establish a Crisis Intervention Team, a research committee, and an office dedicated to handling the work of the research team was written off by the conference in the 1990s.

Now, it is clearly ironic that the bishops in their June 2002 meeting in Dallas essentially accepted the suggestions the manual offered in 1985. The power of the secret system had been breached by the manual. This was never the intent of the report, but the goal of protecting children from abusive clergy was not possible while the secret system held sway. Although belated and somewhat begrudgingly the bishops established a national office of child protection at the USCCB and hired an ex-FBI official, Kathleen McChesney, to head it. They also set up a National Review Board for the Protection of Children and Young People, and an independent lay board. From December 2002 to January 2004, the review board's research committee interviewed eighty-five individuals, including Fr. Doyle and Fr. Richard Sipe, a psychotherapist with extensive experience of treating both victims and perpetrators of sexual abuse of minors, and delivered its report on February 27, 2004. The history of this board is a story in itself and its report lays the blame for the crisis squarely at the feet of the hierarchy. Among its conclusions was the statement that the "absence of fraternal correction compounded the lack of episcopal accountability and further fueled the current crisis" (*A Report on the Crisis in the Catholic Church in the United States,* by the National Review Board for the Protection of Children and Young People, USCCB, Washington, D.C., 2004, page 139).

As a result of the Dallas meeting, the bishops also commissioned a research team from the John Jay College of Criminal Justice to provide a comprehensive description of the extent of sexual abuse of minors by Catholic priests. The tally of offending clergy was arrived at through a process of self-reporting by the dioceses. The majority of dioceses (90 percent) did participate, but a significant number of bishops (3 percent of the total) resisted cooperation. The maneuvering of the archdiocese of Los Angeles and the bishops of California moved the chair of the National Review Board, Frank Keating, to say that the bishops operated like "*la cosa nostra*." He subsequently resigned.

Gerald Lynch, the president of John Jay College and coordinator of the study, could say of the report:

> The findings presented in this report are very disturbing ... we were deeply moved by the recitation of the large numbers of offences committed against children and the seriousness of their nature (Preface to the John Jay College Research Team Report, February 2004).

Even in 2002, the manual still stirred controversy. Several articles appeared in conservative Catholic publications alleging that its authors intended to mislead the Catholic Church by proposing that accused priests be turned over to psychologists who claimed to be able to cure them, when they (the authors of the report) actually knew they could not.[138]

Fr. Peterson, a physician and board-certified psychiatrist, was a colleague and consulted frequently with Dr. Fred Berlin and Dr. John Money. Dr. Berlin and Dr. Money (now retired) founded the Sexual Dysfunction Clinic at Johns Hopkins University and, indeed, Dr. Berlin is one of the world's most eminent researchers and clinicians in the area of sexual abuse. He provided a major resource in developing clinical opinions reflected in the report. Critics erroneously claim that Dr. Berlin and Dr. Money are intent on releasing sexual abusers back on the street and promoting a so-called "homosexual agenda."

No matter how misunderstood, misrepresented, or derided the 1985 manual has been, it stands as testimony to the fact and the awareness within the secret system of the Catholic Church of the ongoing presence of sexually abusing priests and the lengths powerful men within that system are willing to go to protect abusers and themselves from exposure.

Chapter 4
The Doyle-Mouton-Peterson Manual, May 15, 1985

Table of Contents

The Problem of Sexual Molestation by Roman Catholic Clergy: Meeting the Problem in a Comprehensive and Responsible Manner

I. Ominous Signs of a Serious Problem
Forward

This document contains a discussion of an extremely serious situation and a proposal to establish and fund a Special Project to be comprised of a Crisis Control Team and a Policy and Planning Group.

Both the team and the group would work under the direct control and supervision of an ad hoc committee of four bishops, all of whom have civil law degrees. This committee of four would control every aspect of the Special Project, subject to the supervision of a committee formed out of the National Conference of Catholic Bishops, under whose auspices they would be appointed, receive authority, and serve.

The Project itself, both the team and the group, should be comprised of professionals and consultants who possess a significant degree of experience and expertise in their given fields. Some of this group of experts from different disciplines should devote the entirety of their professional endeavor to the Project during its existence. Other experts should be retained as required. However, a group of professionals would be working full time on the Project.

It is contemplated that the minimum life of the Special Project would be five years. It is believed that following the completion of that term, it would be beneficial to retain some of the elements of the Project in place as opposed to dismantling the entire structure.

The cost of the Project is dependent upon the caliber of consultants retained, their degree of expertise and experience, and the portion of their professional life to be devoted to the Project. The cost would be substantial.

A. History of the Proposal

Some extremely serious issues have arisen that presently place the church in the posture of facing extremely serious financial consequences as well as significant injury to its image. As a result of sexual molestation of children by clerics (priests, permanent deacons, transient (sic) deacons, non-ordained religious, lay employees, and seminarians), for many months there has been continuous confidential communication amongst some expert consultants and clergy, all of whom possess hands-on experience with the more serious cases of sexual molestation. Through those discussions, the idea of this Project was born. The scope of the Project has been defined and redefined until it reached the final form presented herein. It is contemplated that the very nature of the Project would cause further redefinition during its existence.

The Criminal Considerations, Civil Considerations, Canonical Considerations, and Clinical Considerations are of such magnitude, not to mention the other substantial considerations such as Insurance and Public Relations, that it was decided that the presentation of these extraordinary issues necessitated an extraordinary response, a response that would affirmatively and aggressively attack the problems. This is a very new and narrow area of legal jurisprudence that is developing with a very adverse effect upon the church's interests. In addition to the legal issues, there are unique Canonical Considerations and extremely complex Clinical Considerations that cannot or should not be addressed in a piecemeal manner.

It is submitted that time is of the essence. At the moment this is being read, problems with which the Project will deal are continually arising. Many of these problems appear to be old problems, and indeed some are. However, all now carry consequences never before experienced.

B. Confidentiality of This Document

The necessity for protecting the confidentiality of this document cannot be overemphasized.

The document was drafted by retained counsel hired for the specific purpose of communicating to the reader. However, though much of the language is that of counsel, the document is reflective of the thoughts of clergy and other professionals in different disciplines, professionals who have worked closely with counsel throughout the development of these ideas.

An effort has been made to have this document afforded the protection and privilege provided under our law for confidential communications. That privilege would not apply should the reader discuss same with anyone other than a recipient of this document.

In an abundance of caution and in consideration of the reader, great care has been given to protect the anonymity of any case mentioned or alluded to, and further there is no specific reference herein below nor is there any allusion to any fact in litigation that has not been publicly reported in the press. This has been done to protect the reader so that the reader may not be placed in a position of having received any specific knowledge not generally known to the public and thereby become the target of a subpoena or other discovery device.

The national press has an active interest in items discussed herein, and, therefore, an abundance of caution is required. It is requested that each reader return the document to the person from whom they received same, without copying. It is requested that no copy be retained by the reader. The rationale for this request is the great interest of the press. Over the last two weeks there has been national press coverage of the problem and that coverage is increasing. Security for the entire Project is extremely important.

C. The Consequences of One Particular Case

Over one hundred million dollars ($100,000,000) in claims have been made against one Diocese as a result of sexual contact between one Priest and a number of minor children. To date the cost of this catastrophe exceeds five million dollars ($5,000,000) and the projected cost of concluding the civil cases in that Diocese alone is in excess of ten million ($10,000,000).[139]

It is not hyperbolic to state that the dramatic description of the actual case contained herein above is indicative that a real, present danger exists. That other cases exist and arise with increased frequency is evidenced by reports of same. If one could accurately predict, with actuarial soundness, that our exposure to similar claims (i.e., one offender and fifteen or so claimants) over the next ten years could be restricted and limited to the occurrence of one hundred such cases against the church, then an estimate of the total projected losses for the decade could be established with a limit of one billion dollars ($1,000,000,000).[140]

A ten billion dollar ($10,000,000,000) class action lawsuit has been threatened, which threat is documented, and others who have not threatened same in writing, including Melvin Belli of San Francisco, are contemplating same. The suit would be brought on behalf of a number of children who are alleged victims of sexual abuse by priests and would be filed against the entirety of the church. The effort would be to embroil the whole structure in the controversy and conduct discovery in each and every diocese in this country in an effort to discover all damaging information.

The financial factors mentioned in the preceding paragraphs are actual and illustrative of what is now occurring in sexual molestation cases across the country.

In the cases cited above, the priest has been charged in a thirty-four count criminal indictment by a Grand Jury and the crimes with which he is charged carry a sentence upon conviction of life imprisonment without benefit of pardon or parole. The estimated cost of criminal defense is one-half million dollars and with the prospect of a lengthy trial.

The priest is presently housed at a private mental institution approved by the court where he would remain pending trial at a cost of ten thousand dollars monthly.

There are a number of civil trials from that case that have been set to commence beginning September 10, 1985.

Each development of that case has carried with it attendant adverse publicity. That publicity was local in nature originally but has now become national.

There are presently a significant number of other sexual molestation cases involving priests that exist in other jurisdictions. This document would not allude to those out of deference to the reader as many aspects of same have not been widely reported.

Presently all three major networks (ABC, NBC, CBS) and subdivisions of same (*20/20, 60 Minutes*), as well as CNN have reporters assigned to developing stories. Some have had crews on location shooting second unit (background) footage for inclusion in segments to be shown later. All national radio networks, as well as CBS Evening News and NBC Evening News have shot filmed reports.

A minimum of six national print publications (*New York Times, Washington Post, National Catholic Reporter, Vanity Fair, Mother Jones,* and *Rolling Stone*) have reporters in place trying to tie the isolated, regional episodes into a national story, presumably one of scandalous proportions. Several of these publications have already published lengthy articles (See NCR 7 June 1985).

Two previously published authors, Mr. Jason Berry (author of *Amazing Grace* and regular contributor to many magazines of national import) and Mr. Chris Segura (author of *Marshland Brace,* which was nominated for the Pulitzer and a former wire reporter covering European affairs) are attempting to place book proposals with publishers on this topic. At least one writer has applied to the Fund for Investigative Journalism for a grant to do a full-length work on pedophilia, priests, and the Catholic Church. All major wire services are now distributing articles and national commentators such as Paul Harvey have done pieces.

The American Bar Association and other groups comprised primarily of plaintiff lawyers are conducting studies, scheduling panel conferences, and devising other methods of disseminating information about this newly developing area of law. Thusfar three plaintiff lawyers representing children who have sued the church have agreed to make a presentation at two national meetings of the Bar to educate other lawyers on methods of successfully suing the church.

Our Diocesan lawyers have themselves addressed this situation and some of its ramifications as recently as their April (1985) meeting in Chicago and there presently exists an ongoing effort by some to study the problems. Though these efforts may produce significant studies, it is believed that the retention of full-time professionals and expert consultants is preferable to relying upon those whose responsibilities are already full time to take this task and exert the requisite effort. It is contemplated that the Project, where feasible, would avail itself of already existing resources and in some instances a coalition between those within the official structure of the church and outside consultants on the Project would be formed, i.e., where competent professionals exist within the USCC and other organizations and have workloads requiring less than their full attention, then, in those situations, it is possible the Project personnel may reach to those resources for assistance.

D. General Discussion

There are many newly developing areas of jurisprudence that deserve our attention. An example is the newly developing area of clergy malpractice. Suits are being filed against Protestant ministers and Catholic clergy. These malpractice cases involve situations where clerics give advice that is considered by the civil courts to be beyond their sphere of expertise or competence. This advice allegedly causes catastrophic consequences (divorce, suicide) resulting in civil suits. This document recognizes that a vast number of such issues exist separate and apart from sexual molestation, and have been discussed in the confidential consultations and meetings referred to earlier. It is contemplated that the Project will deal with those issues, as well as all other issues referred to it. However, this document has largely been restricted to a discussion of what has been perceived as the pressing problem, the possible cost to the Catholic Church of many millions of dollars and the potential devastating injury to its image as a result of inappropriate or felonious sexual activity between priests and parishioners, lay employees of religious institutions and third parties, and related areas involving consequential civil responsibility and criminal sanctions ... which situations give rise to Canonical and Clinical Considerations equal in import to the civil/criminal concerns.

This is the "age of litigation." The potential exposure to the Catholic Church for the continuation of claimants coming forward in legal jurisdictions across the country is very great. Already, a large number of damage claims have been made and more are certain. It might have been unthinkable a few years ago for a Catholic parent to sue the church. Similarly, there was a time when it was unthinkable for a patient to sue a physician. The analogy with medical malpractice is well taken. This area of jurisprudence, i.e., the church's financial responsibility for damages caused by the sexual conduct of a priest, is presently situated where medical malpractice litigation was a quarter century ago. There are absolutely no definitive appellate court decisions that exist at present on the substantive questions. The law is waiting to be made! And it will be made, with or without the church's involvement in the process. Presently the church is prepared to participate in the process through the non-uniform, random actions of individuals (local diocesan lawyers and others) with the result being a divergent application of the Canonical, Clinical, Civil, and Criminal Considerations. This Special Project seeks to rectify that immediately by making uniform assistance available to those bishops and local lawyers who wish to avail themselves of this offered assistance.

In this age of litigation, plaintiff lawyers are constantly breaking barriers down, finding new causes of action, and searching for deep pockets, defendants to sue who possess great financial wealth. The Catholic Church is undoubtedly perceived by plaintiff lawyers to have very deep pockets, to have a very serious interest in its image, and therefore should become the biggest target in this newly developing field of jurisprudence, i.e., seeking compensation for an allegedly abused child from the employer or parent organization of the wrongdoer.

"Pedophilia" and related deviant disorders is an area that has been closeted in Western civilization for centuries. Most individuals and organizations, including the church and bishops, who were ever confronted with the issue of illicit sexual relationships between adults and children responded in a manner they thought to be responsible in an effort to protect the injured child and aid the offending priest. It is now known because of strides in the clinical field that perhaps those actions insofar as they aided, comforted, or enabled the sex offender to continue his secret life were irresponsible and injurious to the sex offender. Though psychological study is still in its infancy in some respects, much more is known about the long- and short-term traumatic injury inflicted on the victim.

In any event, the entire issue of "Child Sexual Abuse," whether same be categorized as pedophiliac, homosexual, or heterosexual, is displayed prominently across the front pages of newspapers where it would remain for at least the balance of the decade (having replaced the sexual issue of the 1970s, homosexuality).

The general awareness and consciousness of the public in regard to sexual abuse of children has reached a previously unattained level and shall continue to escalate with each new revelation of discovered cases of sexual molestation. This increased awareness, widespread publicity, and the excellent educational programs available to children, which we all support, would increase the reporting of such incidents and increase the likelihood that both civil and criminal actions would be instituted against the offender and those sought to be held legally responsible with the wrongdoer.

For well over a decade the news media of this country has exhibited a tendency to attack institutions presently or previously held in high esteem by the public, including the presidency. The tendency is ever escalating, particularly in instances where the press can characterize a situation as scandalous.

Cases of this nature have all of the necessary elements for press reporters and plaintiff lawyers; there is a significant injury, psychological in nature, to a sympathetic victim of a tender age, an odious and heinous circumstance surrounding the infliction of injury that engenders prejudice, and punitive awards from juries against the defendant church, an organization perceived by many to be possessed of great wealth.

Also, the secular press attempts to portray the church as hypocritical, as an organization preaching morality and providing sanctuary to perverts ... the attempts are in evidence today and will escalate.

E. Five Hypothetical Cases

Experience has shown that sexual misconduct by the clergy takes a variety of forms. While the cases have common threads running through them, there are many dimensions and tangential aspects that could occur. All of the elements of each case must be given careful study.

Though many hypothetical cases could be considered, the following are brief descriptions of five realistic (yet hypothetical) occurrences. The listing is illustrative only, and intended to provide a basis for the pertinent questions that follow.

1. Hypothetical Case No. 1

As bishop, it comes to your attention, as a result of a visit from a parishioner, that an associate pastor is suspected of having had sexual relations with one or more children not related to complainant.

2. Hypothetical Case No. 2

As a bishop, you have confirmed a suspicion that a parish priest has, over a long period of time, been involved sexually with juveniles.

3. Hypothetical Case No. 3

As a bishop, you have confirmed a suspicion that a parish priest has, over a long period of time, been involved sexually with juveniles and further that some of the parents have retained lawyers, some have gone to the criminal prosecutor, and others have contacted various media representatives.

4. Hypothetical Case No. 4

A case involving a pedophile priest arises in a jurisdiction where the criminal prosecutor has great animosity against the church. This prosecutor has the most devastating of legal weapons in his arsenal, the Grand Jury Subpoena, which allows him to bring all of the Diocesan records and personnel he desires into a closed room, subject to cross examination, without counsel to advise them. It is the setting for a witch hunt that the vindictive plaintiff lawyer referred to earlier tried to institute in a civil case, i.e., it was his announced intention to prove a pervasive pattern of widespread sexual dysfunction and by implication argue same has been condoned by the clergy. A case is now developing where these explosive elements are present.

5. Hypothetical Case No. 5

A case involving a homosexual priest who has been suspended by a bishop following the discovery of his sexual activity with a juvenile or adolescent. In this hypothet, the priest is a Gay Liberationist and as such retains the services of a gay lawyer, the support of gay organizations … and strikes back at us, suing to show, among other things, all sexual skeletons in our closet across the county. There is a strong gay ministry movement as evidenced by the literature and this hypothetical confrontation can occur.

The following are select questions that should be considered in dealing with these kinds of cases. They are divided into the following categories: criminal law questions; civil law questions; canon law questions; and clinical or medical questions.

II. Asking Questions and Giving Consideration

(A compendium of the questions raised by the clerical sexual abuse of minors raises and a consideration of ways to respond to them.)

A. Questions Seeking Answers

1. Criminal Law Questions

a. Does sexual contact with minor children constitute a criminal offense? Which types of sexual contact are considered felonious (involving maximum imprisonment at hard labor) and which are classified as misdemeanors (involving fines and minimum incarceration)?

b. At what age is a child considered to be an adult? At what young age is a child considered to be so tender as to cause a sexual crime to be considered by criminal law to be an aggravated crime, one that carries the most serious sentences such as life imprisonment?

c. What is the requirement in criminal law for one who has knowledge that a sexual crime has been committed to report that knowledge to the authorities? To which authorities (district attorney, state child welfare agency) must the report be made? What criminal law penalty, fine, or jail term would be given to a bishop who failed to comply with the reporting law?

d. Is there any privilege that attaches to the communication between the bishop and the priest under criminal law? Can the bishop be made to testify before a Grand Jury, give statements to police detectives, or give evidence in a criminal trial against the priest?

e. Does the criminal law provide that the bishop's files or other diocesan records can be subpoenaed and utilized in a police investigation, Grand Jury hearing, or a criminal trial?

f. Is there an obligation to provide constitutional due process to the priest accused of sexual crimes and furnish an attorney for the priest prior to eliciting any incriminatory information? Must the priest be provided this protection and can the priest reasonably refuse to answer questions posed by this Ordinary?

g. Should a criminal lawyer be retained for the priest or by the priest? If so, should this be a lawyer separate from Diocesan Counsel? At what stage should this be done? What financial obligations exist for payment of legal fees, expenses, bonding costs, etc?

2. Civil Law Questions

a. What specific provisions for insurance coverage exist in regard to the civil law consequences of the sexual conduct between the priest and child?

b. What contractual obligation, if any, exists in regard to notification of insurer? At what point should the insurance companies be told of the exposure?

c. What rights, if any, does the bishop have in relationship to the civil law defense of the diocese? Can the bishop either select or reject the particular attorneys to be utilized? Can the bishop dictate any aspect of the handling of the case to ensure that the image of the church is protected from injury?

d. If the bishop is aware of sexual misconduct, or a propensity for sexual misconduct, that took place at an earlier date, does this fact become a critical question in subsequent litigation involving child molestation? In other words, if the bishop has knowledge that a priest sexually abused a child in 1970, does this knowledge affect his liability in the event of a similar incident in 1980? Does this prior knowledge by the bishop constitute negligence on his part independent of diocesan negligence? Can the bishop be financially liable to the suing parties, independent of, or in addition to, liability of the Diocese?

e. What civil law obligations exist toward the child-victim and the family of the child?

f. Can suits be brought against the Corporate Entity, i.e., the diocese, or can the superiors, including the hierarchical superiors (pastors, vicar general, bishop, metropolitan archbishop, papal representative, Holy Father, Holy See) be named in the suits as well with some possibility of success?

g. Can the civil lawsuit be restricted to the one priest and his actions, or will the suing parties be able to expose all other sexual misconduct of every other priest in the diocese? Can the civil law courts cause the bishop to give information regarding all aberrant sexual practices of priests in the diocese? Can all this information be subpoenaed, and will the diocese be forced by civil law to provide the information?

h. Which parties can bring a civil law suit? Will the child be the only person entitled under civil law to a recovery of money? Can the parents sue and recover money?

i. What are the factors in a civil law that determine what damages were incurred by the parties and what sums they would receive?

j. Is there any provision in civil law for restricting the access of the press to the civil proceedings? Will all of the civil law proceedings be reported?

k. Which canonical and clinical procedures instituted at this juncture shall be later viewed favorably by the civil law courts and which shall be viewed unfavorably and why?

l. Which initially instituted measures will later be deemed prudent and reasonable by the civil law courts and which will be classified as imprudent and negligent?

m. In which civil law cases should the diocese attempt to force its insurance companies to either settle cases quietly without public disclosure or, in the alternative, admit liability to prevent public disclosure or damaging information? What are the civil law effects of such settlements or admissions? What are the key factors that cause a bishop to consider these alternatives? What effect will settlements and admissions have on future insurance premiums?

n. Which civil law cases should be defended through trial and appeal courts? What factors are to be considered in determining whether a case should settle or be tried? Most importantly, at what stage should the decision be made?

o. Does the diocesan attorney have expertise and experience in trial law generally, and specifically does the diocesan attorney have civil law and criminal law experience in the area of these sexual conduct cases? Should additional lawyers be hired? Should counsel be sought from lawyers with expertise and hands-on experience in this field?

p. What civil law procedures, if any, exist? What was the experience of prior cases and trial court decisions? What databank, if any, exists that might contain accurate information from prior cases and circumstances in dioceses across the country? Which individuals (lawyers, psychiatrists, canon layers, etc.) have expertise, experience, and information on the civil law cases and how does the bishop contact the people and gain access to the information?

3. Canon Law Questions

a. Should the bishop investigate the incident?

b. Does he have an obligation to conduct an investigation?

c. Does Canon Law provide a format for any type of investigation?

d. Is it necessary that an investigation precede the bishop's confrontation of the cleric?

e. If there is a confrontation, are there any canonical procedures that should or must be followed?

f. If the priest admits the allegations, and he is the only priest in the parish, how should the bishop proceed?

g. Is the bishop limited in any way, because of confidentiality, in his ability or freedom to consult with others concerning the alleged incidents?

h. In studying the source of the allegations, or suspicions, is there a preferable method for assuring credibility/reliability of the source?

i. May/should the bishop delegate the power to investigate to a vicar or some other person?

j. Should a record be kept of the allegation and investigation?

k. Where should such a record be kept?

l. How secure is such a record from civil authorities?

m. Should the bishop confront the priest? If so, should this be done privately or in the presence of someone else?

n. If the priest admits the incidents, what action should the bishop take: transfer, removal, suspension?

o. Can the priest be suspended? Without a process? What are his rights to recourse?

p. Is the bishop canonically responsible for the priest's support while he is suspended? If he is living in another diocese? If he is laicized?

q. Is such a priest suspected of any canonical delicts and liable to canonical penalties?

r. Does the bishop have any canonical/moral/pastoral obligations toward the victims and their families?

s. Should the bishop inform the Metropolitan and/or the Apostolic pro-Nuncio?

t. Does the canon law clearly define the bishop's relationship to his priests and deacons (permanent and transient)?

u. What will the civil law perceive this relationship to be, based on ecclesiastical documentation available to the courts?

v. Should an expert in canon law be retained to assist in the case, possibly by helping prepare witnesses or appearing as an expert witness himself?

w. Where can such a canonical expert be found? Should he be affiliated with the NCCB, Nunciature, Holy See, etc.?

x. Does the law provide for any general method of vigilance over the activities of priests and other church employees?

y. Does the law provide for any method of investigation and consequent action in cases of complaints of misconduct?

z. Is there a canonical entity known as the Roman Catholic Church in the United States?

aa. If a class action were so filed, would the National Bishops' Conference qualify as the canonical entity?

bb. What is the canonical relationship of each diocese and its bishop to other ecclesiastical entities such as the Metropolitan See and Archbishop; the National Conference of Catholic Bishops; the United States Catholic Conference; the Apostolic Nunciature and the Pro-Nuncio; the Holy See and the Holy Father?

cc. What is the canonical authority of the NCCB over individual bishops and their dioceses?

dd. Is there any protection for diocesan files, secret archives, and tribunal records?

4. Clinical/Medical Questions

a. Are psychiatrists, psychologists, and social workers equally qualified, both professionally and legally, to examine clerics who have a suspected problem of sexual molestation of children?

b. If you ask a social worker, psychologist, or psychiatrist to examine and evaluate your cleric, is he obliged under your state law to report this to the district attorney or the child abuse agency?

c. What is the difference between pedophilia, homosexuality, and the sexual abuse of adolescent males or females?

d. Does the age of the offending priest (older or younger) create a significant difference in his diagnosis and treatment?

e. Are there mitigating psychiatric disorders of which it would be important to be aware before proceeding with a decision on a treatment facility or a treatment program?

f. If there is a problem of alcohol or drug abuse complicating the problem of sexual abuse of children or adolescents, would any alcohol treatment center be capable of treating both the alcohol or drug abuse and the sexual abuse issues?

g. Are the treatment centers presently used for Catholic Clergy and Religious, i.e., the Houses of Affirmation, Guest House, St. Luke Institute, the institutions of the Servants of the Paraclete and Southdown (near Toronto) equally qualified to treat both the alcohol/drug abuse and dependence as well as cases of sexual abuse of children or adolescents? Do they all have follow-up programs for two or more years that would monitor the cleric's activity and report to the Ordinary?

h. If the case involves a repeat offender and prior psychiatric or psychological intervention has been useless, what drug therapy would be considered in the treatment of the sex offender, whether or not alcohol or other mitigating psychiatric disorders were present?

i. What constitutes sexual abuse? Does touching the buttocks of a fully clothed nine-year-old child constitute sexual abuse either in the law or from a psychiatrist's viewpoint? Does touching the covered genitalia of a fully clothed youngster constitute sexual abuse? Does masturbation of the child by the priest or of the priest by the child constitute sexual abuse?

j. Does the age of the child at the time of the abuse and the extent of the abuse have any effect on long-term function or dysfunction of this child with adults?

k. At what age would an abused child be expected to fully comprehend and be cognizant of the long-term effects of prolonged and severe sexual abuse by a layperson or by a cleric?

l. If the juvenile were a sixteen-year-old boy, would this imply that the abuse would have a lesser impact in the adult life of this victim?

m. If the teenager appeared to initiate the sexual contact and seemed to continue to enjoy it over a period of time, would this change the offense in the eyes of the law or in the eyes of a psychiatrist?

n. If the sexual contact is mainly with juvenile boys or adolescent boys, does this imply that the boys are more likely to be homosexually oriented in their future adult life as compared to abuse of pre-pubertal children?

o. Clinically, in cases involving cleric sexual offenders, is there a difference if the offender regularly abused children as opposed to adolescents? Is there a difference if the victims are pre-pubertal girls as opposed to adolescent girls?

p. Would there be more likelihood that the adolescent boy or girl would "not tell the truth" as compared to a pre-pubertal child?

q. If there is a "mitigating" psychiatric disorder or psychological disorder, would it make it any difference in where you would send this priest for treatment?

r. Of the facilities listed in number 7, which offers a complete neurological and neuropsychological as well as complete physical and medical evaluations as well as psychological testing? Would the facility and the variety of evaluations be important in determining the presence of mitigating medical or psychiatric disorders?

s. What kind of pre-intervention strategy should the Ordinary consider?

t. How soon should a complete evaluation be done?

u. Should the alleged priest-offender see anyone else before the evaluation?

v. What are the causes of sexual abuse by Roman Catholic clergy?

w. What should an Ordinary look for and expect in an adequate evaluation of a cleric?

x. How can an Ordinary know which treatment center is best for the needs of the alleged offender?

y. Can a priest/cleric ever return and function in the diocese?

z. What should the Ordinary do with regard to the families of the victims?

B. Considering the Questions

(The following criminal and civil law considerations follow upon the pertinent question in the same area, posed elsewhere. These are not to be construed as answers to these questions. Rather, they expand upon the questions and suggest the importance of dealing effectively with the various aspects of these two dimensions of this problem.)

1. Criminal Law Considerations

Every civil jurisdiction (usually by states) has statutes that impose civil and criminal penalties on persons who engage in illicit sexual activities with children and/or adolescents. If a cleric is charged with sexual misconduct, civil lawsuits can be lodged against him and his Ordinary for monetary damages to the victim and families resulting from felonious conduct. The offender could also be charged with criminal activity. If a sworn complaint is received by a police agency or a prosecutor (D.A.) it is inevitable that criminal charges will be filed, causing the press to publish reports of the charges. This would lead investigative reports to delve into the details of the case.

What follows the pressing of criminal charges is this: upon completion of the criminal investigation by the police authorities and the D.A., an indictment is obtained, the priest or cleric will be apprehended and arrested, placed in custody, i.e., jail, pending a bond hearing where it will be required that some individual or entity (Ordinary or Diocese) assume substantial financial obligations that will allow the priest offender to remain free (in treatment) pending trial. A very expensive criminal defense will be required prior to and through the course of the trial. At the conclusion of the trial the priest will either be acquitted or convicted. Upon conviction the priest will be sentenced to imprisonment at a state penitentiary. A judge usually has no choice (depending on the jurisdiction and what the priest is found guilty of) but to sentence a convicted offender to prison.

a. Reporting Requirements

In most or all jurisdictions there are statutes that require that instances of child abuse be reported to the civil authorities. The failure to do so can result in civil and/or criminal penalties.

b. Providing a Criminal Defense

Every instance of sexual molestation of a child is a criminal offense. A judge must sentence a convicted offender to prison. Though this is more the domain of the canon law, an Ordinary has some degree of obligation to provide an offender with a competent trial lawyer in order that he be adequately defended as is his right.

c. Conflict Presented by Civil Cases

The Fifth Amendment of the U.S. Constitution provides the right to all who are accused of committing crimes to remain silent and say nothing to anyone that might later be used against the subject in a court of law. Therefore, should or must the Ordinary provide a criminal lawyer to the priest prior to or in advance of having the initial conversation with the priest about the complaint? Can the priest refuse to answer the questions posed by the Ordinary based on his civil constitutional rights in anticipation of criminal charges being filed against him? Can the Ordinary be forced to reveal or convey any communication he receives from the priest to police or prosecution authorities, including information that would either be utilized to provide corroborating evidence of the priest's guilt or provide the very basis for the prosecution? The basic conflict that exists here is whether or not the priest should honestly communicate with his Ordinary or not.

The accused priest is obviously the one in the best position to provide all of the basic information about the alleged incidents. This essential information is needed in order to determine how best to proceed with such matters as treatment plans for the offender and identifying all of the victims and their families so that adequate intervention can be planned, etc. Nevertheless if the priest, in all good faith, provides this information to his Ordinary it may derogate from his fifth amendment privilege. This could, in some jurisdictions, literally finish him in terms of a defense in criminal prosecution.

The choice of a criminal attorney at the earliest state and the creation of the mutually cooperative relationship between the criminal attorney and counsel in the civil cases as well as insurance counsel is very important.

d. Unavailability of Plea Bargaining Process

Plea bargaining is a process whereby a district attorney and a criminal defense lawyer reach a binding agreement providing that there shall not be a trial. The defendant, as a result of the plea bargain, admits guilt to a crime, and receives a minimal sentence, much lighter than the maximum that might well have been imposed following a trial. Plea bargains are unavailable in criminal cases where there is the commission of a heinous and odious crime against a young and defenseless victim. These cases are very high profile, attracting widespread media attention, and these cases enrage communities, all of which creates obvious and subtle political pressure bearing down on the prosecutor or D.A. This forces him to bring the cases to trial. District attorneys in these cases want to make certain that there is no perception in the public or opinion in the community that because the church was involved that the D.A. has treated the priest in a deferential or preferential manner. To prove his political independence, the tendency of most D.A.'s would be to prosecute fully.

e. Extreme Criminal Law Possibilities for Superiors

There have been situations wherein district attorneys almost pressed criminal charges against the priest's Ordinary, which would have resulted in the indictment, arrest, incarceration, bonding, or trial of the Ordinary. Had this process occurred, upon conviction, the Ordinary would have been faced with the possibility of serving a severe sentence in the penitentiary.

There are a lot of criminal laws that pertain to an Ordinary in instances of sexual molestation of children by their subjects. Primarily there are two broad areas under which this criminal responsibility falls. First, the area of reporting. Failure to report information regarding sexual molestation of a child by a priest when such information is available or in the possession of the Ordinary is considered a criminal offense in some states.

Secondly, to allow a priest to continue to function, endangering the health of children, following the receipt of private, confidential knowledge that this priest victimized a child is considered to be "criminal neglect" (a crime in many states).

The proposal contained herein seeks to deal with this very serious question.

2. Civil Law Considerations

a. Liability of Bishops

Some debate exists in the civil law's understanding of the relationship between a bishop and his priests and major religious superiors and their subjects.

The extent of responsibility a bishop or religious superior has in regard to tortious or felonious conduct of his priests/subjects has not been defined in the original sense by the higher courts of the civil law system, and, thus, the exceptions to such original definition do not exist. There are absolutely no reported civil court decisions on the issues. This body of law is just beginning to develop with the filing of these cases.

The bishop's responsibility beyond the incardinated priest, for the actions of non-incardinated priests assigned for study, special work, visiting (or having been suspended by another) as well as a bishop's responsibility for one whom he has suspended who is residing elsewhere, including a treatment center without appropriate supervision ... the questions await definition.

b. Impact of Code of Canon Law on Civil Courts

The Canon Law shall play an important part of the civil damage cases. The interpretation of Canon Law by plaintiff lawyers in litigation has already been experienced. No court has yet made rulings in this regard.

It is well founded in civil cases that operation manuals, policy and procedure memoranda, and other documents generated as guidelines by the civil defendant may be utilized in evidence.

That the Code of Canon Law actually has the effect of law over our personnel shall make it more relevant than some civil document that constitutes no more than a guideline. The impact may be negative or positive depending on the preparation of the civil lawyer and the participation of a canon lawyer in cases where the issue presents itself.

c. Liability of Larger Entities

Presently there are efforts to sue, successfully, not only a diocese but also a bishop, diocesan vicars, the metropolitan archdiocese, the Holy See's representative in the United States, and the Holy Father himself. These cases are being partially settled by the insurance companies without first attempting to settle the question for the civil jurisdiction in question.

The trend to expand the circle of responsibility beyond the diocese of the priests in question to the National Conference of Catholic Bishops, the Apostolic Pro-Nuncio, and the Holy Father himself shall continue.

In great measure the courts shall look to both the civil law and the canon law to comprehend the relationship of these other ecclesiastical entities with the diocese in question, the bishop, and the priest-offender himself.

It is highly probable (nearly certain) that each and every Ordinary in the United States shall be made a party-defendant in a federal class action suit, the threat of which has been documented in correspondence to the general counsel's office of the USCC-NCCB. In a class action every Ordinary in the country would have to testify about every instance of aberrant sexual conduct in their diocese, produce all records relating to aberrant sexual practices, and defend their actions or inaction in each instance.

The Papal representative in the United States, the Holy Father, and the NCCB will be the primary target of lawsuits seeking to establish their direct responsibility for the grave injury suffered by the child-victims. In these efforts plaintiff lawyers will utilize, possibly to their advantage, the structures set forth in the Code of Canon Law describing the interrelationship and interdependence of these various ecclesiastical entities. The project proposed herein shall address these extremely serious issues and attempt to provide acceptable solutions.

d. Responsibility for Seminarians

The responsibility for seminarians is two-edged in that there is a responsibility on the part of the Ordinary for things done by the seminarian and things done to the seminarian.

Depending on the geographic location of the seminary as well as the canonical and corporate structure, more than one bishop may be involved in answering the questions of responsibility. It is also possible that the wider ecclesiastical entities may be involved if the seminary has some direct connections to the Holy See (i.e., a Pontifical seminary, inter-diocesan seminary, etc.).

e. Responsibility of Bishops for Visiting Clergy

A bishop may extend hospitality to a priest who is not incardinated to his diocese and allow said priest to live and work as a priest in his own diocese. If the priest has a history of problems involving sexual misconduct and the bishop is aware of this and allows the priest to live and work in his diocese anyway, there are serious questions regarding his responsibility to act in the event of a subsequent incident.

A legal agreement between the host bishop and the priest's own Ordinary may provide a partial remedy to problems pursuant to an incident.

f. Maintenance of Diocesan Records

A paramount concern is the security of diocesan records and the limits of confidentiality that may be successfully claimed by church authorities. This issue is governed by complex discovery decisions in the state and federal law. In civil law the courts allow lawyers who bring suits to use the process called "discovery" to make the defendant (in these cases, bishops and/or dioceses) produce records and personnel who may be compelled to give sworn testimony.

In the event of a class action suit such as the one that is threatened, the lawyers bringing the suit shall try to obtain records from each and every diocese in the country. They shall also try to obtain testimony from each and every bishop. All this shall be an attempt to document each and every known instance of sexual misconduct by a priest.

It is important to know what matter should be contained in a priest's personnel file, considering the very probable discoverability of these files.

The idea of sanitizing or purging files for potentially damaging material has been brought up. This would be in contempt of court and an obstruction of justice if the files had already been subpoenaed by the courts. Even if there has been no such subpoena, such actions could be construed as a violation of the law in the event of a class action suit. On a canonical level, to sanitize the personnel files could pose a problem of continuity from one diocesan administration to another.

One other suggestion regarding files has been to move them to the Apostolic Nunciature where it is believed they would remain secure, in immune territory. In all likelihood, such action would ensure that the immunity of the Nunciature would be damaged or destroyed by the civil courts.

The canon law speaks of secret archives. Are these safe from the civil discovery whereas ordinary files might not be? Thus far it appears that the secret archives afford no more security from discovery than regular diocesan archives.

g. Uniformity of Case Management

At this time there is no uniformity of case management. It is desirable that such uniformity be developed in order to provide optimum assistance to bishops and diocese lawyers. The same issues are present in similar cases in the different dioceses such as:

(1) The confidentiality of diocesan records

(2) Legal arguments against liability

(3) The criminal defense posture to be developed for a priest-offender

(4) The responsibility of insurance companies to act in a manner that is not detrimental to church interests

(5) Legal pleadings to be filed on behalf of all defendants and their contents

(6) Potential conflicts between defendants and with insurors

(7) The public posture of all parties in relationship to the general public and the wider church community as presented in press announcements and stories, statements of the bishop and other authorities related to the case, as well as pulpit announcements.

All of these legal efforts and the many others that arise should be coordinated so that a single, carefully choreographed theme is presented. This theme or posture should be consistent in character and design and produce a result that is advantageous for the church, victims, and the public.

h. The Discovery of Information That Is Circulated About This Problem

If all of the possible questions related to this problem are posed and a suitable and complete set of answers drawn up and set forth in the form of a policy manual or procedural guideline, it would not be advisable to release such a manual/document to the bishops of the country or the diocesan lawyers.

Such information could fall into the hands of either the plaintiffs or the press and the document itself could be deemed discoverable and used as evidence.

Nevertheless it is virtually impossible at this time to compose a document or manual that a) adequately addresses the problem with all of its vitally important aspects and b) would not cause damage if it fell into the hands of the press or plaintiffs.

Only two major insurance considerations and eight civil law considerations have been noted for the sake of brevity. This is because the purpose of this entire document is to provide a basis for understanding both the enormity and the gravity of the total situation. To continue to list the hundreds of civil law considerations and the many issues would expand this document beyond its intended format. Accordingly a limited listing of the criminal law considerations, clinical and medical considerations, and canon law issues follows.

3. Canon Law Considerations

Because of the nature of canon law, as opposed to Anglo-American Common Law, there is a perceived closer relationship between the proposed canon law questions and the following discussion of canonical issues. This discussion is not an attempt to provide definitive answers to these important canonical issues. This information on the canonical dimensions of these problems provides a general context within which to work with each specific case.

a. Investigation of Complaints

When a bishop receives a complaint that a priest or deacon has engaged in sexual misconduct with a minor child, this complaint should be discreetly investigated at once.

(1) The obligation rests with the bishop himself and should not be delegated to another person. This bishop may see fit to involve trusted advisors in the process, but he should supervise and directly participate in the investigation himself. (A private response from the prefect of the Congregation of the Clergy in 1983 referred to the bishop's obligation to directly involve himself in disputes regarding priests. The response stated that this duty is not to be delegated.)

(2) The Code of Canon of law provides a basis for an investigation in Chapter I, "The Preliminary Investigation," of Book VII, Part IV, "The Penal Process." The canons (Canons 1717–1719) offer wide discretion to the bishop in the investigation of complaints. The second chapter, "The Course of the Process" (Canons 1720–1728), outlines the manner of proceeding if the preliminary investigation shows that there is a probability that a canonical delict was committed.

(3) If the bishop follows the basic procedures outlined in Canons 1717–1719 he need not move to the next phase, a trial. He may simply want to go on record indicating that the canons provide for a process whereby complaints may be investigated. Such a course of action could be advantageous if the civil courts require proof of responsible action by the church authorities in light of complaints. Following the canons to some extent shows two things: the church has a mechanism for protection of rights of the faithful (Cf. Canon 221).

(4) The *notary:* canon law allows laypersons and non-ordained to hold the office of ecclesiastical

notary, yet canon 483, 2 stipulates that in any case that *could* involve the reputation of a priest, the notary must be a priest. Consequently, the person keeping the record of a preliminary investigation or indeed any process, including the penal process, involving these cases must be a priest.

b. Canonical Delicts

For those bound to perpetual continence and in sacred orders, a number of canonical delicts (crimes) may be committed in the course of sexual misconduct

(1) Canon 277 refers to the cleric's obligation to perfect continence as well as his obligation to act and relate prudently to persons.

(2) Canon 285, 1: The obligation to shun anything that is unbecoming the clerical state.

(3) Canon 1395: This canon refers to offense against the sixth commandment by clerics. It deals with concubinage and sexual intercourse with women and related scandal in the first paragraph, and with other related offenses, including those involving force, threats, and offenses with children. The canon sets no specific penalties but merely refers to "just penalties up to and including dismissal from the clerical state."

(4) Canon 1387: Solicitation in the confessional. A priest who solicits in the confessional or under the pretext of confession for a sexual act is to be punished with penalties up to and including dismissal from the clerical state.

(5) Canon 1378: This canon refers to canon 977 (the absolution of a partner in a sexual sin is invalid except in case of danger of death). A priest who commits this delict is automatically excommunicated and the absolution is reserved to the Holy See.

(6) Canon 1389: This canon deals with the general abuse of ecclesiastical office or power. The crime is to be punished in relation to its severity.

Clerics who have sexual intercourse with women, men, or children are obviously liable to canonical penalties since such actions constitute the matter for canonical crimes. There are other issues related to these crimes, however, and the fact of commission of a crime should not be isolated as the major issue.

The canonical legislation of sexual misconduct indicates that such actions are contrary to the cleric's essential obligations. The law makes no distinction between performance of such acts while carrying out ecclesiastical duties and those perpetrated at other times. These actions are contrary to the cleric's very way of life and consequently he is obligated at all times to comply with them.

c. Canonical Penalties Applicable

Although canonical penalties are ordinarily applied at the conclusion of a trial or process, the unique nature of certain forms of sexual misconduct, especially sexual abuse of minor children, should preclude such an approach under most circumstances.

In certain cases, the perpetrator might find himself excommunicated automatically, such as when he absolves an accomplice.

The preferred method of applying appropriate canonical penalties in such cases would be by way of administrative decree, issued by the bishop. The penalty referred to is suspension of the priest from all sacred functions, ecclesiastical offices, and duties.

(1) *Administrative Leave* (See Canonical Revision 7-28-86): After the initial report has been made and the Ordinary has decided that an investigation is justified, he should proceed according to Canons 1717–1719. The accused is simply that ... his guilt

has not yet been determined. The canons provide for a kind of "administrative leave" (Canon 1722) whereby the priest or deacon may be asked to leave his residence and cease all public ministerial functions. This type of action by the bishop is not only advisable but should be routine. At this point the priest or deacon should *not* be suspended. Suspension is a canonical penalty that leads to a presumption of guilt. This could be misconstrued in civil courts and used to the disadvantage of the church. The priest or deacon has been accused of a delict, which is an actual manifestation or result of a highly compulsive disorder. Although the actual effects of involving Canon 1722 may be similar to suspension, the act whereby these effects take place is not a suspension. There is no process required beyond that mentioned in the canon. It would be advisable to explain to the accused that such action is for his benefit.

(2) *Suspension* as canonical penalty may be imposed by decree for a period of time, following the procedures outlined in the Code, or it may be imposed perpetually but not by decree. A perpetual or indefinite suspension can be imposed only after a canonical trial. In any case, suspension should only be used after the priest or deacon's guilt has been determined. If the accused is convicted and imprisoned, he could well be suspended for the duration of his incarceration. Such action might be advisable to avoid the appearance of tolerating the actions of pedophiles (but at the same time treating them with compassion). If it is determined, in conjunction with clinical advisors, that a priest or deacon can and should not exercise in the ministry again because of the nature of his affliction or its severity, then laicization must

be seriously considered. In the meantime it would be well to suspend the priest or deacon.

(3) *Removal from office:* Although removal from office (associate, pastor, etc.) or transfer is not penal procedure but an administrative procedure, the law provides for such actions if the Ordinary believes that he has sufficient reason and that it rebounds to the good of the faithful. Canons 1740–1752 set out in detail this procedure as well as the recourse against a decree or removal or transfer.

The Ordinary, upon encountering a case of sexual misconduct, might give consideration to invoking the canons regarding removal in conjunction with those pertaining to penal procedures.

Nevertheless it is imperative to clearly understand that transfer or removal isolated from any other action is far from adequate and could in fact lead to a presumption of irresponsibility or even liability of the diocesan authorities by civil courts. In short, those presumed to be guilty of sexual misconduct, especially if it involves child molestation, must *never be transferred* to another parish or post as the isolated remedy for the situation.

(4) *Laicization:* Canon 290 states that although sacred ordination, once validly received, never becomes invalid, a cleric (priest, deacon, or even bishop) loses the clerical state in three instances:

> (a) when a judgment of a court or administrative decree declares the ordinations to be *invalid*
>
> (b) when laicization is lawfully imposed as a penalty
>
> (c) when laicization is imposed by rescript of the Holy See.

Declaration of the invalidity of ordination is extremely rare and quite difficult to prove since it involves the intentionality of both the recipient of Holy orders and that of the ordaining prelate. Allegations of lack of fitness for celibacy would not constitute solid basis to pursue such a matter.

Although the law includes dismissal from the clerical state (laicization) as a possibile penalty for the offenses mentioned in Canons 1387 and 1395, this penalty may not always be imposed on those guilty of sexual crimes not excluding pedophilia. Canon 1324, 1, 10, 20, 30 indicates that the penalty prescribed by law or precept must be diminished if the culprit had only imperfect use of reason; lacked use of reason because of culpable drunkenness or other mental disturbances of a similar kind; acted in the heat of passion which, while serious, nevertheless did not precede or hinder all mental deliberation and consent of the will, provided that the passion itself was not deliberately stimulated.

As is obvious from the last paragraph, it is possible to dismiss a cleric from the clerical state if he committed canonical crimes involving sexual misconduct. Yet if he acted under the influence of one or more of the conditions mentioned in Canon 1324 it is not possible to impose the extreme penalty allowed, namely dismissal.

Dismissal may be prudently considered when it is obvious that the cleric in question will not be able to fulfill the duties of the clerical state and sacred orders, even to a minimal degree, because of his compulsion for illicit sexual activity. In such cases this course of action might prove to be the most beneficial for the person and for the church. It would effectively lighten the liability and responsibility of church authorities for the actions of a clear pedophile who is proven to be completely incorrigible. The decision to proceed toward dismissal should be made in conjunction with expert canonical counsel as well as well-founded clinical advice on the man's suitability for the clerical state.

It may happen that situations arise when dismissal is seen to be the only viable course of action but when, at the same time, a court process is ill-advised or impossible. In such cases only the Holy See has the power to issue a rescript whereby a priest or deacon is reduced from the clerical state. It is possible for the Holy Father to *ex officio* laicize a man when it appears that no other course of action is advised. In such cases the cleric's local Ordinary should prepare the petition for laicization and send it, together with all pertinent material, to the Congregation for the Doctrine of the Faith. The relative urgency of the case will determine the alacrity with which the case is handled in Rome. Laicization requests arising from pedophilia will be given serious consideration by the Congregation for the Doctrine of the Faith (for priests) and the Congregation for the Sacraments (for deacons). See Canonical Revision 7-28-86.

d. Ecclesiastical Records

Canon law refers to two types of archives or records: the Ordinary diocesan archives and the Secret archives. In fact, there are numerous types of records kept in most, if not all, diocesan curias. These include financial records, lay personnel records, insurance records, priest-personnel records, tribunal acts, etc. In most dioceses the priest-personnel records are kept in a separate file. What is contained in each priest's file can vary greatly with the dioceses and its policy. Usually seminary records, transfer indications, letters of commendation and complaint, and other related matters are kept in the priest's file. In some instances, recorded conscience matters that would include such matter as sexual misconduct are also contained in the priest's file.

(1) *The Diocesan archives:* Canon 487 states that only the bishop and chancellor may have keys to the archives and permission for entry must be obtained

from the bishop, the moderator of the curia, or the chancellor. This is a broad canon that implies that the wide range of materials that could be placed in the archives enjoy a degree of security and confidentiality. The same canon also states that persons concerned have a right to receive copies of documents that concern their personal status and are by nature public. Thus access to certain documents about persons could be restricted if these are not considered public by nature. Complaints about sexual misconduct would not be considered public by nature.

Canon 488 states that documents may be removed from the archives only for a short time and then with the permission of the bishop, moderator of the curia, or chancellor.

While the canon law on diocesan records may be clear and may be presumed to guarantee security of files and confidentiality, the fact remains that in certain civil courts in the United States, decisions have been handed down that have held that the contents of diocesan records, including priest-personnel files and even tribunal files, are not absolutely confidential and thus may be discovered in a civil court process.

(2) *The Secret archives:* Canons 489 and 490 refer to the secret archives of the diocese. The canons describe this as a secure place that is either separate from the other archives or, if this is not possible, is a place in the diocesan archives that is secure. Only the bishop is to have the key to the secret archives.

The canons do not describe in detail what is to be kept in the secret archive. Yet Canon 489, 2 states that documents of criminal cases concerning moral matter are to be destroyed if the guilty parties have died or ten years after the sentence if the case has been pronounced. This implies (an implication confirmed by commentaries on the similar canon in the 1917 Code) that cases involving moral and criminal matter are by their very nature the matter of the secret archives. They are secret when actually in the place of the archives or not. Canon 1719 clearly states that the acts of the investigation of the penal process, the decrees of the Ordinary by which the investigation was opened and closed, and all other matter that preceded the investigation are to be kept in the secret archives. By this canon it is clear that all documents related to a penal process, even though this process may not be concluded by sentence, are to be kept in the secret archives.

If, for instance, complaints of sexual misconduct are investigated by the Ordinary, every document pertaining to the complaint could be construed to be related to the preliminary and formal investigation of the penal process and thereby part of the secret archives.

Although the inviolability of the secret archives is clear in canon law, it is not so certain that such is to be respected by the civil law. Random legal opinions indicate that even the serious matters contained in the secret archives could be subpoenaed in the civil courts. The matter is still under research.

As a possible manner of distinguishing between the diocesan archives and the secret archives that pertain to priest-personnel problems, the bishop could have all material related to conscience or matter of a moral nature placed in separate files that he personally would keep, at his residence for instance. These could be labeled "conscience" files or something similar, which would indicate that they contain matters that only the bishop, in keeping with his unique relationship to the priest, had access to.

(3) *Recording sexual abuse:* Reports of alleged sexual abuse or sexual misconduct, as well as records of investigations, should be kept in the secret archives and certainly not in the diocesan archives or the Ordinary priest-personnel files.

e. The Limits of a Bishop's/Superior's Responsibility

The question involves the limits of a bishop's responsibility for those clerics who are working or living in his diocese. This responsibility is looked upon differently in civil law and canon law, yet the civil law might well look to the canon law to clarify questionable areas.

(1) *The relationship to incardinated clerics:* It is clear that a bishop is responsible for clerics who are incardinated to his diocese. This includes diocesan priests, transient deacons destined for ordination to the priesthood, and permanent deacons. Canon 273 states that clerics have a special obligation to show respect and obedience to their own Ordinary and to the Supreme Pontiff. The bishop also assigns ecclesiastical offices in his diocese, including pastorates and associate pastorates, by free conferral (Canons 157, 523, 547, 682). This means that the bishop alone has the power and the right to confer an ecclesiastical office or, in other words, to make an assignment. In those dioceses that have personnel boards or officers, these have no power nor can they be given the power to make assignments or confer offices. These canons are based on the nature of the episcopal office and the continent relationship of the bishop to his cleric-subjects.

(2) *The relationship to visiting clerics:* It is common for clerics, especially priests, to work or study in dioceses other than their own by incardination, for temporary periods of time of varying length. The usual custom is to seek the permission of the local bishop

for such a cleric to live and work in the host diocese, with the permission of his own bishop. This possibility is outlined in Canon 271, 2, 3.

Such a cleric working in a diocese other than his own is responsible to the host bishop for the apostolic work he does and for his actions while carrying out his clerical duties. Because the bishop is the head of the local church, his responsibility for *all* clerics living and working under his jurisdiction is comprehensive, as is the responsibility of these clerics to the bishop. Although the law does not mention it, the cleric's proper Ordinary would seem to have an obligation in justice to inform the host Ordinary of any problems the cleric might have that would possibly have an effect on his life and work in another diocese.

(3) *Religious clerics:* Clerics who are members of religious institutes have their own major superiors as their proper Ordinary. The superior is usually called a "provincial." He is not the local superior of the community in which the religious lives but the superior over the territorial grouping of religious of the same institute. The major superior's responsibility to his clerics is similar to that of the bishop to his clerics.

Religious living and working in a diocese are subject to the local bishop in those matters that involve education, public worship, or the apostolate (Canon 678). In most cases they are not subject to the bishop in the internal ordering of their lives. This is known as the privilege of exemption, which applies to most clerical religious institutes (known also as orders, congregations, and, in some cases, societies). Nevertheless if the local bishop becomes aware of serious internal abuses he may intervene if appeals to the proper religious superior prove to be ineffectual (Canon 683, 2).

In matters of sexual misconduct, a religious cleric is responsible both to his own superior and to the bishop of the diocese in which he lives/works/resides. If the bishop becomes aware of an alleged incident he is within his rights to notify the religious' proper Ordinary and also to conduct his own preliminary investigation. The law gives the local bishop the right to impose a suspension on a religious cleric by reason of penalty (Canon 1341–42) and by means of an administrative decree or precept (Canons 48–58).

A bishop may also forbid a religious to remain in his diocese for grave reasons (and alleged sexual misconduct would certainly be one) provided the cleric's major superior has been informed and has failed to act. The latter is to be reported to the Holy See (Canon 679).

(4) *Suspended clerics:* Is the diocesan bishop responsible for priests or deacons whom he has suspended (or someone else has suspended)? It is clear that such clerics are merely suspended and are not dismissed, thus they remain clerics and the local bishop is still responsible for vigilance over such clerics. Similarly the clerics are responsible to their bishop. If, for instance, a bishop were aware of an act of sexual misconduct by a suspended cleric, he could not absolve himself of responsibility or possible liability by the fact of the cleric's suspension.

(5) *The bishop's financial responsibility:* The nature of the bishop's relationship to support his clerics has changed from the 1917 Code. The 1983 Code (Canon 281, 1, 1) refers to the support of priests and transient deacons and non-married permanent deacons in some circumstances. Essentially a bishop is obligated to provide remuneration to the cleric as

benefits his condition taking into account both the nature of the cleric's office and the condition of time and place. The second paragraph states that suitable provisions be made for such social welfare as the cleric may need for infirmity, sickness, or old age.

Also, Canon 1350, 1 says "In imposing penalties on cleric, except in the case of dismissal from the clerical state, care must always be taken that he does not lack what is necessary for his worth support." To arrive at the canonical nature of the bishop's financial responsibility one must study the two canons in context.

First, it is clear that the bishop responsible is the bishop of incardination. Secondly, he is obligated to support his cleric but not unrealistically. The bishop may not withdraw all support for a cleric who is withdrawn from an assignment pending an investigation into sexual misconduct. If the allegation is proven and the cleric is suspended the bishop must study the cleric's needs and his capacity to support himself and, if necessary, he (the bishop) is obligated to assist in supporting the cleric.

This support includes provision for psychiatric and medical care. A bishop cannot waive his obligation to such support by explicitly excluding clerics involved in sexual misconduct. Is the bishop bound to provide legal assistance to clerics in trouble? Strictly speaking he is not, however he may choose to do so out of charity and with a view to the impression that could arise if refused to assist a cleric in trouble in such a manner.

The second paragraph of Canon 1350 states that if a cleric is dismissed and is truly in need, then the bishop is obligated to provide for him in the best way possible.

The matter of financial support is most important since clerics involved in sexual misconduct, especially pedophilia, will most probably be suspended and will need extensive psychiatric care as well as legal assistance. The cleric may have little means of outside support and will therefore depend on the bishop or diocese for help. Like a cleric suffering from cancer, a pedophiliac suffers from a serious emotional/mental disorder. Unlike the cleric suffering from a physical disease, the symptoms of the pedophiliac's illness are also criminal actions.

(6) *Responsibility for Permanent Deacons:* A permanent deacon, married or not, is a cleric and not a layman. When the code refers to clerics, it includes both deacons and priests with no distinction between transient and permanent deacons. Married deacons are not obligated to continence but are obligated to chastity, which precluded sexual relations with anyone other than their wives. In the event that permanent deacons committed sexual misconduct, the bishop would have a responsibility to investigate the incident and to take appropriate action. The permanent deacon may also be suspended as can a priest. In the event that it is necessary to laicize a permanent (or transient) deacon, this too is possible, yet the process is handled through the Congregation for the Sacraments rather than the Congregation for the Doctrine of the Faith, which handles laicization of priests.

The bishop is responsible for just remuneration for permanent deacons who work for the church *full time.* In the United States, most permanent deacons have full-time professions or employment and work for the church on a part-time basis. Canon 281, 3 state that married deacons (and presumably single permanent deacons) who support themselves and their families from secular employment are not entitled to support from the bishop as well.

It appears from a reading of the canon that a bishop is not obligated to provide for medical or psychiatric care or legal expenses for permanent deacons involved in sexual misconduct.

f. The Canonical Nature of the Bishop-Cleric Relationship

The civil law will look to canon law as well as theology to aid in understanding the nature of a cleric's relationship to his bishop and to his diocese.

A cleric is bound to his diocese through incardination, which takes place at the time he received the sacred order of the deacon. Under the 1917 Code a cleric became incardinated at the time he received first tonsure, probably two or three years before ordination to the diaconate. By incardination the cleric is bound to the diocese in a special manner. He is not simply a resident but is a kind of ecclesiastical public servant. This pertains to permanent deacons as well as other clerics.

The priest especially is bound in a special way to the diocese because he is called by Vatican II a "collaborator" with the bishop. His life's work, calling, or occupation is ordered to the work of the church, ordinarily in his diocese. A priest or deacon may live and work in another diocese yet remain incardinated to his own diocese and responsible primarily to his own bishop.

The cleric owes reverence and obedience to his bishop. Here the law (Canon 273) refers to the bishop of the diocese of incardination. At the time of ordination to the diaconate and again to the priesthood the cleric makes a promise of obedience to his Ordinary and the Ordinary's successors. By this promise the cleric owes the bishop obedience in all things that are neither sinful nor illegal.

The relationship of the bishop and his priest differs theologically and canonically from that of the bishop to a deacon. This difference would have little impact on the civil law understanding of the overall relationship of history to cleric. Nevertheless since most of the problems exist with priests this special relationship should be well understood.

The bishop-priest relationship is unique. Clearly the bishop is much more than an *employer* since the priest is responsible to him for all areas of his life and not merely those hours during which he is exercising priestly ministry. The priest owes complete obedience to his bishop and it is the bishop alone who has the power, by reason of office, to transfer or assign a priest.

The priest is also referred to as a *cooperator* with the bishop. One of the post-Vatican II documents says: "All priests ... share and exercise with the bishops the one priesthood of Christ. They are thus constituted providential cooperators of this episcopal order. The diocese clergy have however, a primarily role in the care of souls because, being incardinated in or appointed to a particular church, they are wholly dedicated in its service ... and accordingly form one priestly body and one family of which the bishop is the father" (*Christus Dominus*, n. 28). Likewise says the conciliar document on the priesthood: "All priests share with the bishops the one identical priesthood and ministry of Christ. Consequently the very unity of their consecration and mission requires their hierarchical union with the Order of Bishop ... Bishop will regard them as indispensable helpers in the ministry and in the task of teaching, sanctifying and shepherding the people of God" (Presbyterorum Ordinis, n. 7).

The essential responsibility of a bishop for his priests is rooted in their common sharing of the same priesthood:

"On account of this common sharing in this same priesthood and ministry then, bishops are to regard their priests as brothers and friends and are to take the greatest interest they are capable of in their welfare both temporal and spiritual" (Ibid., n. 7).

Most priests are either pastors or associate pastors. Others may be teachers, preachers, administrators, etc. The canon uses a technical term to describe the special and unique authority and responsibility that certain offices hold in relation to the pastoral ministry: *cura animarum,* or "care of souls." This term is directly connected with the office of bishop and the office of pastor. Others share in it or participate in it but do not have it in its fullness. According to Canon 519 the pastor "exercises the pastoral care of the community entrusted to him under the authority of the bishop whose ministry of Christ he is called to share. ..." A pastor must be a priest according to Canon 512, 1.

A diocesan priest (pastor, associate pastor, etc.) is not automatically a *vicar* of the bishop, that is, one who represents the bishop and functions on power delegated by the bishop. The law provides for vicars in special places. The pastor has his own authority that he obtains by reason of his office, conferred on him by the bishop, his basic pastoral powers come to him by the very office he holds.

Parish priests are not paid directly by the bishop but are paid from parish funds. The IRS considers priests to be self-employed.

g. The Church's Canonical Understanding of Its Identity

In lawsuits against employees of the Catholic Church it is not uncommon for the person to be named along with other authority figures in the hierarchical structure of the church. This includes local ordinaries, metropolitan archbishops, papal representatives, and the Holy Father himself in some cases. Because of this tendency it is helpful to clarify the canonical dimension of the relationship of church entities.

(1) *The Diocese:* Canon 368 refers to a particular church, the diocese being the principle example. A particular church is a portion of the people God entrusted to a bishop (Canon 369). Only the Holy Father has the power to establish, alter, or suppress a diocese (Canon 373) or any other type of ecclesiastical authorities.

The diocesan bishop, also referred to as the local Ordinary, has all of the ordinary, proper, and immediate power required for the exercise of his office in the diocese except in those matters that the pope has reserved to himself or to other ecclesiastical authorities.

The diocese is composed of parishes that are erected or suppressed by the authority of the diocesan bishop. He has complete authority in his diocese including the power to enact legislation to a certain extent and according to the norms of the universal canon law. Canon 391 states that the bishop governs the diocese with legislation, executive, and judicial power. In all juridical transactions the bishop acts in the person of the diocese (Canon 393).

The bishop's immediate superior is the Holy Father. The pope alone has the authority to name a bishop, appoint him to a diocese, remove him, or ask for his resignation.

Each diocese is to have its own administrative officers and organs and its own court, called a tribunal. A diocese is not dependent in any way for its ongoing existence on other dioceses. The bishops of the world belong to what is known as the "college of bishops." This is a union of the bishops as successors of the apostles with the pope at its head. It functions in solemn form when in ecumenical council.

(2) *The Metropolitan and the Province:* Dioceses are arranged according to geographical areas called provinces. The majority entity in a province is called the archdiocese. The other dioceses are called suffragan dioceses. The head of the archdiocese is known as the Metropolitan Archbishop. He has no power of governance over the suffragan dioceses but can celebrate sacred functions in churches in these other dioceses (Canon 436).

The metropolitan archbishop is not the superior of the bishops of the province. He can exercise moral suasion over them but they are not bound to obey him or accept his advice unless the metropolitan is delegated by the pope in particular occasions. It is clear that the individual bishops do not report to the metropolitan nor is the metropolitan responsible for the decisions or actions of the bishops. The only power given to him by law is to appoint an administrator of a diocese if the see is vacant and if the diocesan consultors have failed to duly elect one. Also, he may conduct a visitation of a diocese if needed but only with the permission of the Holy See.

(3) *The Episcopal Conference:* The episcopal conference, an entity that grew out of Vatican II, is the assembly of all of the bishops in a country. Conferences are established, altered, or suppressed only by the Holy See (Canons 447 and 449). The conference can enact legislation or decrees only when this is provided for in the universal law of the church (Canon 455). The conference is not a legislative body nor does it have executive or judicial power over the individual bishops of the country. It exists

primarily as a service organization to assist the bishops in their pastoral work. The size and complexity of each individual conference's permanent staff varies from country to country.

The Episcopal conference in the United States, as in other countries, does not have authority over the individual bishops nor does it have a right by church law to intervene in diocesan affairs. The president of the conference is elected for a set term by the bishops. He has no authority over the individual bishops nor over the national church as a whole. The law allows the conference or the president to speak in the name of all of the bishops only when each and every bishop gives his consent (Canon 455, 4).

The national conference of bishops is not the equivalent of a national Catholic Church. The dioceses do not form a federation. Their identity in the law would remain the same with or without the conference.

(4) *Juridic persons:* Aggregates of persons or things that are directed to the church's mission in some way may be given the status of a juridic person either by provision of the law itself or by an act of a superior competent to create a juridic person. A juridic person is similar but not entirely analogous to a corporation. Dioceses are juridic persons.

(5) *The Apostolic Pro-Nuncio:* The papal representative in the United States is known as the Apostolic Pro-Nuncio. He is the personal representative for the Holy Father to the American Church and the ambassador of the Holy See to the United States. He enjoys power or authority, which is given to him by law (since he usually is an archbishop) or is delegated by the Holy See.

The papal representative has no direct authority over the individual bishops. He assists the bishops by action and advice while leaving intact the exercise of their lawful power. The papal representative may act only upon instructions of the Holy See. He may not interfere in the internal workings of a diocese nor may he remove or censure bishops in any way.

Similarly bishops are not bound to report to the papal representatives concerning their personnel nor the internal workings of the diocese except in cases specifically defined by law. By weight of his office, the papal representative can exercise a certain degree of moral authority over the individual bishops but has no direct, canonical authority.

Finally, the papal representative enjoys diplomatic immunity. While he may be a citizen of this or that country, he carries a Vatican diplomatic passport for the duration of his services with the Holy See.

h. The Advisability of Reporting Incidents to Church Authorities

Although the diocesan bishop is bound to report only to the Holy See in just about every case, it is advisable that incidents of sexual misconduct among the clergy be reported to certain ecclesiastical authorities. This, of course, would depend on the nature of the incident, the amount of publicity attending it, and possible civil law ramifications. Naturally there is a difference between an action that has moral culpability only and an action that is morally wrong but also constitutes matter for criminal prosecution or civil liability.

When an incident of alleged child molestation is reported to a bishop he may have an obligation in civil law to report it to the civil authorities. No such obligation exists in canon law. Nevertheless, if the incident and the cleric's identity remain confidential, the bishop may wisely refrain from widespread reporting. It may be advisable in every instance to report the incident to the papal representative in the event of a subsequent inquiry from the Holy See. Rather than communicate directly to the Holy See, a bishop could communicate through the papal representative.

A bishop is not bound to report incidents to the Metropolitan archbishop or to the president of the episcopal conference or the conference staff, including the office of the general council.

i. Vigilance in the Seminaries

No man has the right to enter a seminary nor a right to remain in the seminary. The law states that the bishop is to admit to a seminary only those candidates whose human, moral, spiritual, and intellectual gifts as well as physical and psychological health show that they are capable of dedicating themselves permanently to ministry (Canon 241, 1).

The bishop who sponsors the candidate is responsible for him, yet the seminary may not be in the same diocese. The bishop then depends on the seminary rector and staff to assist him in determining if the candidate is suitable for ordination. A seminary rector or staff may dismiss a candidate yet a bishop still may place him in another seminary or ordain him.

Seminaries fall under the authority of the bishop of the diocese in which they exist. If the seminary is an interdiocesan seminary by decree of the Holy See, all of the bishops involved share authority.

A seminarian may be dismissed from a seminary by the rector if the statutes of the seminary provide for this, or by the bishop. He need not be told why he is being dismissed and he has no right of appeal of any kind. Canon 1029 stipulates that those who are to be ordained must, in the judgment of the bishop, be motivated by the right intention, enjoy a good reputation, have moral probity, and the physical and psychological qualities appropriate to the order to be received. If the bishop even suspects deficiencies in a candidate he may refuse to ordain him even without indicating why. There is no recourse or appeal since there is no right to ordination.

Canon 1041, 1 states that no one who suffers from any form of insanity or from another psychological infirmity is "irregular" for receiving orders. Experts are to be consulted to determine if the person's infirmity will make him incapable of exercising orders properly. By irregularity is meant a kind of impediment that must be dispensed from either by the bishop or the Holy See depending on the circumstances.

j. Religious Clerics

The canonical consideration listed earlier pertain equally to clerics who are members of religious institutes. Since there are different kinds of religious communities, it is important to understand the differences.

(1) *Religious institutes:* This is the canonical term for groups of men or women who take public vows and are recognized and erected as a religious institute. These were commonly known as Orders, Congregations, or Societies in the past and still are to a certain extent.

(2) *Secular institutes:* These are recognized organizations of clerics or laity who belong to a group without taking public vows or living a common life.

(3) *Societies of Apostolic Life:* These organizations lead a common life, pursue an apostolate, but do not take public vows.

The major superiors of religious institutes of men are known as Ordinaries. Their power and authority as well as responsibility for their subjects are similar to that of a bishop. In some ways, because of the vow of obedience, the religious superior may have even greater authority over his subjects.

Religious institutes are usually divided geographically into provinces with members living in religious houses. A religious Ordinary is responsible for those subjects assigned to his province or those assigned to another province but living in his province. The method of assignation and the terms used differs from one community to another.

4. Clinical/Medical Considerations

The section entitled "Clinical/Medical Questions" posed many of the important questions that face an Ordinary in dealing with a cleric who is alleged to have committed sexual abuse or a related act on a child or adolescent. The following considerations cover this same area expanding on the problems that the alleged offense poses to the Ordinary. It is intended that they provide essential information at the outset. These considerations in no way replace all of the pertinent questions.

a. Pre-Intervention Strategy by the Ordinary

The Ordinary, rather than a subordinate or vicar, should confront the cleric as soon as an allegation of sexual offense is made about the cleric. The bishop-priest relationship, for instance, is a very special one and should be utilized to the fullest both canonically and psychologically, to intervene immediately if there is a suspicion or allegation of sexual abuse by a priest.

Prior to speaking with the priest (or cleric) the Ordinary (usually the bishop except in the case of religious clerics) should speak with a priest-psychologist who is knowledgeable about this particular problem. This should be done before the bishop confronts or speaks with the priest so that the bishop can obtain some "pointers" on the intervention itself. The priest-psychologist can also assist the bishop in designing some personalized strategies according to the nature of the allegations made and the personality of the priest involved.

The Ordinary should make it clear to the priest before even stating the allegations that it is vitally important that truthfulness exist between them. The Ordinary should reassure the priest or cleric that he will support him legally and financially and that he will also help him to obtain evaluation and treatment for his problems. However if the priest chooses not to be fully honest in the initial intervention, the Ordinary may still be obliged to be helpful but he could/should let the priest know that he would be disturbed by the lack of truthfulness in the initial interview.

This initial conversation between the Ordinary and the priest may be one of the most important moments in the sequence of events that will follow. It is assumed that most Ordinaries in the United States have not had a great deal of experience with child abuse by the clergy and for that reason they need some professional reassurance for the initial encounter with the accused. Each priest or cleric brings a different set of problems and a different set of circumstances concerning the sexual abuse. The initial intervention should be tailored accordingly.

b. What Are the Causes of Sexual Abuse by Roman Catholic Clergy?

Once the priest or cleric admits to any type of sexual contact with children or adolescents it is not appropriate for the Ordinary to delve into the causes of this sexual abuse. This is best left to the professionals who have had a good deal of experience in this area and who understand Roman Catholic clergy.

Nevertheless, it is important that the Ordinary have some idea as to what these causes are so that an appropriate place can be chosen for the evaluation and treatment of the priest.

A concrete example best illustrates the question. A 32-year-old priest had been seen by a psychiatrist in private outpatient therapy for 2 years, which included the administration of psychotropic medications. Over a three-year period this priest had inappropriately committed sexual crimes in a public grammar school yard in three different locales. He was on his way to jail. He had been evaluated by two "excellent" mental health centers that stated that the inappropriate sexual behavior was due to early childhood experiences that required intense psychotherapy and perhaps group therapy.

When the priest was sent to another evaluation center with the capability of looking at medical, neurological, and substance abuse problems as well as psychiatric and psychological problems, it was found that the priest had been drinking over one quart of bourbon a day over the past five years but was unable to admit to having an alcohol problem. In such a case it would have been inappropriate to have this priest continue to see the private psychiatrist. Rather alcoholism, the primary disorder, would have to be treated and then the inappropriate sexual behaviors evaluated after the patient had been sober for a number of months.

Statistically, at least in regard to adolescent sexual abuse by priests, drugs and alcohol are the primary complicating problem or "mitigating" factor that the treatment professionals must deal with. Even though alcohol or drug abuse is present it does not mean that the sexual problem will necessarily disappear following treatment. There is, however, a greater likelihood that the individual will be able to exert control and prudence if he is sober and is monitored over a prolonged period of time. Naturally, treatment should be given for the sexual issues as well as the substance abuse issues.

Further, there a number of rarer disorders that can cause unusual behavior over a prolonged period of time. These include such disorders as manic-depressive illness, frontal lobe dysfunction, temporal lobe epilepsy, brain tumors, etc. The problems will never come to light if a priest or cleric is evaluated at a center that looks only at the psychological dynamics of the patient's family and his adult and religious life as the source of all problems, using the same model for treatment. Refer again to the 32-year-old priest with two competent evaluations, neither of which uncovered the problem of alcohol abuse.

c. How Soon Should the Evaluation Take Place?

Immediately. As soon as the Ordinary has ascertained that there is some truth to the allegations of sexual abuse by a cleric, arrangements should be made the same day or the following day at the latest for the priest's transfer to an evaluation center. The Ordinary may be familiar with a competent evaluation center or may have discussed such a center with the priest-psychologist.

It is especially important to understand that evaluation centers may be located in states with laws that might prove problematic for the Ordinary. For example, some states have enacted legislation that does not extend privileges of communication between a patient and his psychologist or psychiatrist to cases involving child abuse, including sexual abuse of children. In Massachusetts, a therapist, no matter what his training, must report the incident to local authorities if there is any indication that the incident occurred within the state of Massachusetts. It is also possible that this extends to people who were involved with other adults who were involved with the incident in the state of Massachusetts. For this reason this state would be a hazardous area to send a priest for evaluation because of the stringency and extent of the reporting laws. Almost all states require and suspend the privileged communication between mental health professionals and the child if the child is the patient. A sexually or physically abused child seen by such a mental health professional must be reported in all fifty states along with the names of the persons offered by the child.

The point here is that the Ordinary should determine the reporting laws in the states of possible evaluation centers. It would be wise to consult with attorneys knowledgeable of these issues prior to sending the priest for evaluation.

The nature of the disorder dictates why the evaluation should be *immediate.* We are dealing with compulsive sexual habits that the priest may temporarily suspend in the face of legal or canonical pressure, but not in all instances. There are many examples wherein sexual abuse took place very soon after the confrontation between the priest and his Ordinary had taken place. The priest must clearly be seen as one suffering from a psychiatric disorder that is beyond his control. For this reason—the compulsion of the disorder—evaluation of the disorder and the separation from temptation should be immediate and state as much to the priest by the Ordinary without the Ordinary experiencing any feelings of misplaced guilt or lack of charity. This will emphasize to the priest the importance of his being truthful both to the bishop and to the evaluating mental health professionals.

d. Should the Alleged Offended See Anyone Else Prior to Evaluation?

The Ordinary may perceive, as he converses with the priest, that the latter is not taking the allegations very seriously. If this is true it is strongly urged that the Ordinary have the priest meet with competent attorneys conversant in dealing with the issue (whether or not there is an immediate legal threat). This should be arranged immediately. The attorneys should outline in detail all of the possible consequences in criminal law as well as the civil law liability of the priest and the diocese. This will also be helpful to the evaluation center since the priest will have a better appreciation of the significance and consequences of his behavior and perhaps even of the effect it may have on the victims.

e. What about Canonical Suspension?

A suspension of the cleric, especially if he is a priest, should happen in all cases. This makes a clear separation between the Ordinary and the cleric. It is a statement that the man is not capable of carrying out his sacred functions of ministry until an evaluation is completed and a determination of his fitness for ministry is made.

f. How Long Does an Evaluation Take?

Some mention should be made of the open-ended nature of the evaluation. Many times it takes a week or two for the evaluation center to arrive at a good picture and feel for the total situation involved with the priest as well as his diocese or religious community. Most centers will do an evaluation in five days but usually will extend it in order to better get to know the priest and his diocese/community. Thus they are in a position to make a better recommendation to the Ordinary when the evaluation is completed.

g. What Should an Adequate Evaluation Include?

This is a very important question. In the final report the following should be looked for as part of the evaluation from any competent center:

(1) Clear evaluation by the psychologist or psychiatrist who has had experience in dealing with sex offenders of different types.

(2) An evaluation by a chemical dependency counselor or someone with equivalent experience in substance abuse to make certain that the person does not have a history of abuse of alcohol or drugs that would be contributing to sexual problems.

(3) A complete physical and neurological examination completed by an internist or neurologist.

(4) A electroencephelogram done both in the sleep state and with nasopharengel leads.

(5) A CT brain scan with and without contrast dye study to rule out the possibility of intercerebral tumors or other cerebral pathology.

(6) Blood and urine laboratory tests that rule out the presence of alcohol and/or illicit substances. The lab test should include an evaluation of liver, kidney, endocrine, lung, heart, and other vital functioning, all of which may give clues as to the presence of mitigating problems that must be explored.

(7) Some neurological assessment including intelligence test that will give an idea of the "functional" capacity of the patient.

(8) Appropriate psychological tests including projective testing that may give clues as to the stability of the character structure of the priest or the pathology of the character structure.

This is not an exhaustive but a basic list of tests that should be completed on a priest who is accused of sexual offenses. In other words, it is important to have a holistic approach to the problem that helps to discover mitigating factors that will assist in moving in the correct direction for the appropriate modality and treatment facility.

h. How to Choose an Appropriate Treatment Center?
This is the most difficult and at the same time important question for the Ordinary. He may have a center where he has been pleased with the treatment of priests with other problems. However the "favorite treatment center" may not be the appropriate center for clerics with sexual problems, especially if the problem is pedophilia. The following is a partial list of appropriate questions to be answered.

(1) Have the therapists and other professionals of the center had significant past experience in dealing with sexual abuse/sexual offenders/pedophiles? Will the priest be supervised by professionals with such experience?

(2) What kinds of physical and environmental restrictions will be placed while the priest is in therapy? Will he be allowed use of a car at any times? Will there be non-supervised periods in a 24-hour period each day? Will he be allowed to go out to dinner, entertainments, churches where he might encounter children in the course of his treatment program?

(3) Will he be allowed to consume alcohol of any kind? No sex offender should ever be allowed use of alcohol or drugs in a recreational or social setting because of the possibility of relaxing inhibitions or relapse of sexual acts. Total abstinence is a must in order for there to be hopes for abstinence and control of the sexual problem.

(4) What are the criteria used to determine the fitness of the priest for discharge, or the possibility of a return to ministry? How are these criteria tested during the treatment program?

(5) What self-help group will the priest be required to attend while in the treatment program (as well as after he leaves)? It is essential that there be some form of mandatory self-help group such as AA or a sex offender group for the rest of this person's life. This should be started during in-patient treatment and encouraged, to the degree that the patient is taken to the group if necessary.

(6) What concrete follow-up plans are made for the patient after treatment is concluded? Does he return on a period basis for an after-care program? What kind of after-care programs are set up in the diocese

if the priest is to return to function there? What are the guidelines that will be given to the Ordinary with reference to future functioning in the diocese?

All of these plus many more questions must be answered. Every treatment center is not the same nor do all have the same treatment philosophy. It must be stated unequivocally that a pure psychoanalytic or psychodynamically based program is inadequate for the treatment of sex offenders. There must be a multi-disciplinary and multi-dimensional approach to the treatment of these very special people and it is essential that the Ordinary find out exactly what is offered in and by the different treatment programs and centers before a decision is made to place the priest in a center for a prolonged period of time.

i. Can the Priest Ever Return to Ministry in the Diocese?
Individual factors, the extent of the sexual abuse, the extent of the notoriety involved and the extent of knowledge of the problem are but some of the factors that go into this question.

The treatment center chosen should be one that works on a "family model" approach. This means that members of the religious family involved with the priest prior to treatment should be involved in the treatment and in the post-treatment plans. There should be close communication and coordination with the diocese or religious community so that when this question arises during in-patient treatment, it can be answered directly and specifically and the treatment program moved in such a way as to assist the priest in looking at his fitness for ministry or finding new ministries or occupations.

It is inadequate to treat a sex offender in the diocese on a private psychotherapy model. It should be emphasized that in-patient treatment, preferably with peers, is the most preferable model and the one that will have the best results.

j. What about the Families of the Victims?

This is a very delicate area. While the welfare of the priest-offender is considered very important to the church officials, the welfare both at the time of the abuse and well into the future of the victims is most important and should be given priority by Ordinaries. The effects of sexual abuse of children by adults are long-lasting and go well into adulthood. This is well documented, though it may be difficult to predict the extent of the effects in particular cases. We are speaking not only of psychological effects but also the spiritual effects since the perpetrators of the abuse are priests or clerics. This will no doubt have a profound effect on the faith life of the victims, their families, and others in the community.

A rather direct approach should be made to the family (in conjunction with consultation with competent civil attorneys). Psychological help and other needed assistance should be offered to the victims and their families. If the family seems opposed to such a move, there should be some form of healing, if possible, between the priest and the family, possibly in terms of monitored communication or perhaps even a family meeting with the priest at some point when the priest, Ordinary, and family are disposed to it.

We have been rather ignorant of the effects of sexual abuse of children by Catholic clergy over the years because it has never been investigated or studied in a systematic manner. However from a professional viewpoint, enough adult persons who have been in therapy in the past several years have discussed abuse by priests that it seems clear that such abuse has a profound effect even when it does not come to the attention of parents, family members, of the civil or church authorities.

The extent and degree of the sexual abuse, the age of the child at the time of outset of the abuse, when it was discovered and finished, the manner in which it was discovered, any other dimensions of relationship of the priest with the family ... these are all factors involved in treating the victims and their families. Special mental health professionals, trained and competent in this particular area, should be called on by the Ordinary to provide help and support as soon as is feasible. This is also a healthy preventative measure with respect to civil litigation since most families are eager to help their children and themselves in these embarrassing and complex psychosocial problems.

5. Insurance Considerations

a. Loss of Liability Insurance Coverage for Dioceses

It is highly probable that specific, exclusionary language shall begin to appear following a few years experience in all diocesan liability policies that shall exclude coverage to the diocese, the bishop, vicars, clergy, and other personnel for "coverage of claims arising as a result of sexual contact between a priest and parishioner, an employee and any member of the public ... "

Such an exclusion was adopted as an insurance industry standard on January 1, 1985 for the psychiatric and psychological profession. Coverage for those professions and the entities, partnerships, corporations, and associations that employ them is no longer available for "claims arising as a result of sexual contact between patient and therapist or other employee."

The exclusion was a reaction to payment of large claims by insurance companies over several years and an inability actuarially to predict the risk that a physician might have sexual contact with a patient.

The estimated cost of the loss of coverage correlates to the remarks contained in the introduction. The cost could be hundreds of millions.

This threatens the very economic viability of the church's mission in many areas.

b. Interim Increased Cost of Liability Insurance Coverage

Following the experience by insurance companies of a number of claims resulting in large monetary court awards or cash settlements involving insurance funds and prior to the cancellation of coverage, a significantly higher actuarial value would be assigned to the risk, resulting in a significant increased premium cost.

One diocese that experienced insurance losses as a result of a priest sexually molesting children has been notified that the insurance premium shall increase more than 25 percent.

According to *Time* magazine (June 3, 1985) a day care center that suffered a child molestation experience was forced to pay a liability premium that increased nearly 750 percent, from $600 dollars per year to $8,000 dollars per year.

This individual increase to each diocese, weighted in aggregate, will cost many millions.

6. Spiritual Considerations

In addition to other effects of sexual abuse on children and their families, since the perpetrators are priests or members of the clergy, there will also be serious "spiritual" consequences. Those affected include the victims, their immediate families, as well as others in their circle of friends and acquaintances. There will also be serious spiritual consequences for the wider church community. Spiritual concerns encompass the cleric-offenders and other members of the clergy in the diocese and in other areas.

a. Sexual abuse of a child by a cleric, especially a priest, can have a devastating effect on the child's short- and long-term perception of the church and its clergy. How will the child be able to perceive the clergy as authentic, unselfish ministries of the gospel and the church as the body of Christ?

b. The victim's capacity to develop trusting relationships with adult clergy will be impaired.

c. The abused child's faith in the sacraments as sources of grace and communications with Christ, through the ministry of a priest, will be seriously weakened.

d. Depending on the manner with which church authorities deal with the case, the victims and others may quickly develop a perception of church leadership as ineffective and unauthentic vis-à-vis its commitment to all of its members and not simply its commitment to its leaders and the clergy.

e. Church attendance by the victims, their families, and other members of the faithful may decline.

f. Help must be given to priest-offenders to discern the nature of their commitment to the priesthood, the reasons for their choice of this vocation, their hopes and plans for the future, and the real possibility that they are almost totally unfit to be priests.

g. Other priests and clerics who are not affected with sexual problems may perceive a severe hampering in their ability to minister, particularly to and with children. They might become very fearful of even touching children such as blessing them, making normal signs of affection, etc.

h. In addition to the overall problem of the image of the church as a haven for homosexuals and sexual perverts, the image of the priesthood is severely hampered and the faith of many in the priesthood is threatened by the fact of priests who are sex offenders as well as by the way the problems are handled or mishandled by church authorities.

i. The victims and possibly even their families may develop unwarranted feelings of guilt because of the contact with priests. This can be complicated by an unwillingness to accept a priest as the minister of forgiveness and absolution with consequent inability to alleviate the guilt feelings through the traditional channels of absolution.

7. Public Relations Considerations

a. The necessity for careful consideration of this aspect of the problem is self-evident. The negative impact of widespread sexual abuse of children and involvement in other forms of illicit sexual activity by Catholic clergy and religious cannot be underestimated nor can the full import be realistically assessed. One initial indicator is provided by the most recent attention given to the problem in the secular press as well as the National Catholic Reporter.

b. The first objective, of which one must never lose sight, is to maintain, preserve, and seek to enhance the credibility of the church as a Christian community. The church should be presented as a sensitive, caring, and responsible entity that gives unquestioned attention and concern to the victims of misconduct by priests. The church should not be presented as or identified with only the hierarchy or the governing structures or the clergy. The P.R. approach can emphasize positive programs utilizing imaginative and creative thinking that converts adversity to advantage.

c. A second objective of the media policy should be the public separation of the offender from the church authorities. In appropriate cases the offender must be made to accept the consequences of his actions and the public must be made to understand that the offender's acceptance of this responsibility indicates that the church authorities could not have done anything to prevent the incident (in cases wherein this assertion is true). Separation does not mean that the church authorities abandon the offender. It means that his action will be portrayed not as an action of the church or an action even indifferently condoned by the church but an action that the church views as profoundly unfortunate.

d. A third objective is to adopt a policy that will in all cases carefully control and monitor the tonal quality of all public statements made about particular cases or the general problem. This will include statements to and in the secular and Catholic press, letters of bishops to their clergy and faithful, remarks of church authorities, pulpit announcements, etc. All statements, including written legal pleadings, must be entirely consistent and aligned with the image of the church in the minds of the general public, the Catholic community, jurors, judges, prosecutors, and plaintiffs.

e. The church must remain open and avoid the appearance of being under siege or drawn into battle. All tired and worn policies utilized by bureaucracies must be avoided and clichés such as "no comment" must be cast away. In this sophisticated society, a media policy of silence implies either necessary secrecy or cover-up.

f. Policy analysts and media consultants can construct sound, specific targeted policies to be utilized in response to localized or regional publicity that may be adverse to the church's best interests. Broad general policies of a national scope can be put in place. Most important, very specific thematic policies can be developed for each phase of a developing problem from its discovery to its conclusion.

III. Project Proposal

A. Project Components

It is proposed that the appropriate body of the National Conference of Catholic Bishops authorize and fund the following described Project.

1. The Committee

A Committee of the NCCB would be fully authorized and empowered to allocate authority and funding at its discretion, within predetermined bounds, to a group of four to five bishops, holding degrees in Civil Law and/or Canon Law, to be named by the Committee. This Group of Bishops would be fully authorized, subject to the supervision of the Committee, to contract services of consultants and otherwise do any and all things necessary to conduct and carry out the mission of the Project, within the budget guidelines set in the grant of authority.

2. The Group of Four

These bishops would act immediately to contract the services of consultants in forming two distinct and separate entities: (1) a Crisis Control Team and (2) a Policy and Planning Group.

Thereafter, these bishops would act as an Ad Hoc Committee of the whole, in administering and supervising the efforts of the team, which would primarily be concerned with assisting in developing cases in different dioceses where requested, and the group, which would be engaged in long-term planning in an effort to put together competent and comprehensive policy recommendations to ultimately be considered by the Committee and in certain circumstances by the body of the National Conference of Catholic Bishops.

3. The Crisis Control Team

Initially, the Crisis Control Team should include a full-time trial lawyer with experience and expertise in the civil and criminal aspects of the problem. This trial lawyer would close his private practice, if he has one, and anchor both the Team and Group of Four, which is more fully explained in the following material.

The second position on the Crisis Control Team should be occupied by a canon lawyer who would give priority to duties with the Team.

The third position should be filled by a psychiatrist.

In time, this core group would expand its personnel resources. However, this expansion should not be rapid, as it is critical to maintain the level of expertise and experience specifically, and overall competence generally.

The expansion of resources should ideally occur on a regional, geographic plane. An effort should be made to recruit and work closely with others, giving them the benefit of the civil, criminal, canonical, and clinical experience and expertise, so that they should be equally suited to respond to a request for assistance.

All actions of this team are subject to the authority of the Group of Bishops that created the Team.

4. The Policy and Planning Group

This group would be made up of: the Group of Four Bishops, members of the Committee that created the Group of Bishops, and members of the Crisis Control Team.

In addition, it is contemplated that a wide array of consultants with expertise in different disciplines would be consulted to perform services for this Policy and Planning Group.

Thus, in addition to those listed in the preceding paragraph, the Group should also consist of, either temporarily or permanently, the following, non-exclusive listing of personnel:

a. Psychiatrists and psychologists with expertise in evaluation and treatment of offenders as well as victims and their families.

b. Psychiatrists and psychologists with expertise in screening, testing, and evaluating emotional stability and vocational suitability.

c. Directors of Seminaries and/or other similar religious houses of formation.

d. Consultants with expertise in Insurance Planning, Institution of Self Insured, single risk programs.

e. Policy Analysts with expertise in loss management.

f. Attorneys with expertise in Uniformity in Case Management in multiple jurisdictions.

g. Attorneys with specialized expertise in either narrow constitutional areas or broad-based areas such as Federal Class Actions.

h. Representatives of religious and lay medical treatment facilities.

i. Persons with expertise in area of personnel, i.e., religious personnel directors from Orders or the personnel directors of large, medium, and small dioceses.

j. A scholar in canon law to provide specific information required by the group.

k. A Policy Analyst with expertise in media management, formulation, implementation, and administration of general media policy as well as a specific, targeted media policy designed to deal with a single issue.

l. An administrative assistant would work with both the Team and the Group to provide support services and facilitate the flow of information among the members.

B. Scope of Services

1. The Crisis Control Team

First, the Team would not replace any individuals on either the national or local scene. Their function, where requested, would be to supplement the efforts of others and assist those who are presently positioned nationally and locally, and to devote their full time exclusively to the Project and problems encountered.

Second, their on-site involvement at a local level would only be in response to requests from a bishop or religious ordinary to provide advice, assistance, guidance, or active participation in the problem-solving process.

Finally, a mechanism would immediately be put in place so that any bishop or religious ordinary confronted with a problem would have knowledge on whom to contact for assistance. Once contacted, the scope of services rendered would range to and include any of the following:

a. Perform legal and factual investigations on-site, with the cooperation and assistance of local parties, compile results and report assessment of the situation to the local bishop, with recommendations if requested.

b. Arrange for and/or conduct evaluations of persons accused and process persons for treatment at an appropriate facility.

c. Assist in satisfying any canonical requirements that may be scrutinized in civil proceedings.

d. Assist in researching all applicable criminal and civil statutes with diocesan lawyers and gaining compliance with all.

e. Advise local parties, priests, and psychiatrists in regard to drawing a plan for immediate intervention with families of victims with least possible negative fallout.

f. Where civil litigation is probable, examine all evidence and assist in setting strategy that contemplates all possible courses. Particularly in these cases, force insurers to act immediately in appointing counsel and meet with insurers to explore settlement or set strategy.

g. Where criminal action is contemplated, assist in interviewing and selecting criminal counsel to be retained, seeking cooperation if feasible.

h. In all matters where court cases are anticipated, assist in drawing pleadings to protect the confidentiality of the process. In criminal cases, such orders are recognized by the U.S. Supreme Court, silencing all participants and cutting off flow of information to press. In civil cases, the efficacy of such a court order varies from one jurisdiction to another. However, such orders have been recognized to protect the identity of a juvenile.

i. In all such court cases, all uniform information and pleadings that are particularly important, such as suppressing or quashing subpoenas for Diocesan Records, should be furnished to local counsel.

j. Where the press is already involved or it is anticipated they would be involved, assistance should be rendered in formulating a media policy for every stage of the proceedings from discovery of the occurrence through settlement, judgment, or conviction.

k. When requested, Team members would become active participants in the process locally. Particularly, the trial lawyer, if requested, should enroll as co-counsel and assist in the handling of the entire case, including preparation of witnesses, taking of testimony, and conduct of trials.

l. In the interim, when not involved in assisting in the management of a crisis, the team, among other things would:

(1) Coordinate and assume responsibility for searching out, interviewing, and recommending the retention of experts in other geographic regions in an effort to expand the resources of the team.

(2) Commence and complete a study of the available treatment facilities in each state, the statutory laws in each state relating to the situation, and all other relevant data to be compiled and catalogued on a state-by-state basis.

(3) Commence and complete the compilation of all works of legal scholars and medical experts in the field, continually adding to the databank and refining the sample pleadings and other legal and medical advice to be offered.

(4) Continually monitor those situations in which the team has been invited to intervene, developing standard monitoring procedures to be utilized in tracking developments.

(5) Remain responsive on a twenty-four hour basis, year-round, to render assistance when requested.

(6) Work with the Policy and Planning Group.

2. The Policy and Planning Group

There is no necessity for a detailed discussion of the scope of services to be provided by this group. A perusal of the personnel who would comprise the group, coupled with an understanding of the nature of the problem is self-explanatory of their purpose. It is contemplated that very comprehensive and competent policies and procedures would be produced by the group for consideration by the Committee.

C. Strategy to Be Employed

In order to protect and provide a privilege to both the team and the group, it is contemplated that:

1. A base contract would be executed between the Group of Four Bishops and the trial lawyer that, among other things, would provide that a client-counsel relationship exist between (a) the Group of Four and the lawyer, (b) the National Conference of Catholic bishops and the lawyer, and (c) each diocese and the lawyer.

This should be done in an effort to avoid discovery of any information transmitted by any of the clients to counsel to any of the clients, providing as free a flow of information as possible without the discovery of plaintiffs or press.

2. All consultants who work on the team or with the group should be retained under contract with the trial lawyer and not with anyone else. All of their fees and expenses should be paid by the trial lawyer and the entirety of their work product should be performed for him.

This is an effort to legally shield from discovery all of the sensitive studies and other materials that might be generated during the existence of the Project.

3. The only official evidence that this Project was ever proposed or in fact existed, assuming each of these documents is returned without copying, would be the base contract between the bishops and the lawyer—a document that by its very nature is private, privileged, and may not be discovered.

4. In the confidential discussions mentioned herein, it was the consensus that this work might best be performed by an

ad hoc group in a method and manner whereby only the final product is officially provided to an existing Committee of the National Conference and in the interim, perhaps forever, subpoenas would be avoided.

5. It is the intention to locate this Team and center the Group in a large metropolitan area where required resources (university faculty, etc.) are readily available.

IV. Conclusion

Though each case of felonious sexual misconduct is bound to be different with regard to circumstances, notoriety, and possible liability, there is also a set of common threads that weave through all such cases. The very fact that these cases involve clerics of the Roman Catholic Church who have committed acts that are considered by society to be despicable and heinous and that have received a very high degree of publicity in the media of late (not necessarily those cases involving priests but child molestation in general) makes it imperative that there be comprehensive planning and specialized strategy for handling all such occurrences among the clergy. There is simply too much at stake for the church—its leaders, its clergy, and its faithful—not to attempt to provide the best possible response to the overall crisis.

In their developmental stages these crises are so fluid and move so swiftly that it is impossible to contrive on-the-spot plans and strategies that will adequately anticipate most if not all of the adverse developments and complex considerations that arise. It is equally difficult to attempt to implement a plan put together by an unknown author. Frankly, when faced by these crises for the first time very few in authority know what to do. It often seems to those in charge that everything that might be done could well go wrong, so the temptation is to do nothing, which is worse than wrong.

It seems that the best approach to ensure affirmative and aggressive action is for an Ordinary facing such a crisis to have available to him the support, assistance, guidance, and advice of personnel experienced in all aspects of the problem. A crisis control team, set to work with all aspects of the problem, can fill the need in providing immediate and short-term solutions.

The long-term solutions to the problems in general, their causes, and possible remedies, can effectively be addressed by a policy and planning group that can offer definitive consideration to all of the nuances and subtleties of these situations as well as the very obvious problems that have been discussed in this document. In short, there are several dimensions to the problem of multiple instances of sexual misconduct by Catholic clergy, the most offensive type being molestation of children. The individual cases and the effects on clergy, victims, their families, and the local church are deep: the image of the Catholic clergy projected throughout the country and the world as a result of these cases; the determination of causes such as improper seminary screening, etc.; the true clinical nature of certain of the actions, especially pedophilia. All of these dimensions demand a concentrated degree of attention by the church of its own good in the short term and for the sake of its role in the wider society in the long term.

Those who drafted this document as well as those who have contributed to its content—all those whose thought are represented herein—have been directly involved, with various degrees of intensity, in each aspect of these problems. It is from this vantage point that this document is written.

The questions and considerations should provide not the answers to the problem but a source of valuable information for the Ordinaries of the country. This work has been undertaken in the hope of contributing in some way to a solution in dealing with probably the single most serious and far-reaching problem facing our church today.

Respectfully submitted by:
Rev. Michael Peterson, M.D.
Mr. F. Ray Mouton, J.D., Esq.
Rev. Thomas P. Doyle, O.P., J.C.D

Part Three

The Church in Court

If any of you put a stumbling block before one of
these little ones ... it would be better if a great
millstone were fastened around your neck and
you were drowned in the depth of the sea.

—MATTHEW 18:6

The Church gets involved with politics when she
ceases to produce enough saints.

—FRANÇOIS MAURIAC

Chapter 5

The Perils of Courtroom Exposure

Although more than two thousand civil and criminal cases alleging the sexual abuse of minors have been lodged against the Catholic Church and its representatives in the United States over the past two decades, few have made it to trial. The custom throughout the country is to settle victims' claims before they come to a court trial. Trials generate a good deal of publicity—often national—and most of it reflects badly on the Catholic Church. The facts laid out before judges and juries with all the corroborating documented evidence projects a portrait of churchmen mired in conspiracy and neglect. The church is always eager to contain these negative images as much as it possibly can. Although settlements have been as high as $5.2 million and $7.5 million for some individual victims, settlements rather than court hearings are generally more economical and preferred by bishops.

A May-to-July 1997 trial in a Dallas, Texas, courtroom was a monumental case, the facts of which were reported by Brooks Edgerton in the *Dallas Morning News*. The history of the case, known as the Rudi Kos case, is significant for two reasons: 1) The facts of the case reveal the pattern and practice generally employed by dioceses throughout the country to cover up for offending priests, and 2) the startling amount of punitive damages jurors are willing to award for what they see as reprehensible behavior on the part of the church authorities.

The saga began in 1993 and 1994 when victims of three Dallas priests, Fr. Rudi Kos, Fr. William Hughes, and Fr. Robert Peebles, approached a Dallas attorney, Sylvia Demarest, to file cases against the priests, the bishop of the diocese of Dallas, Charles Grahmann, and the diocese itself. The seven plaintiffs would have settled their claims for less than $1 million when negotiations began. However, the church's lawyers dug in their heels and refused to settle. They also refused to consolidate the three cases for one trial.

The cases were divided and the Fr. Kos trial proceeded first. It ended in 1997 with the jury awarding $119.6 million to twelve plaintiffs. Despite the fact that the award was mediated to $32.5 million, that sum was remarkable for its time. Since then, the diocese of Louisville, Kentucky has settled multiple cases for a total of $25 million, Boston for $85 million, and in 2004, Orange, California for $100 million. In California, eight hundred cases of abuse were pending settlement in 2005. More remarkable, however, at this time was the message that the *vox populi* no longer held the church above the law. The Catholic Church could not be trusted. Indeed, even when it spoke in court about the sexual behavior of its priests, the church was not deemed credible.

On a national level, where the 1983 trial of Fr. Gilbert Gauthé caused interest and amazement, the 1993 admission of guilt by Fr. James Porter raised the visibility of victims and organized advocacy. The 2003 conviction of Fr. Goeghan incited disgust and outrage. The 2005 trial of Fr. Paul Shanley unveiled the complex defense of a notoriously sexually active priest against allegations of torture of abuse and its power over behavior that is out of conscious control. It was the legacy of the Kos trial to expose the way the church conspired to hide abusers and how abuse really operates. The height and breadth of the church's denial and its prevarication even under oath continued to astound ordinary concerned Catholics and not only in Dallas. For instance, on November 23, 2004, Cardinal Roger Mahony of Los Angeles swore in a deposition that while he was bishop of the dioceses of Fresno and Stockton, California, he knew "of no priest between 1962 and 1985 who violated his celibacy." He said this in defiance of reason and common sense, and despite three egregious cases of sexually abusive priests under his jurisdiction during that time period. One priest spent time in prison; another was sent back to his native county; and the third left the Stockton diocese when Cardinal (then a bishop) Mahony was in charge. Cardinal Mahony said he had forgotten the two cases when he denied, on the witness stand, knowing about any abusers at the trial of the third priest, Fr. Oliver O'Grady, in 1998. When faced in 2004 with his hand-written documents to police and others, he simply said he had forgotten these incidents and his involvement with them.

Celibacy Scrutinized

Not many people, not even Catholics, understand the dimension and workings of celibacy. The cases recorded in the press raise questions not merely about sex with minors, but priest's sexuality generally. Not only, "What is it?" but, "How do they do that?" Those questions are raised both with disbelief and skepticism. The courtroom puts celibacy on the line. The obligation of celibacy binds a Catholic priest to behave himself not only when he is fulfilling some official duties within his parish, but at all times regardless of where he is. A priest is always a priest, 24 hours a day and 7 days a week. He is also obliged to avoid any situations that would cause scandal, wonderment, or possibly lead to inappropriate situations.

Priests are charged with representing Christ and the church to the people whom they are called to serve. They are charged with treating all people with respect and kindness. The Second Vatican Council's decree on the *Life and Ministry of Priests* urges them to model themselves on Jesus and treat everybody with the greatest respect and kindness (Par. 6).

The Code of Canon Law—both versions, 1917 and 1983—makes it abundantly clear that priests are to refrain from any kind of sexual activity with men and women, regardless of their age. Taking any kind of sexual advantage of a person is in no way consistent with the standards of conduct expected of a priest.

The 1917 code and the 1983 code state that the abuse of a minor under the age of 16 is certainly a violation of a priest's obligation of celibacy. Because sexual acting out with a minor by a cleric is particularly heinous, it has also been enumerated as a crime or delict in canon law. This crime is mentioned in the 1917 code in Canon 2359.2 and in the 1983 code in Canon 1395.2. These canons state that clerics guilty of sexually abusing minors are to be punished with appropriate penalties, not excluding dismissal from the clerical state. The legislation—specifically mentioning sex with minors because of its particularly reprehensible nature—is not new; it goes back to the earliest days of the church and is found repeatedly in collections of ecclesiastical laws.

The code does not mention homosexuality or homosexual acts. However, it is clear that homosexual acts, whether with age-appropriate or underage people, are forbidden by the obligation of celibacy. The 1917 code stated that clerics who committed any crime against the sixth commandment, especially if they had care of souls, were to be punished with severe penalties. The phrase, *care of souls*, is ecclesiastical parlance for priests who have pastoral duties as pastors or assistant pastors.

The church has not always recognized a clear distinction between homosexuality and pedophilia (or other sexual disorders for that matter). In the past it was common to refer to priests who had sexually abused male children as homosexuals when in fact "pedophiles" would have been the more scientifically accurate term. Obviously not all homosexually oriented priests are pedophiles; nor are all pedophiles homosexuals. A man who is sexually attracted to young boys may be a homosexual. But his attraction is not necessarily exclusive in the sense that he may also be sexually attracted to males his own age. The same may be said of heterosexually oriented men.

Canon law states that the bishop's primary duties are to see that the laws of the church are obeyed by all and that abuses, particularly moral abuses, are to be prevented. He has what amounts to absolute authority over the priests incardinated in (officially attached to) his diocese. He alone can decide if they can be ordained priests and he has the final word on assignments. The 1983 code specifically states that bishops are to see that priests fulfill the obligations of their clerical state (Canon 384).

Another way of looking at the bishop's supervisory duty is within the context of his obligations toward all the faithful. He is obliged to see that faith and morals are protected. In selecting priests for ordination, and, after ordination, in assigning them to parishes and other ministerial positions, the bishop is to first make sure that the candidate possesses all the requisite intellectual, spiritual, and moral qualities. With regard to pastors and assistant pastors, the bishop is obliged to be sure that the requisite qualities are present in those he appoints. These include "good moral character, learning, zeal, prudence" (Canon 454).

The bishop's duties are also mentioned in the section of the code dealing with Catholic education. They are to watch that in any schools in their diocese nothing is done or taught that is contrary to faith and good morals (Canon 1381.2).

Finally, it is most important to understand that the Catholic Church's governmental and judicial system is fundamentally different from that of a democratic society. The church's government is hierarchic with power descending from the top down, and vested in people assigned or appointed to various offices by superiors. Power is not obtained by election to an office by the laity. There are no checks and balances. Legislation may be drawn up by consultative bodies, but it comes into force or has meaning only when enacted or put into force by individuals with legislative power (the pope and diocesan bishops).

The Obligation to Investigate Celibate Practice

Nowadays, however, the influence of certain corporate bodies (especially the national bishops' conferences) cannot be discounted. The USCCB, for instance, a corporate body composed of the American bishops, can vote on legislation as allowed by canon law. It can also propose and vote on legislation not specifically contained in the law. But such legislation would require the approval of Rome before it takes effect in a U.S. diocese.

Similarly, the judicial system contained in the code reflects the hierarchical nature of government. The bishop is the first judge of his diocese. He appoints judges and other judicial officials. He has the power to initiate judicial inquiries, investigations, and trials.

Sexual misconduct by a priest with anyone—but particularly with a child—is an especially serious offense. It causes extremely grave harm to the child, his or her parents and family, and to the community in general (both church and secular community). Because of this harm, allegations of sexual abuse within the church must not be dismissed without thorough investigation. This obligation is especially onerous on other priests since they have a special obligation toward the laity and toward children.

Pastors are responsible for the spiritual and moral welfare of all in their charge. If serious harm is caused to someone because of the actions of an assistant priest, for instance, it is the pastor's duty to report it to higher authorities (or vice versa by extension). This obligation can be deduced from general legislation dealing with a pastor's responsibilities to the people in his charge (Canon 464, 470).

The 1917 code was more specific than the 1983 code in regard to the pastor's supervision of his assistant pastors. Canon 476 stated that the pastor is to "paternally instruct and direct them (assistant pastors) in the care of souls, watch over them and send each year a report to the bishop concerning their conduct."

With regard to canonical crime, the 1917 code had explicit reporting mandates. Canon 2209 stated that a person who, because of his office ("office" here refers to any official church position, including pastor or bishop, but also vicar) failed to prevent an offense or sheltered an offender shared in the responsibility for the offense itself. This liability also includes carelessness in supervision by a religious superior over a subject.

Canon 383 of the 1983 code states that a bishop has a grave obligation to safeguard the spiritual welfare of all those who are under his care. These include Catholics who reside in his diocese as well as those who may be simply staying there temporarily. Several post-conciliar instructions of the Second Vatican Council reinforce this obligation: *The Dogmatic Constitution on the Church* (November 21, 1964), *The Decree on the Pastoral Office of Bishops in the Church* (October 28, 1965), The Apostolic Letter implementing certain aspects of this decree, *Ecclesiae Sanctae* (August 6, 1966), and *the Directory on the Pastoral Office of Bishops* (1974).

A bishop's obligation to investigate an accusation made against a cleric can also be deduced from the nature of his relationship with his priests. The 1983 code says:

> The diocesan bishop is to attend to the priests with special concern and listen to them as his assistants and advisers; he is to protect their rights and see to it that they correctly fulfill the obligations proper to their state and that the means and institutions which they need are available to them to foster their spiritual and intellectual life (Canon 384).

Because this is such a close and all-pervasive relationship, the bishop can hardly absolve himself of responsibility for what a cleric under his authority does, whether the action takes place while the priest is actually performing ministerial duties or not.

It follows then that a bishop is required to investigate allegations of child molestation on two counts: his obligation to respect the laity's right to have their spiritual welfare taken care of, and his obligation to see to it that the priests observe their obligations in regard to chastity. The code also requires church authorities to take seriously allegations of sexual offenses by clerics and punish them when appropriate:

> Apart from the case mentioned in Can. 1394 (attempted marriage), a cleric living in concubinage, and a cleric who continues in some other external sin against the sixth commandment of the Decalogue which causes scandal, is to be punished with suspension. To this end other penalties can progressively be added if after a warning he persists in the

offense, until eventually he can be dismissed from the clerical state. (Canon 1395.1)

A cleric who has offended in other ways against the sixth commandment of the Decalogue, if the crime was committed by force, or by threats, or in public, or with a minor under the age of sixteen years [after 2001, 18 years], is to be punished with just penalties, not excluding dismissal from the clerical state if the case so warrants. (Canon 1395.2)

By the "sixth commandment of the Decalogue" is meant the traditional Sixth Commandment, "Thou shalt not commit adultery," which is used in the law as a catch-all for any sexual activity outside of marriage.

The code, in the same section on penal law, contains canons that outline the manner in which an allegation is to be investigated. If there is reason to believe that a canonical crime was committed, there is a procedure to be followed for a judicial examination with the possible application of penalties. However, problems can arise when priests hear the confessions of sexually abused victims. They are not allowed, under any circumstances, to divulge anything revealed to them in confession (Canon 983.1).

Another problem can arise with regard to information revealed to a spiritual director or mentor by a victim of sexual abuse. This, too, may fall under the umbrella of confidentiality, and it should not be expected nor would it be ethically appropriate for such information to be revealed to a third party. In this case, the spiritual director should advise the person aggrieved to report such actions to the proper diocesan authorities. It would also be possible for the spiritual director to obtain the specific permission of the victim to disclose the information to third parties.

Ordinarily in sexual misconduct cases involving priests, the preliminary investigation of the incident should take place very quickly after the report is received. The canons concerning the preliminary investigation (Canons 1939 to 1946 of the 1917 code and Canons 1717 to 1728 of the 1983 code), say that if information about an offense comes forward from any source—a report, a rumor, a complaint, or public knowledge—an investigation is to take place. This investigation is initiated by the bishop and is to be documented. After the evidence has been examined, the accused is to be confronted and the bishop is to take judicial (a canonical trial) or administrative action. The action can result in the imposition of a canonical penalty.

The canons do not mention a specific penalty for the commission of the crime of sexual abuse of minors. The gravity of the penalty depends on the gravity of the offense and attending circumstances such as force. Transfer of a priest from one parish to another is not a penalty nor is it an acceptable administrative action in the light of a confirmed commission of an ecclesiastical crime.

The bishop is not obliged to impose a penalty, but should do so once it is clear that the damage resulting from the crime has not been repaired nor the offender reformed. In any event, the bishop is obliged to conduct an investigation according to the norms of the law and following the procedures outlined in the norms of the law, prior to making any decision.

The Rights of the Laity

Although the church is a hierarchy with no checks or balances and is not accountable to the laity, the Second Vatican Council decreed that "the People of God" have rights that deserve to be recognized and included in the church's legal system.

Cases of sexual abuse that come to trial often reveal how victims and their families have been treated by the church. Sometimes the picture does not reflect a deep regard for the rights or respect of laypeople. Reporting abuse and confronting bishops or superiors has resulted in a "revictimization" at the hands of the bishops and church lawyers who do not shy away from accusations, humiliations, and impugning motives so that the victims can be made out to be the criminals. The imbalance of the ratio of the hierarchy to the laity suggests why legislation to protect laypeople is appropriate. There are 67.3 million Catholics in the United States at the present time. Of this number there are 43,000 priests, 14 cardinals, 48 archbishops, and 373 bishops. Even including 14,000 deacons the leadership of the church amounts to about .09 percent, 9 ten-thousandths of the total. However, Vatican II teaches that the church is the "People of God" and not simply its government, hierarchy, or clergy.

The 1983 *Code of Canon Law* contains a significant section on the rights of the faithful. Canons 208–223 cover both clerics and laity, and Canons 224–231 cover the rights of the laity alone. These rights are grounded in the new understanding of the meaning of "church" as defined in Second Vatican Council documents, especially the *Constitution on the Church* (*Lumen Gentium*). This constitution makes clear that the church is not to be identified with the hierarchy. Rather, the church is to be understood as "The People of God." The church is all of the people who profess belief.

The significance of this understanding in the context of sexual abuse is that church officials have frequently requested victims and their families to avoid scandal and not to make an issue of their plight "for the good of the church." The good of the church they wanted to protect was no more than the good of the power structure or hierarchy. Whereas the true good of the church is best served by holding accountable clerics and office holders who abuse the laity in any way.

Indeed, Canon 221 states that all the faithful have the right to vindicate their rights before a competent ecclesiastical court according to the norms of law. Basically this is the right to due process. This would be the canon to which one would appeal in arguing that a person alleging sexual abuse by a cleric has a right to some form of redress. In short, the code gives members of the laity the right to be heard when they approach the hierarchy with a complaint about sexual abuse.

How the hierarchy responds in reality is a different matter. In recent years, reports of the sexual abuse of children by priests were handled in a secretive way. Church officials feared that public knowledge of abuse would severely harm the church's credibility, the image of the priesthood and, in general, result in serious scandal.

It is ironic that while church officials believed that child abuse by clerics is so offensive that it should be kept secret at all costs, they often tried to excuse their failure to follow due process on the ground that they never realized how destructive a problem it is. Sexual abuse of children is a felony that is abhorred by society. It is understandable that no organization would want it be known that its own officials are guilty of such abuse, yet the harm done by the abuse far outweighs the bad reflection awareness might cast on the institution.

In the past, priests confronted with accusations of sexual abuse were admonished by their superiors. Often the shame of the event would prompt promises that it would never happen again. The church usually appealed to a kind of "spiritual" approach to remedy the problem. Priests were reminded of their vows, and of the potential for scandal and harm to the church. Sexual abuse was treated primarily as a moral problem that some form of spiritual conversion could take care of. Although confession may absolve the moral guilt, it does not cure the sexual disorder. In some instances, priests were sent away for psychiatric or other medical treatment after they had acted out more than once.

However, the church has held a certain degree of mistrust for the psychiatric profession. The belief that all sexual problems were a matter of the will held sway for decades, if not centuries, and is still held in some circles. The church has often been reluctant to accept the assistance of the medical profession in dealing with sexual abuse, and then only as a last resort after it had become apparent that other methods of control had failed.

Priests were quietly transferred from one parish to another, one diocese to another, or even to another country, in an effort to give the accused a new start and avoid the possibility of added problems and exposure in the parish where the abuse had taken place. Some bishops sent priests away to study, or on retreats, or to psychiatrists, or special rehabilitation centers. Priests would be deemed unsuitable for ministry in the home diocese yet recommended for ministry in another diocese. The evidence of rampant recidivism should have indicated to church leaders that transfers do not solve the problem. Juries and the court of public opinion judge that church leaders are negligent because of this behavior.

The media exposure of the case and trial of Fr. Gauthé (Lafayette, Louisiana) in 1984–1985 brought the secret operations of the church to the attention of the public. What really changed, however, was not the church officials' knowledge of the problem, but the widespread public awareness of it, and the realization that the problem was not simply a case of secular press "Catholic bashing." Child victims were believed where before they were not. Many adults came forward alleging that they had been abused in their youth by priests and religious brothers. Cases of sexual abuse popped up all over the United States. The media exposure and the threat of lawsuits forced church officials to take a radically different approach to the issue.

Whether and to what degree there had been a conscious and organized cover-up of the abuse problem is speculative. However, there is little doubt that on a diocese-by-diocese basis, common strategies were adopted to make sure that sexual abuse cases never became public. Transfer of priests with little or no public explanation, reassignment of priests with sexual problems with no advance warning to parishes, assertions that internal investigations had found no evidence of wrong-doing, and public denials of problems are all factors that have contributed to the problem over the past several years. There is little evidence that church officials followed state reporting statutes or reported incidents of child abuse to civil authorities. All of these patterns and practices have been attested to in civil procedures.

In order to protect the officials' complicity, the language of church documents referring to sexual problems of priests has been code-like. Sexual problems may be cryptically referred to as "moral problems," "over familiarity with youngsters," "stress," "unfortunate incidents," or simply as "problems." Minor abuse has been commonly referred to by some as "identity concerns" or "homosexuality." Two Latin phrases that often crop up are offenses or problems *"de sexto"* meaning problems with the sixth commandment and actions *"in re turpi"* (literally, matters that are morally disgraceful or foul), another Latin phrase used is acts *"contra naturam."*

Bishops are used to being in control. Their notion of power and authority is traditionally bolstered by the belief that bishops are descended from the apostles. They are the official teachers of the church truth and responsible for all that happens in the church. This attitude predisposed bishops and other ecclesiastical leaders to think that they could control the problem of sexual abuse of children. When issues of abuse come before the courts, however, bishops consistently deny that they had any knowledge or control. There was a feeling that somehow the church was above the civil law. The 1917 *Code of Canon Law*, which forbade the laity from taking clerics before a civil court, partially supported this belief. Church law decreed that problems with clerics should be handled from within, using the church's own canonical system. Unfortunately, the system has not adequately responded to the sexual problems.

Although there have been hundreds of allegations of sexual abuse by priests brought to the attention of the church over the past decades, we do not know of a single instance of an allegation being pursued and satisfactorily settled using proper due process as prescribed by canon law. In many instances, evidence obtained through civil litigation has demonstrated that even the canonical regulations concerning proper investigation of complaints were not followed.

The system of canon law fails when it comes to sexual abuse problems because plaintiffs in church tribunals (and before church authorities) allege not only that priests have sexually abused them, and by implication, that church authorities failed to act. There is a conflict of interest when an allegation or charge is made against the central authorities of a diocese because the responsible person is the bishop. The bishop is also the "first judge" (in canon law terms) of the diocese. In short, the bishop is put in a position of judging himself. Moreover, officials of a diocese who would be able to handle such a canonical process are also part of the diocesan governing structure. Again, there is a conflict of interest here. Historically there has been a reluctance on the part of diocesan officials to pursue cases against the very system that employs them.

Much of the recent civil litigation concerning clerical sexual abuse demonstrates that bishops in numerous dioceses throughout the country knew about the sexual abuse of young people by priests as far back as the early 1960s, and in some cases before that. The Paraclete Fathers say that by 1976 they had already treated a large number of priests for sexual problems. The fact is that there was sufficient information available for the body of bishops to initiate procedures to deal with this problem. Claims that there was no corporate awareness of the existence of the problem prior to the mid-eighties are groundless.

Recurring Issues, Problems, and Questions

There is no standard or rule in canon law stating that the reputation of the institutional church is to be preserved at all costs. There is no policy that requires suspected criminal activity be concealed from public disclosure, or that priests suspected of criminal acts (in the canonical and civil law sense) not be subjected to proper investigation and due process, even if to do so would result in an embarrassment to the church. Whatever the motivations of diocesan officials, it is simply incredible and indefensible that an ecclesiastical crime as serious as the sexual abuse of children not be thoroughly investigated and perpetrators disciplined in every case. It is even more astounding that priests known to have sexually abused minors (or others for that matter) be allowed to continue in pastoral ministry as long as there is even a suspicion of their sexual activities.

The question is sometimes asked: What kind of notice of a complaint warrants an investigation? Church law does not stipulate or restrict the sources of information. If sexual abuse by a cleric is brought to the attention of church authorities, an investigation, (not a trial at this stage) should be initiated. It is not required anywhere in church law or practice that there be two or more accusers, two or more witnesses, or first-hand knowledge of an offense before an inquiry can start. Repeatedly, legal proceedings show that offenses were disregarded with excuses of lack of witnesses or more than one accuser.

In dioceses throughout the country, when cases of sexual abuse by priests have surfaced, the same recurring problems have surfaced. Sometimes the existence of records is denied, only to be produced after repeated demands. In some cases, officials have even stated that the church does not keep personnel records or have a record retention policy.

Priests accused of sexual molestation are often found to have raised suspicions early in their careers and in some cases even in the seminary. In many cases, after reports of sexual impropriety, priests were simply transferred from one parish to another without supervision.

It is rare that allegations of sexual abuse of minors by priests is reported to civil authorities. And sometimes, victims have not been believed, or have been coerced into not making complaints, or have been urged to remain silent. In too many instances, victims have received little or no pastoral attention from church officials.

Diocesan Mishandling

Civil actions taken by numerous victims of sexual abuse by the clergy have brought to light many incidents of diocesan mishandling of the perpetrators and the investigations that should have been—but were not—undertaken when complaints were made. The Dallas cases of Fr. Peebles, Fr. Hughes, and Fr. Kos are examples but, sadly, not the only examples on record.

Even before Fr. Peebles was ordained in April 1977, he had received two negative evaluations from pastors of parishes where he had served as a temporary deacon. Neither of the evaluations contained reports of sexual activity, but concern was expressed about his drinking. There appears to have been no significant follow-up with Fr. Peebles regarding this red flag and he was ordained to the priesthood.

Fr. Peebles' known history of sexual molestation began in 1979 when he was suspected of taking indecent liberties with a young boy at the parish where he was an assistant pastor. Reports of this were made to a Dallas pastor, Fr. Raymond Scott, who in turn relayed the information to Msgr. Robert Rehkemper, the vicar general. This pattern of reports of behavior rising very quickly to the top of the administration ladder is common. The reports were not investigated nor was Fr. Peebles confronted. Although these reports came by way of rumor, the diocese, through the bishop, had an obligation in canon law to investigate them. No investigation took place and the bishop, in defiance of logic, appointed Fr. Peebles diocesan Director of Boy Scouts on June 29, 1981. Over and over, a reason given for appointing potential abusers to roles as [Catholic Youth Organization] CYO or Boy Scout directors is "they get along so well with youths."

However, five months earlier—and despite knowing about Fr. Peebles' sexual activity—the diocese had allowed him to enter the military chaplaincy program of the U.S. Army, and the Military Vicariate endorsed him for the inactive reserves. At this time (February 1981), he was referred to a counselor, Dr. Ted McCandish. The following February, Fr. Peebles was endorsed by the Military Vicariate for active duty.

Had the diocese disclosed the fact of his counseling and the suspicion of sexual abuse to the Military Vicariate, or had the Military Vicariate conducted a more detailed investigation into Fr. Peebles' suitability (given the vicariate's awareness at the time of such problems with other chaplains), the endorsement would not have been granted.

In May 1982, Fr. Peebles took a young boy with him to a retreat house for his orientation course for new military chaplains. He kept the boy in his own room where he sexually abused him. How Fr. Peebles got away with having the boy stay in the same room with him is not known. The fact of the boy's presence should have been questioned. The boy should have been sent home and Fr. Peebles investigated. However, no questions were asked.

Eventually, Fr. Peebles was apprehended at Fort Benning, Georgia, for attempted rape after the boy ran naked from Peebles' quarters and was found wandering around the base. The diocese put pressure on the boy's family to urge the military not to prosecute him. The diocese itself, through the bishop and the judicial vicar, also put pressure on the military authorities not to proceed with a prosecution. The military officials, all the way up to the secretary of the army, were convinced by church officials of the Dallas diocese that a court martial would cause more harm than good. This is another common pattern of activity that conceals abuse.

In a December 1973 letter, Fr. Joseph Marbach, a senior military chaplain, stated the church's policy of dealing with priests accused of sexual impropriety:

> Yes, we prefer that a chaplain resign—we very rarely withdraw an endorsement as this would be a black mark on his official record. On the other hand, a "resignation" is the proverbial umbrella which covers many things and no one will ask questions.

Ironically, after being accused of and confessing to what amounts to a felony crime and facing the possibility of a lengthy term in prison, Fr. Peebles was reassigned as an assistant pastor at St. Augustine's parish in the Dallas diocese on May 21, 1984. This assignment was made not only with the knowledge of what had happened at Fort Benning, but also with the knowledge that Fr. Peebles had been tentatively identified as a child abuser as early as 1981, and this was known to diocesan officials. The people in the parish were not informed of his background. This too, is part of the pattern that kept priests' known offenses "secret" from other priests and parishioners.

Even more ironically, Fr. Peebles was appointed pastor of St. Augustine's in June 1985. One year later it transpired that Fr. Peebles had acted out again with teenage boys. He resigned from the pastorate on August 27, 1986, and was sent to St. Luke Institute for evaluation. The bishop subsequently decided that Fr. Peebles would not attend St. Luke's for therapy.

On November 21, 1986, Fr. Peebles was suspended and, five days later, he petitioned the pope to be laicized. The diocese loaned him $11,000 per year for law school tuition and continued paying his monthly stipend of $800 for living expenses.

The case of Fr. Peebles was mishandled by the diocese of Dallas in many respects: When rumors first surfaced in 1979, he should have been investigated but was not. The military and Military Vicariate should have been told about these rumors, but were not. The vicariate did not ask any questions about prior drinking or sexual problems. After the Fort Benning incident the diocese concentrated its efforts on damage control by convincing the parents that prosecution would be harmful to the victim and promising strict control of Fr. Peebles and therapy. Instead, it appointed Fr. Peebles to another pastoral position. This appointment and the appointment as pastor were both uncalled for and ran directly contrary to the standard of care the diocese is called to with regard to the appointment of priests to pastoral (or any) positions.

Taking all the evidence into consideration, it becomes clear that the diocese of Dallas was primarily concerned about its image and a possible backlash from a prosecution, and not the impact of the assault on the victim or the future activities of Fr. Peebles. Regrettably this practice of dealing with priest abusers has been repeated in more than 180 dioceses throughout the country.

Fr. William Hughes

Fr. Hughes was ordained a priest for the Dallas diocese on April 29, 1982, and assigned to a parish as an assistant pastor shortly after. It was there that he first got to know and eventually sexually abused a young girl. She came from a devout Catholic family that held priests in high esteem. Although Fr. Hughes became a fixture in the family home and spent inordinate amounts of time with the fourteen-year-old girl, her parents could not bring themselves to believe that a priest would be romantically interested in her. They had seen the two together more than once in situations that would cause alarm in most parents, but they shrugged it off, based on their conviction that a priest would not do those kinds of things.

It was not until a number of love letters were found by the girl's mother in July 1984, that her parents began to believe that something was wrong. The girl's mother immediately told Fr. Robert Cloherty, the diocesan vocations director. Fr. Cloherty reacted with alarm and suggested that the letters be destroyed.

By this time, knowledge of the alleged abuse was known by Fr. Cloherty, who reported it to the vicar general, Msgr. Rehkemper, and to the bishop, as is typical of the way the awareness of abusive behavior of priests is communicated within the secret clerical system. There is no evidence to indicate that anything was done about it. Since the plaintiff was fourteen at the time, the disclosure by the mother constituted a valid report of a possible canonical crime (sex with a minor, Canon 1395.2). This should have triggered the investigation mandated by Canon 1719, but it did not.

Fr. Hughes was reassigned to another parish the following month and appointed director of parish youth groups. In September, the girl's mother met with the bishop and Msgr. Rehkemper. This was a meeting she sought out and not one that was initiated by the diocese. The bishop and his vicar general did not appear to have believed the story nor did they appear to have instituted any kind of follow-up with the girl, her family, or Fr. Hughes.

In May 1988, Fr. Hughes was reassigned to another parish as a resident priest so that he could attend school. In February 1989, he was appointed to the Priest Personnel Board of the Diocese. Both actions indicate that no credence had been given to the girl's family's concerns or, if credence was given, the actions of the diocese were irresponsible.

Finally, in July 1990, the family met with the new bishop and told him their story. It is not known what action the bishop took at the time, but it is known that Fr. Hughes petitioned for and was granted a leave of absence in July 1990.

There seems to be little doubt that the diocese failed to act when the initial report of the abuse was made in 1984. Fr. Hughes was still a risk to young people and to the young girl when he was simply reassigned. Moreover, there is little if any evidence that any adequate pastoral care was extended to the plaintiff or her family. The diocese paid for some counseling for the girl in 1990. However, documents in the case indicate that when the subject of providing counseling was first brought up with Msgr. Rehkemper, he suggested that the girl's family insurance pay for it. It remains a mystery why the histories of scores of abusing priests record promotions within the system after they have been reported for abusive behavior.

Fr. Rudolph Kos

Fr. Rudy Kos had been married in the Catholic Church in 1966 and received a civil divorce in 1971. In 1975, he expressed an interest in becoming a priest of the Dallas diocese and in February 1976, the diocese granted him an annulment of his marriage. As part of the annulment process the diocese had contacted his wife, Kathy, the previous December. She told the diocesan representative, Fr. Duesman, that their marriage had not been consummated and her husband should not be ordained because he had a problem with boys when he was in the military. According to Fr. Duesman, Kathy implied that the FBI had investigated an allegation that her husband had abused a military officer's son.

There is no indication that the diocesan officials ever contacted Kathy about her allegations concerning her husband, or that her statements to Fr. Duesman were ever taken into account in the process leading up to his ordination.

Fr. Kos was ordained, but it eventually emerged that he had been sexually abusing young boys or attempting to abuse them prior to his ordination. He continued to abuse boys through his stints as assistant pastor and pastor, and even when he was supposed to be in therapy with the Paraclete Fathers. In 1986, as an assistant pastor, Fr. Kos had boys staying overnight at the rectory. His pastor, Fr. David Clayton, reported this to the vicar general, Msgr. Rehkemper, and he spoke to Fr. Kos about the matter, seemingly to no avail.

Fr. Kos was appointed a pastor in 1988. Another priest, Fr. Robert Williams was also living at this parish, and he documented Fr. Kos' behavior and reported it to Msgr. Rehkemper, who recommended Fr. Kos see a psychiatrist, Dr. Richard Jaeckle.

In April 1992, Fr. Williams and Msgr. Rehkemper met with a pedophilia expert, Dr. Brenda Keller, who recommended that Fr. Kos be immediately removed from all contact with boys. He went to St. Luke Institute for evaluation, (their report was inconclusive) and further testing was recommended. He returned to his parish in Texas and, finally, in October 1992, he was sent to the Paraclete facility for treatment. He was suspended by the bishop in November 1993.

Fr. Williams was the hero of the trial of Fr. Kos because he was willing to testify about his messages to the chancery office concerning Fr. Kos' activities. He produced the documents he had written to diocesan officials at the time. Few priests have had the courage to withstand the pressure that the church structure exerts on them to keep silent about the sexual violations of their confrères.

However, the officials of the diocese of Dallas consistently failed in regard to Fr. Kos and his victims. They failed to properly investigate reports that he had a problem prior to his ordination. After he was ordained they failed to properly investigate rumors, suspicions, and reports of inappropriate activities with boys. They failed to act on detailed complaints given by at least two priests who observed his suspicious activities. They failed to provide Dr. Jaeckle with adequate information upon which to evaluate Fr. Kos, and they failed to take action when Dr. Keller advised that he not have any contact with boys.

There appears to be no rational excuse for this succession of negligent acts by the diocese. The diocese had already been dealing with the problem of Fr. Peebles, so it cannot claim ignorance of the problem of sex abuse of children by priests on that score alone.

There were significant warning signs present prior to Fr. Kos' ordination to indicate that he never should have been ordained. Hence, the diocese violated its canon law obligations to the community by failing to properly screen him. Perhaps the two most egregious errors were the failure to take into consideration the information provided by his former wife, and the failure to give proper attention to the report a seminarian made to Msgr. Rehkemper about improper sexual advances Kos made in March or April of 1981 prior to his ordination.

Canon law contains numerous provisions aimed at protecting the common good, that is, the good of the faithful. Among these provisions are some related to the ordination of men to the priesthood. The provisions refer to circumstances in the candidate's life that could prevent him from properly performing the duties of a priest. Indeed, the 1917 code, which was in force at the time of Fr. Kos' ordination, states that the bishop must have positive proof of the candidate's suitability. This means that he possess not just an absence of negative factors but positive proof of capability, and moral and spiritual suitability.

Canon 984 refers to irregularities for ordination. These are circumstances in the candidate's life that constitute an impediment. This canon mentions two irregularities that apply to this case: the irregularity of insanity and the irregularity of infamy of law. The compulsion to have sex with minors is and has been generally considered a form of emotional or mental illness and would fall under the umbrella of insanity as defined by the code. The other irregularity, infamy of law, is a unique canonical term. In short, it is a penalty that is automatically incurred at the time a person commits one of the crimes specifically set forth in the code. One of these is the crime of impurity with minors (Canon 2359). On both counts, the diocese of Dallas failed to observe church law when the bishop ordained Fr. Kos.

A Paradigm of the Pattern and Practice

These three cases in one diocese constitute a paradigm of the pattern and practice of the American Catholic Church in dealing with sexually abusive priests and their victims. The exposure of a myriad of cases in Boston and Los Angeles (more than five hundred) refines and demonstrates the extent to which the church bypasses and ignores its own guidelines, directives, laws, and wisdom.

The notoriety of civil and criminal cases of abuse has been a painful education for the clergy and laity alike. There have been church reactions, but it still remains to be seen how thoroughly the widespread public knowledge of the church's secret system, which has been exposed only because of court pleadings, judgments, and settlements, has spurred the authorities to initiate effective and lasting reform.

Chapter 6

How the Bishops Knew and When They Knew It

When victims of sexual abuse launch civil suits against priests, they often sue the alleged perpetrator's bishop as well, reasoning that he, as the priest's supervisor, shares responsibility for the harm they have suffered. Such a claim naturally begs the question: How did bishops know about sexual abuse? The answer is: They knew about abuse from many sources, but especially from their membership in the secret society of clerics bent on preserving their public image above everything else. As to the questions: What did they know, and when did they know it? The answer, in a nutshell is: All about it and all along.

It is abundantly clear from the evidence that a great deal was known about the prevalence and pervasiveness of the sexual activity of priests within the clerical system, but it has been kept under wraps. The laity were certainly not made aware of it, at least not until relatively recently, and then only through the efforts of victims, lawyers, and, pre-eminently, the media.

Priests know about the clerical abuse of minors from hearing the confessions of other priests, but of course can do nothing about an individual case, being held by a most sacred obligation to observe the seal of confession at all costs. Spiritual directors know about the abuse from priests who come to them for counseling. Priests also know about it from hearing rumors from other priests about priests who have young boys stay with them or develop inordinate friendships with minors—boys and girls. Many seminarians know about the homosexual and heterosexual behavior of other seminarians and faculty members. Bishops and religious superiors know about clerical sexual activity from conversations and preliminary investigations of reports about priests in their charge who misbehave. Although bishops and religious superiors are expected to observe confidentiality with reference to their subjects, this presumption is not absolute as is the obligation to observe the seal of the confessional. Indeed, for this very reason, bishops and religious superiors are forbidden by church law to hear the confessions of priests in their charge (Cf. Chapter 7).

Three questions occur when considering the widespread knowledge of sexual abuse by clergy concomitant with an equally extensive blindness to its reality. Why do exemplary clergy keep silent about abuse in their midst? Why do laypeople and even the parents of abused children often not respond to rational indicators of priests' misbehavior? What paralyzes victims of abuse into speechlessness about the abuse they have witnessed and endured?

What accounts for these conundrums? Clergy exist and perpetuate a cult of secrecy. Lay Catholics are reared in a culture of the unimaginable and unspeakable sexuality of all Catholic clergy. And victims of clergy sexual abuse are cowed into silent submission by religious duress.

Cult of Systemic Secrecy

Secrecy is an unwritten, but strict, code within the clerical system, and like any other closed trade or professional group clerics tend to stand up for one another. However, the closeness of this brotherhood lends itself to creating a system with an aura of secrecy that withholds at all costs the knowledge of sexual violations by its members from the laity. This system acts as though rumors, hearsay, and even direct evidence of sexual violations by its members should be treated as though they were entitled to the confidentiality guaranteed by the seal of confession.

This aura of secrecy is nurtured by the church. The oath that cardinals take, for instance, never to divulge anything confided to them that "might bring harm or dishonor to Holy Church" creates a template for everybody else to keep scandals under wraps. The oath reads:

> I (name) cardinal of the Holy Roman Church, promise and swear to remain, from this moment and for as long as I live, faithful to Christ and his gospel, constantly obedient to the Holy Apostolic Roman Church, to the Blessed Peter in the person of the Supreme Pontiff (name) and of his successors canonically elected; to preserve always in word and deed communion with the Catholic Church; never to reveal to anyone whatsoever has been confided to me to keep secret and the revelation of which could cause damage or dishonor to the Holy Church; to carry out with great diligence and fidelity the tasks to which I am called in my service to the Church, according to the norms of law. So help me Almighty God.

When one bishop was chided by a priest for denying the existence of sexual abuse when he did, in fact, know about it, he replied: "I only lie when I have to." And as recently as May 2002, a judge of the Holy Roman Rota, the highest court in the church, wrote in a Vatican-approved article that bishops should not report sexual violations of priests to civil authorities. The reasoning: lest the image and authority of the church be compromised and victims harmed instead of protected (Ghirlanda, previously noted).

Although many of the laity in the church have not even allowed themselves to think about the extent of sexual abuse by members of the clergy, individual people have known about individual cases. They would hear rumors, second-hand or even third-hand, about priests violating their vows, and sometimes they would defy their training to remain silent and report them to the church authorities. The records of the investigations that bishops were required by law to initiate, but may or may not have been undertaken in fact, are not available to the general public. There is no shortage of evidence to suggest that many of them did nothing in a large number of cases. Yet, canon law requires all bishops to investigate even rumors and suspicions of sexual misbehavior by priests in their charge.

The reasons for bishops' and priests' inaction may be that so many of them themselves are sexually active, although not necessarily with children. The evidence of the widespread sexual abuse of minors by Catholic clergy in the United States is only one facet of the evidence for the short-comings of celibate practice among Catholic clergy. Four times as many Catholic priests and religious are involved with women than are involved with children, and nearly three times as many are involved with adult men. Broad-based sexual activity (most of it legal from a civil law point of view) within the clerical system provides protection for priests who abuse minors. Priests who abuse minors are part of a much larger group, an anonymous network of the clergy who are aware of each other's sexual proclivities, behaviors, and activities and are capable of blackmailing each other. Reports from four grand juries (Rockville, New York; Boston, Massachusetts; New Hampshire; and Phoenix, Arizona) present a pattern of the hierarchy neglecting to investigate, supervise, discipline, and report priests who abuse minors to the civil authorities. All four juries concur that the church authorities are not capable of dealing with the problem of sexual abuse of minors by their clergy.

The Unthinkable: The Unspeakable

The paper trail of church and civil documents provides only a partial record of the sexual activity of bishops and priests. Even written records present a mystery: How is the reality of clergy sexual violation and crime kept relatively secret—at least for long periods of time?

Catholics rightfully do not think of themselves as "inmates." But church documents provide a description of the dynamics of an institution-like communication that provides protection of the sexual secrets of the clergy. Things are known, but remain unspoken because they are unthinkable. Irving Goffman in his classic analysis of patterns of communication in prisons, mental hospitals, and monasteries provides a template for thinking about the mysterious way in which clergy sex is protected by the celibate/sexual system of the church.[140a]

Catholic celibate doctrine restricts thought or consideration about any sexuality in regard to its clergy. Priests and bishops become asexual or non-sexual entities. Catholic education inculcates in various ways, verbal and non-verbal, that it would be sacrilegious to think or speak about papal sex, and just a bit less so to think of bishops or priests in sexual terms. The height to which these sexless men are elevated is above the angels. The spiritual powers they possess are truly supernatural—over salvation and eternity.

And yet, bishops and priests are considered to be the experts on sexual behavior and morality. This image of authority and proficiency is reinforced in schools and from pulpits. Official pronouncements about marital relations,

contraception, pre-marital sex, and sexual morality generally leave no doubt that the church holds itself as the final
arbiter on all sexual values and behaviors. Beyond that,
Andrew Greeley, priest, sociologist, and fiction writer,
who has conducted surveys on the sexual lives of
Catholics (but not priests) claims that women have better
sexual relations with their husbands when they have a
celibate priest confidant.[140b]

Where do priests get their knowledge and sexual expertise? A study of moral theology provides guidelines, but their
practical knowledge is acquired primarily from laypeople in
the sacrament of confession and in counseling. Sacramental
confession is a weekly requirement for men studying for the
priesthood. Each seminarian is required to have a regular
confessor to whom he confides his inner life, concerns, and
aspirations. Laypeople are required by church law to go to
confession at least once a year. It is the custom of many people to go more frequently.

Sacramental confession is the core social and psychological element that relegates all sexuality to a secret system.
Within it sex can be acknowledged and examined. The
unspeakable and the spoken are bound together and controlled in one ethic that permeates Catholic teaching and
family custom. Church documents that focus on sexual violations in and around the sacrament of confession (Cf.
Chronology) are written witness to the tradition of priests
using this privileged setting to impose on its ambiguity.

The ultimate power of the code of silence is manifested
in religious duress (Chapter 8) when direct experience of
sexual violation becomes unmentionable and a taboo subject. But the code of silence is bridged in important ways
that give clues to sexual secrets, and if appropriately followed and investigated, can break the cycle of clergy abuse.

Rumors of sexual activity by priests have frequently
been dismissed as idle gossip when, in fact, they are an

important means for the Catholic community to protect itself from the prevailing power system. Even legitimate suspicions of abuse are often suspended because of the unthinkable and unspeakable culture that surrounds clergy. Only reluctantly can many Catholics bring themselves to complain about mistreatment or report abuse, again because they have to speak about what they were taught was unthinkable: namely, that a priest would involve himself in any way with sex, let alone in acts that are illegal or abusive.

Sexual violations by their nature are difficult to document because the actions are commonly executed without a third-party observer. This is why rumors, suspicions, complaints, and reports of inappropriate sexual behavior by priests must be taken seriously, without prejudice, but free from the cultural presumption that has protected clergy violations and persecuted untold numbers of innocent minors for centuries.

The wholesale trust given to clergy in sexual matters must be reexamined. Sexual trust must be merited on a rational not a magical basis. Sex must not be relegated to a secret system.

Not a New or Local Phenomenon

Catholic Church authorities often allege that the problem of sexual abuse of young boys and girls by priests is a new problem. The authorities claim it is so new that they are only now beginning to realize how serious it is and only now beginning to figure out how to deal with it.

The evidence shows, however, there is no valid reason why they should be able to say that. The historical evidence dating from the fourth century demonstrates that mandatory celibacy has been consistently violated by Catholic clerics through sexual abuse of minors and vulnerable adults.

Activity in the United States to treat sexually troubled clergy is not recent. The work of Fr. Thomas Verner More at the Catholic University of America and Mount Hope Retreat (Seton Psychiatric Institute) from 1924 on, and evidence from the earliest days of the Paraclete Fathers, demonstrate efforts that were well-known to the hierarchy (Cf. Fr. Fitzgerald letters 1952). Sufficient research has been presented to the bishops—some of it under their sponsorship—to demonstrate that they knew of the existence and prevalence of sexual abuse by the clergy, but did not respond as they were obliged to.

The large number of sexually active homosexual priests further complicates the issue of the sexual abuse of minor boys because of the potential for confusion between sexual orientation and object of attraction. They are distinct and can be easily distinguished when a thirty-five-year-old man abuses a thirteen-year-old girl. Homosexual orientation is the subject of public controversy and disapproval of any same-sex behavior—particularly in view of the church's own disparagement of homosexual orientation as an "inherently disordered condition." But homosexual orientation and behavior has never been secret among the ranks of the clergy. Although training for celibacy has been lacking or seriously deficient in all Catholic seminaries, seminarians and young candidates for religious life have been warned, from time immemorial, about "particular friendships." This caution, plus all the rules that control association between students in rooms, after hours, and even during recreation (always 3, never 2), is motivated by the awareness of the homosexual impulses that prevail within the seminary atmosphere. The Vatican directive of 1961 clearly addresses the question of homosexually oriented persons who present themselves as candidates for the priesthood or religious life (Cf. Chronology).

In 1980, a study of homosexual priests conducted by a Catholic priest at the Institute for Advanced Study of Human Sexuality found that of a sample of fifty gay Catholic priests ranging from 27 to 58 years of age, only two, or 4 percent, were abstaining from sex at that time. The number of previous same-sex partners for that sample ranged from 500 or more for 11 of the participants in the study, to fewer than 10 for 9 participants, and an average of 227 for each of the entire group. A total of 49, or 98 percent of the survey sample, stated they intended to continue living a gay lifestyle. In addition, 88 percent stated that, despite their sexual activity, they would again take a vow of celibacy. Although this is not a representative study, it is indicative of a problem in the clergy. It is, however, one of many survey examples that confuse the "happiness" of priests with their lifestyle as if they were practicing celibacy.

Some knowledgeable observers, including authorities within the church, estimate that 40–50 percent of all Catholic priests have a homosexual orientation and that a majority of these are sexually active. The psychotherapist, Richard Sipe, estimates that 30 percent of Catholic priests have a homosexual orientation and that half of these are sexually active (Cf. Lothstein, [1994] 34 Catholic Law Rev. p. 89).

The vast majority of homosexually oriented priests do not abuse minors. However, the question of homosexuality is sometimes confused with the issue of sexual abuse of minors also because a disproportionate number of the victims of clerical sexual abuse are male minors. Some clinicians report that 90 percent of the sexual victims of priests are male; others put the percentage at closer to 70 percent. Whatever its exact size, it seems by all accounts that priests molest a larger percentage of minor boys than do abusers in the general population (Cf. Lothstein, ibid.).

Abuse Itself Is Systemic

It is now an undisputed fact that sexual abuse by priests is neither simply a current aberration nor a passing phenomenon: It has deep systemic roots. In 1976, Sipe estimated that 6 percent of Catholic priests involved themselves sexually with minors. In 1985, he reaffirmed the accuracy of that number with the completion of an ethnographic study on the basis of his twenty-five years experience collecting data and treating priests, many of whom had sexual concerns. The data from the John Jay study between the years 1960 and 1985 exceed Sipe's estimate. When individual Catholic institutions or dioceses are considered, the proportion of those alleged or indicted for the sexual abuse of minors frequently runs higher than these estimates. For example, in several Catholic dioceses in the United States, more than 10 percent of priests have been sexually involved with minors.

An extensive study of a Santa Barbara, California, minor seminary (student ages 13–17) was conducted in 1993 by an independent review board consisting of religious and lay professionals in the field of social work, psychology, law, and medicine. They found that 25 percent of the religious faculty (Franciscan friars) had inappropriate sexual contact with minor students over a twenty-three-year period. A similar pattern of misconduct was documented in a Midwestern minor seminary (also ages 13–17) where, between the years 1968–1986, fourteen boys suffered sexual abuse by six priest faculty members, all Capuchin friars. Between 8 and 10 percent of a Benedictine community in Minnesota were listed as alleged abusers by 2004. Additional complaints were registered against three superiors of the community between 1972 and 1992.

In 1992, Fr. Greeley estimated that between 5 and 7 percent of Catholic priests involve themselves with minors and that there were between 100,000 and 150,000 victims of sexual abuse by Catholic priests and religious in the United States.

The histories of many priest abusers record that they were abused in their childhood by an adult, and a large number of those adults were priests or religious brothers. A significant number of priests introduce candidates for the priesthood to sex. In fact, 10 percent of priests report that they had some sexual contact with a priest or fellow seminarian in the course of their studies. Such activity forms a basis for a network of priests aware of each other's personal sexual proclivities and behavior. This forms a formal and informal tangle of possible blackmail.

The revelation of the thousands of cases of clergy sexual abuse since 1985 indicates that the hierarchy had a standardized method of responding to reports and accusations of clergy sexual abuse. With rare exceptions, perpetrators were surreptitiously moved from one assignment to another with no warning to the receiving parish or community. The documentation on thousands of cases from the past two decades shows also that such cases were never reported to Child Protective Services or its equivalent.

Catholic Church officials who knew about the existence of clerical abuse of minors have either been culpably ignorant of the compulsive dimension of the sexual disorders that afflicted the abusers, or they have ignored the warnings of rumors, suspicions, and reports that would alert the average concerned citizen. They may not have been aware of the scientific nature of the different sexual disorders or of the clinical descriptions of the emotional and psychological impact on victims, but they cannot claim ignorance of the fact that such behavior was destructive in effect and criminal in nature.

Public Pressure Works

The intense public pressure brought to bear on the hierarchy from early in 2002 caused U.S. Catholic bishops to propose a policy that ruled out a return to ministry for perpetrators of sexual abuse. This policy, with its widely discussed "Zero Tolerance" clause, went into effect in 2002. That same year, the bishops commissioned two reports, one—a survey—by the John Jay College of Criminal Justice, another by the Bishops' National Review Board, and these were released on February 27, 2004. The John Jay survey found that almost 4,500 clergy perpetrators had been reported by U.S. dioceses since 1950 and there were at least 10,000 victims. An additional 1,093 complaints of abuse were registered after the report was issued. Although some of the complaints were about previously reported priests the total number of reported abusive priests in 2005 stands at over 5,000. The National Review Board report placed blame for the widespread scandal directly on the bishops' negligence. Both reports confirmed that members of the hierarchy were aware of the existence of sexual abuse since the 1950s, and the church leadership's consistent mishandling of individual cases.

The John Jay 2004 report concluded that 4 percent of Catholic priests abused minors over a fifty-year period, (10 percent in the 1970s and 8 percent in the 1980s). The investigators recognized that the overall estimate was low because of the under-reporting of violations. They postulated that between 3 percent and 6 percent was a more likely constant proportion of priest sexual abuses. The count in Boston came to 7.6 percent, and in New Hampshire, 8.2 percent. In the diocese of Tucson, Arizona, 24 percent of its entire priest population was involved in the abuse of minors in 1986; and in the diocese of Belleville, Illinois, 13 percent in 1995. The

Los Angeles Archdiocese harbored 56 sexual abusers among its 710 priests in 1991.

Highly placed Vatican and church officials have confirmed knowing about sexual activity by priests. Cardinal Franjo Seper said in 1971, "I am not at all optimistic that celibacy is in fact being observed." Cardinal Jose Sanchez, head of the Vatican Congregation for the Clergy said, in 1993, when he was confronted with documents stating that between 45 percent and 50 percent of priests do not in fact practice celibacy, "I have no reason to doubt the validity of those figures." Fr. Timothy Radcliffe, the former Master General of the Dominican Order said in 2003 that the practice of celibacy had "collapsed" in the United States, among other places.

Chapter 7

Files, Secrecy, and Confidentiality: The Ongoing Debate

Hardly any issue has been more contested in legal proceedings in cases of sexual abuse by clergy than access to documents held in church files. Many times these files have proven to hold incontrovertible evidence of the knowledge bishops had of the complaints, allegations, and records of clergy violations.

Although the John Jay investigation concluded that nearly 4,500 priests and bishops had abused minors over a 50-year period and 700 priests were removed from active ministry between 2002 and 2004 because of credible evidence of sexual abuse, fewer than 150 priests have been incarcerated. The release of church files from court protection in Boston was key to finding a way through the labyrinth of secrecy that has protected thousands of priests across the country from criminal and civil prosecution. The statutes of limitation have saved most priest perpetrators from criminal prosecution. This is no vindication. Grand juries have declared dioceses responsible for covering up sexual abuse and conspiring to keep abuse by clergy secret.

The church's own files have been the single most powerful element in proving its pattern and practice of protecting abusers, concealing offenses from those who had a right to know, neglecting to warn and protect parishioners, and failing to report crimes.

Nowhere in the United States has the debate and fight over access to court files of offending priests been more prolonged and hotly contested than in the Archdiocese of Los Angeles. This is a jurisdiction that has admitted that it has received credible complaints against more than 244 priests. More than 50 percent of its parishes have had at least one offending priest serve on its staff. Even in 1991, 56 of its active priests have been shown to be credibly alleged abusers. In 2005, more than 540 civil cases against the archdiocese and its priests were still pending or mired in prolonged mediation.

In a 2004 court case, Cardinal Roger Mahony, archbishop of Los Angeles, asserted the so-called "Formation Privilege" as a basis for refusing to reveal the contents of files dealing with allegations of sexual abuse of children, adolescents, and adults by priests in his diocese.

Cardinal Mahony himself, in a declaration he made (n.19, p.12) in February 2003, stated:

> Confidentiality is essential to the pastoral work of the Vicar for the Clergy and the Archbishop; and, therefore, essential to the free exercise of the Roman Catholic religion. All of the types of communications identified herein to which I seek confidentiality are communications made in confidence, in the presence of no third persons, to a member of the clergy who, in the course and discipline and practice of the Catholic Church, is authorized or accustomed to hear such communications and, under the discipline of the Catholic Church, has a duty to keep secret.

Internal and External Forum

According the *Code of Canon Law*, the church exercises its power to govern on two levels or areas: the internal forum and the external forum. The internal forum is the forum of conscience. It is here that the most sensitive information is shared between a person and a priest or bishop. The most common example of the internal forum is the act of sacramental confession of sins. Information shared in this forum cannot be revealed by the priest who receives it, for any reason. This absolute privilege of total confidentiality belongs to the penitent and has its roots in canon law going back over a thousand years. This privileged relationship has given rise to what is commonly referred to in Anglo-American Common Law as the "Priest-Penitent Privilege." Matters pertaining to the internal forum should never be recorded in any way.

Matters handled in the external forum include all investigations into allegations of impropriety and the commission of canonical crimes, and all judicial or administrative processes related to such allegations. The present code, revised and promulgated in 1983, respects a centuries-old legal tradition in the church with a section, Book VI, titled *Sanctions in the Church*. This section describes actions that are to be regarded as canonical crimes and the penalties to be imposed on people who commit them. Some of these crimes are also considered criminal by the civil law of many countries. Canon 1395 deals specifically with sexual contact by the clergy with minors under the age of 16.

Judicial matters such as penal investigations are not matters of the internal forum by the very fact that a record of the investigation is mandated by the law. Similarly, the contents of a personnel file are not presumed to be matters of the internal forum.

The communications between religious superiors and their subjects, and bishops and their clergy are not presumed to be internal forum matter unless it is a question of communications received in the course of sacramental confession or spiritual direction or a communication that is explicitly understood to be in the non-sacramental internal forum.

The code also dedicates an entire book (Book VII), to procedural law and Part VI of this book deals with penal procedure. All procedural matters, administrative and judicial, civil and penal, are matters of the external forum. The ability and the power of the church to prosecute behavior that the code deems criminal is directly related to its obligation to protect not only its own and its officials' power and prestige, but most importantly, the common good of all the faithful (Canon 223.1). In some instances, this obligation clearly extends to the church's obligation to the society of which it is a part.

What the Code Has to Say

Cardinal Mahony, Sister Judy Murphy C.S.J., and Msgr. Craig Cox have spoken of allegations of sexual improprieties by the clergy that were received by the Los Angeles archdiocese. These allegations constitute possible violations of Canon 1395, which deals directly with sexual abuse by a cleric, and Canon 1389, which deals with abuse of power or function.

Canon 1395.2 states that if a cleric has committed an offense against the sixth commandment with force or threats, or publicly, or with a minor below the age of sixteen, he is to be punished with just penalties, including dismissal from the clerical state if the case warrants it.

Canon 1389.1 states that a person who abuses ecclesiastical power or an office is to be punished according to the gravity of the act or the omission, not excluding deprivation of the office, unless a penalty for that abuse is already established by law or precept.

Paragraph 2 states that a person who, through culpable negligence, unlawfully and with harm to another, performs or omits an act of ecclesiastical power, or ministry, or office, is to be punished with a just penalty.

The codes also provide a procedure for conducting investigations into reports of possible offenses. While confidentiality and sensitivity is required by the code, the information arising from these investigations remains in the external forum and is not covered by privilege.

Canon 1717 requires the bishop to conduct an investigation into concerns about sexual violations either personally or through a suitable person whom he delegates. The proceedings of this investigation are to be recorded in writing and then kept in the secret archive (Canon 1719). After the investigation is concluded, the information is given to the bishop who then decides whether to proceed with an administrative procedure, a judicial procedure, a pastoral admonition, or nothing at all (Canon 1718).

Although Canon 1717 states clearly that "care must be taken lest anybody's good name be endangered by this investigation," this cannot be construed to mean that the investigation and the information obtained through it are considered privileged as though protected by the highest degree of secrecy. The entire matter, from the beginning of the investigation through the judicial or administrative process, is in the external forum and not covered by any kind of extraordinary confidentiality or privilege. It would be erroneous to equate this level of confidentiality with the total confidentiality demanded by the confessional privilege.

Failure to carry out such an investigation, or carrying out an abbreviated or secret investigation with no documentation constitutes a deviation from the procedural law of the code. Although bishops have the power to dispense from disciplinary laws of the church, Canon 87 explicitly states that bishops cannot dispense from procedural or penal laws.

If an investigation is carried out, it must be documented and the documentation must be placed in what are known as the "secret archives." Information contained in the secret archives is sensitive and should be treated with confidentiality, but it is not privileged and can be revealed to outsiders including secular or civil law enforcement or judicial authorities. In fact, this information is routinely subpoenaed and surrendered to the civil authorities

Communications between Bishop and Priest

Msgr. Cox, the archdiocesan vicar for clergy, said that reports of priests misbehaving in Los Angeles are referred to him. If there is a potential for litigation arising from a priest's conduct, he said, an investigation is made under the direction of and on behalf of the general counsel of the diocese.

To illustrate the relationship between a priest and his bishop, Msgr. Cox referenced a variety of official church documents, including documents that originated at Vatican Council II, and from the *Code of Canon Law*. Except for the canons, all citations are theological in nature and are not from legal sources; they use a variety of terms to describe the bishop-priest relationship: father, brother, collaborator, and friend. None of these citations state that all communications, either oral or in writing, between a bishop and a priest are covered by the privilege of absolute confidentiality.

Neither the 1917 nor the 1983 *Code of Canon Law,* nor the Acts and Decrees of the Second Vatican Council, nor the *Corpus Iuris Canonici* (a fourteenth-century fundamental canonical source) create a special privilege of confidentiality for communications between a priest and a bishop.

Bishops communicate with their priests on a variety of levels. A priest can conceivably ask to speak with his bishop about matters of a deep, personal nature, and in his conversation, he might share matters of conscience with the bishop and ask that these matters be held in strict confidence. It is also possible that a priest would go to confession to his bishop. However, priests are ordinarily discouraged from going to confession to their own bishops, to the vicar for clergy, or to other priests in supervisory positions over them. This practice is actually forbidden in some religious orders and may well be forbidden by local norms in some dioceses. The reasoning is obvious: The bishop is the priest's superior and his employment supervisor. Although the relationship may be described in theological language, the bishop is, in actual practice, the priest's employer. If the bishop were bound by the seal of confession every time he spoke with or admonished a priest, he would hardly be able to take administrative action whenever the behavior addressed demanded it.

However, both Cardinal Mahony and Msgr. Cox stated that all communications between a bishop and a priest are bound by an equal level of confidentiality. This cannot be. Different scenarios require different levels of confidentiality. In one scenario, a priest shares deeply personal information with his bishop, outside the confessional: In this case the bishop, if he sees fit, would be free to share this information discreetly with others. In another scenario, information regarding sexual abuse by a priest is communicated to another priest, who shares it with the bishop or his vicar—as is the case in the Archdiocese of Los Angeles—the

Vicar for Clergy, who passes it on to the cardinal and the general counsel.

Sexual abuse is illegal in civil and canon law, both of which prescribe the imposition of significant penalties on perpetrators. A report of sexual abuse would probably result in a meeting of the priest and his bishop to discuss the allegation. This scenario can hardly be described as an exercise in the priest's formation process. It is the investigation of a crime. It involves the public, and several people are involved in sharing information about the priest and even given by the priest. Any hope of assuming that this information is privileged is lost for a number of reasons, not the least of which is the fact that so many people are privy to the allegation.

Bishops to Oversee the Behavior of Priests

Canon 384 states that the bishop is to see that priests fulfill the obligations proper to their state. This, of course, includes the obligations attached to celibacy. This can be done in a variety of ways since the canon does not restrict its application. Msgr. Cox stated that a priest is encouraged to communicate freely and openly with his bishop about his "deepest psychological and sexual issues, to undergo psychiatric evaluation and treatment, and to share the results of his therapy with the vicar and bishop. All of this is for the purpose of the ongoing formation and sanctification of the priest." In fact, such psychiatric evaluation and treatment cannot be automatically shared with the vicar or bishop unless the subject releases it. Moreover, such treatment is not mandated by canon law nor can it be imposed on a priest. It is not done on a routine basis for all priests and only happens in cases when an allegation has been made against a priest or when some other set of circumstances requires that such an evaluation take place.

This is not a routine event in a priest's formation of spiritual life. In other words, the connection between psychiatric evaluation and treatment and the normal ongoing formation of a priest is illusory.

Some bishops have gone so far as to assert that it is within their power to decide when to cloak a conversation with the "confessional privilege." This power is purely fictional and has no basis in any canon law or theology. There is no parallel to be drawn between the seal of confession and the confidentiality of information given to a bishop outside of confession. The seal of the confessional must be observed at all times by the priest confessor—he has no discretion in the matter—but the penitent is free to disclose at any time what he or she confesses to the priest. Outside of confession, however, a bishop could be obliged, for the good of society, to disclose information about a priest. No right has been given him to claim that all communications with his priests can be kept confidential for the free exercise of religion. The opposite is true: If a child is being abused, the bishop who hears about it is obliged by civil law to report it to the civil authorities.

It is important to note also that the 1917 *Code of Canon Law* had a canon (Canon 2209) that explicitly forbade anyone using his ecclesiastical office to actively or tacitly condone the commission of a crime. The same legislation is contained in Canon 1329.2 of the1983 code. Hence, a bishop who knows about the sexual abuse of a minor by a priest is bound by canon law to take whatever steps are necessary to ensure the abuse is not repeated.

There is no question that some communications between bishop and priest can and should be covered by strict confidentiality, depending on their nature and context. It is also true that priests may discuss matters of personal sexuality and celibacy with their bishops. This is quite apart from documentation covering allegations of sexual abuse, which is not only a potential canonical crime if proven, but a crime in civil law as well. When a bishop becomes aware of such an allegation and confronts an accused priest, the bishop is not acting as his confessor but as his superior. For the sake of good order in the Catholic community, the integrity of the sacrament of orders, and the spiritual and moral welfare of the same community, such communications must be disclosed to other parties with a "need to know" so that appropriate actions might be taken.

The theoretical intimate relationship between a bishop and a priest and the exercise of the Catholic religion do not require that a bishop withhold files that may contain information related to the commission of a crime.

No Constitutional Right to Conceal

The free exercise of the Catholic religion does not exempt bishops and priests from the due process of the civil law in criminal cases. The duty to report suspected cases of child abuse is not a violation of the First Amendment rights of church leaders. In fact, the systematic neglect by church leaders to follow the procedures outlined by Canon 1717 constitutes a violation of the procedures by the very officeholders who have the primary responsibility to uphold the law.

Sister Murphy, who oversees investigations of allegations of sexual abuse in the archdiocese, stated that the records of sexual abuse, along with other highly confidential matters, are kept in a computer. The archdiocesan general counsel for civil matters controls access to this computer. On the face of it, record keeping in a computer that is not kept locked up in the secret archives of a diocese violates Canon 1719 of the *Code of Canon Law*. Of itself, a computer does not constitute a secret archive.

Sister Murphy seems to imply that the investigation of allegations of clergy sexual impropriety are handled under her direction. If this is true, then the sanctity of the bishop-priest relationship championed by the cardinal and Msgr. Cox in their declarations is destroyed because the pertinent information is, by Sister Murphy's own admission, shared with a number of people, many of them not clerics. Msgr. Cox himself states that the investigation is made under the direction and on behalf of the general counsel, a lay civil lawyer. As stated, this procedure is a violation of Canon 1717 since only the bishop can direct and mandate such an investigation. It is also noteworthy that Canon 483 states that the office of notary, required in all judicial proceedings, including the investigation of a Canon 1717 violation, must be a priest if the subject of the investigation is a priest. It is possible for a cardinal to delegate his vicar in individual cases to conduct the investigation.

Chapter 8

Religious Duress: The Power of the Priesthood

When people begin to realize the harm done to a victim of sexual abuse by a member of the clergy, they frequently ask: How could the victims and their families have allowed such abuse to begin and continue? The answer lies in the concept of "religious duress."

A large proportion of victims of clerical sexual abuse come from devout Catholic families—practicing Catholics involved in the day-to-day life of their parishes. These families believed that they would be saved if only they remained loyal to their priest and the church. They were taught not to question the wisdom and decisions of a priest, not to question his lifestyle, and to presume only the purest motives for his actions. In many cases, Catholics also believed it was a serious sin to question the authority of a priest or to speak ill or gossip about him.

It was common for devout and dedicated Catholics to yearn for one or more of their sons to enter the priesthood. The attentions of a priest toward a child were seen as honest and pure, and they hoped that his attention toward their child might lead him to choosing a religious vocation. Parents would allow their children to be alone with priests, to accompany them on trips, and to stay with them in their quarters. The idea of a priest sexually abusing or otherwise harming a child was totally alien to them;

however, the reality was that the victims were overwhelmed by the power of the priest.

It was beyond the imagination of a young boy or girl that a priest who was a friend, confidant, mentor, and spiritual father would do or attempt something evil or wrong. The church taught the virtues of purity and surrounded expressions of sexuality with sin and guilt. Young boys and girls at the beginnings of puberty received these messages from their church through the priests and often reacted to their awakening sexuality with fear, shame, wonder, and guilt. Victims accepted advances by a priest with total incomprehension that a priest could do evil. As the abuse developed, many priest perpetrators continued to use their power by convincing their victims to believe that no one would believe them if they disclosed what was happening. In fact, prior to the widespread media attention to such abuse in the eighties, rarely would parents, church authorities, or others believe a young boy or girl who claimed that a priest was doing strange things to them. The victims, in a very real sense, were caught between a rock and a hard place: The awe and respect they held for the priest induced a fear of harming him or his reputation in any way. Victims were trapped and powerless to step forward and report the abuse.

Religious duress is a real but very special kind of fear. The ultimate source of this fear is a belief in an unseen but all-powerful supreme being who requires obedience, without which the believer is punished. This fear can create a moral pressure on people to behave in such a way as to placate rather than displease the deity; they perform actions that they might not otherwise perform, or omit actions that they would.

From prehistoric times, men and women have created religious systems as a means of communicating with their unseen gods. Some of these systems arose in the wake of recurring but natural phenomena; others have arisen in the wake of overwhelming catastrophes, tornadoes, tsunamis, hurricanes, and the like. In their naïveté, ancient peoples often attributed such events to angry gods and, for safety's sake, sought ways to control or at least influence them. In his book *Religion Explained*, the scholar Pascal Boyer sums up the theories of many:

> Most accounts of the origin of religion emphasize one of the following suggestions: human minds demand explanations, human hearts seek comfort, human society requires order, human intellect is illusion-prone.[141]

Anthropology asserts that religion is a fabrication of mortal men and women and not a creation of the unseen deities, imposed by them on humans. Religions are found throughout history and in every culture in many different forms. As people share their ideas about these deities they are led to wonder about their nature and their powers.

Although religious systems have been created to relieve or displace the fear engendered by the unknown, these same systems have, themselves, often been the origin of fear. In some instances fear is provoked by well-intentioned religious leaders to influence people to avoid wrongdoing. In other cases, however, fear is induced not to coax people to obey an angry god, but to control their behavior.

Thus the world of some organized religions can be every bit as terrifying as a world controlled by unseen angry supernatural forces. The gloom and fear that seem fundamental to some religions, including some expressions of Christianity, can be as mysterious as the unseen supernatural powers. These attitudes have been explored by the philosopher Søren Kierkegaard writing about the psychological tenor of Christian revelation in works such as *The Concept of Dread* and *Fear and Trembling*.[141a]

Religious concepts are connected to human emotional systems. These systems react to life-threatening situations such as the power of nature or any other force that threatens a person and cannot be readily controlled. Indeed, according to Boyer,

> It is probably true that religious concepts gain their great salience and emotional load in the human psyche because they are connected to thoughts about various life-threatening circumstances. So we will not understand religion if we do not understand the various emotional programs of the mind.[142]

As people speculated on how to influence the superhuman entities in order to avoid their wrath and to gain their benevolence, the practice of *sacrifice* began and became a basic component of ancient religions as well as Christianity. Mortals gave their first and best crops, the fatted calf, their money, and various promises of good behavior—not to mention human lives—to the gods, in return for their benevolence. Priests, a special caste of people to conduct sacrifices, came into being.

Priesthood, like the *Witch Doctor*, is the most ancient form of religious office. The priest is the special person deputed by the community and favored by the gods to lead worship services and, especially, to offer sacrifices on behalf of individuals and the community. Because of their closeness to the deities, the priests themselves, traditionally males, were believed to have special powers.

The Catholic Priesthood

Catholicism is the oldest and, in many ways, the prototype of all Christian denominations and central to Catholicism is the belief that the Eucharist, or Mass, is the only acceptable sacrifice to God, having replaced all forms of sacrifice that preceded it. As it has taught down through the ages, the official church statement of belief, contained in *The Catechism of the Catholic Church* (1992), continues to stress the centrality of the Eucharist to Catholic life:

> The Eucharist is 'the source and summit of the Christian life.' The other sacraments, and indeed all ecclesiastical ministries and works of the apostolate, are bound up with the Eucharist and are oriented toward it. For in the Eucharist is contained the whole spiritual good of the Church, namely Christ himself, our Pasch (*The Catechism of the Catholic Church, No. 1324*).

The Eucharist is also a sacrifice, and the means by which the faithful, by participating in the sacrifice of Christ, are made pleasing to God.

> In the Eucharist the sacrifice of Christ becomes also the sacrifice of the members of his Body. The lives of the faithful, their praise, sufferings, prayer, and work, are united with those of Christ and with his total offering, and so acquire a new value. Christ's sacrifice present on the altar makes it possible for all generations of Christians to be united with his offering (*ibid., No. 1368*).

The Catholic Church has traditionally taught the radical distinction between a special office of priesthood bestowed on selected men through the ceremony of ordination, and the "priesthood of the laity" shared by all who profess a belief in Jesus Christ. To the special office of priesthood are attached the powers that are essential for Catholics to attain the fundamental goal of Christianity, a safe deliverance of the soul to the afterlife.

The two major powers of Catholic priests are the power to celebrate the Eucharist and the power to forgive sins in the name of God. The church claims that the priesthood and the powers attached to it—derived from Christ himself— are essential for salvation and fundamental to the nature and life of the church. When the validity of these claims were denied, for instance by the Protestant Reformation, the church responded:

> If any one shall say that in the New Testament there is no visible and external priesthood nor any power of consecrating and offering the Body and Blood of the Lord, as well as of remitting and retaining sins, but merely the office and bare ministry of preaching the Gospel, let him be anathema (*Council of Trent, No. 961*).[143]

The same council also taught that, although priests in all ages have been held in the highest honor, Catholic priests far exceed all others and that the power conferred on them is unequalled in human understanding or reason. (*The Catechism of the Council of Trent*, translated by McHugh and Callan, 1923.)

Concept of Sin

Sin, which Christian theology defines as an offense committed by a mortal against God, has always been and continues to be fundamental in maintaining the stature of the priest. Catholicism speaks of three kinds of sin: *Original sin* which is a negative spiritual condition into which all are born and which is "washed away" by baptism normally administered by a priest. The traditional teaching held that those who died in original sin would never enjoy heaven but would be consigned to a bland state called limbo where they remained for eternity without the possibility of enjoying the presence of God. *Venial sin* is defined as a less-serious offense against God that results in a temporary sentence in purgatory, a milder version of hell, but from which there is hope of eventual release into heaven. Finally there is *mortal sin* which is a grave offense against God and which results in eternal damnation in hell if the sinner dies without absolution. Venial sins are absolved through confession and future penalties attached to them can be reduced or eliminated by carrying out a variety of good works or performing various spiritual exercises. Absolution from the effects of mortal sin requires remorse, a purpose of amendment, and the intervention of a priest.

Fear of divine wrath and everlasting damnation motivates believers to change their ways, avoid sinful acts, and seek the ministry of a priest. Added to the already powerful role of the ordained cleric is the fact that the church's leadership—all male clerics—defines which acts constitute mortal or venial sins. Although the reality of the leadership's role in defining sin is complex, the fact remains that this claim to power has been exaggerated in the minds of believers for centuries. The popular belief has invested bishops and especially popes with the God-given authority to determine which human actions are or are not serious sins.

Like their historical counterparts from pre-Christian societies, Catholic priests and bishops are cloaked with an aura of mystery and power. Traditionally they have lived apart from the laity. They have dressed differently and been held in a unique form of esteem by religious and secular society. There is no question but that the institutional church has created and sustained this priestly mystique by its official teaching, its regulatory or legal system, as well as by a complex collection of mythical stories, legends, and traditions concerning priests and bishops. Mandatory celibacy has served to reinforce the mystique that Catholic priests are somehow removed from and above the laity.

When a man is ordained priest, the church teaches, he is joined to Christ in such a way that he is substantially different from other men.

> This sacrament configures the recipient to Christ by a special grace of the Holy Spirit, so that he may serve as Christ's instrument for his Church. By ordination one is enabled to act as a representative of Christ, Head of the Church, in his triple office of priest, prophet, and king (*Catechism, No. 1581*).

The catechism restates a doctrine that has been an essential part of Catholic belief for centuries, namely that priests represent Jesus Christ in a very special way.

> In the ecclesial service of the ordained minister, it is Christ himself who is present to his Church as Head of his Body, Shepherd of his flock, high priest of the redemptive sacrifice, Teacher of Truth. ... It is the same priest, Christ Jesus, whose sacred person his minister truly represents. Now the minister, by reason of the sacerdotal consecration which he has received, is truly made like to the high priest and possesses the authority to act in the power and place of the person of Christ himself (*virtute ac persona ipsius Christi*) (*Catechism, No. 1548*).

Before 1992, when this catechism was first issued, church teaching was built on statements from the Council of Trent (1543–1545) that reacting to the Reformation had put the priest on a pedestal alongside the angels and close to God himself. Having admonished the faithful to respect the dignity and excellence of the priesthood, the Catechism of the Council of Trent went on to say:

> Bishops and priests being, as they are, God's interpreters and ambassadors, empowered in his name to teach mankind the divine law and the rules of conduct and holding, as they do, His place on earth, it is evident that no nobler function than theirs can be imagined. Justly therefore are they called not only angels, but even gods, because of the fact that they exercise in our midst the power and prerogatives of the immortal God. ... For the power of consecrating and offering the body and blood of our Lord and of forgiving sins, which has been conferred on them, not only has nothing equal or like it on earth, but even surpasses human reason and understanding.[144]

Before 1992, when the most recent catechism was issued, Catholic religious education relied on *The Baltimore Catechism*, which was first published in 1891 and is still the preferred text in some circles today. The question-and-answer formula with which most adult Catholics are familiar had the following to say about priests:

> Question 280: How should Christians look upon the priests of the Church?

> Answer. Christians should look upon the priests of the Church as the messengers of God and the dispensers of His mysteries

> Q. 999: Why should we show great respect to the priests and bishops of the Church?

A. We should show great respect to the priests and bishops of the Church: (1) Because they are the representatives of Christ upon earth, and (2) Because they administer the Sacraments without which we cannot be saved. Therefore, we should be most careful in what we do, say or think concerning God's ministers. To show our respect in proportion to their dignity, we address the priest as Reverend, the bishop as Right Reverend, the archbishop as Most Reverend, and the Pope as Holy Father.

The official church teaching was reflected in popular literature that supported the belief that the priest was a man set apart who was entitled to deference and respect. Popular Catholicism encouraged the exalted role of the priest and surrounded it with an exaggerated form of piety and respect. The writings of St. John Vianney, a nineteenth-century French pastor who is considered the patron saint of all parish priests, are an example:

What is a priest? A man who holds the place of God—a man who is invested with all the powers of God. When the priest remits sins, he does not say, 'God pardons you;' he says, 'I absolve you.' At the Consecration, (of the Mass) he does not say, 'This is the Body of Our Lord;' he says, 'This is My Body.' ...

If I were to meet a priest and an angel, I should salute the priest before I saluted the angel. The latter is the friend of God; but the priest holds His place. St. Teresa kissed the ground where a priest had passed. When you see a priest, you should say, 'There is he who made me a child of God, and opened Heaven to me by holy Baptism; he who purified me after I had sinned; who gives nourishment to my soul.' At the sight of a church tower, you may say, 'What is there in that place?' 'The Body of Our Lord.' 'Why is He there?' Because a priest has been there, and has said holy Mass.[145]

The *Code of Canon Law* promulgated in 1917 put into legislation the practical application of traditional teaching on the priesthood. In the first place, only clerics could hold the power of jurisdiction, or actual power, in the church, and several canons or sections of canons point to this exalted position.

All the faithful owe reverence to clerics according to their various grades and offices; and they commit a sacrilege if they do real injury to a cleric *(Canon 119)*.

The following canon said that clerics could not be summoned before civil courts unless special permission had been obtained beforehand.

The sentiment by John Vianney is still alive among Catholics today. It is expressed in a variety of popular writings including utterances of Pope John Paul II:

The ordained ministry, which may never be reduced to its merely functional aspect since it belongs on the level of 'being,' enables the priest to act 'in persona Christi' and culminates in the moment when he consecrates the bread and wine, repeating the actions and words of Jesus during the Last Supper. Before this extraordinary reality we find ourselves amazed and overwhelmed, so deep is the humility by which God 'stoops' in order to unite himself with man! ... We can only fall to our knees and silently adore this supreme mystery of faith.[146]

The church has long maintained that the division between clerics and laity is itself of divine origin. This stratified and unequal society has served to protect the belief that priests are special, removed, and exempt from much of the social and legal accountability expected of laypeople. The stratification of the ecclesial society has been an integral part of Catholic teaching for centuries and is well summed up in an excerpt from a 1906 encyclical letter issued by Pope Pius X (later declared a saint):

> It follows that the Church is essentially an unequal society, that is, a society comprising two categories of persons, the Pastors and the flock, those who occupy a rank in the different degrees of the hierarchy and the multitude of the faithful. So distinct are these categories that with the pastoral body only rests the necessary right and authority for promoting the end of the society and directing all its members towards that end; the one duty of the multitude is to allow themselves to be led and, like docile flock, to follow the Pastors.

Even the most recent *Code of Canon Law* (1983) defines the church as a society made up of the laity and, by divine origin, the hierarchy.[147] That hierarchy is made up of deacons, priests, and bishops who, in order to function as such, must be members of the clerical state.

The accepted understanding of the hierarchy, as is evident from theological and catechetical writings, church law, and liturgical practice, is that bishops are direct descendants of the apostles and both bishops and priests are ontologically different from laypersons because they have been singled out by God to take the place of Jesus Christ on earth. Despite the lack of concrete historical evidence to support this contention, this theology developed in the church, filling the scriptural gaps with such assertions as "it is the constant tradition that ..."

This isolation of clerics into a special caste within the church formed the basis for clericalism, the belief that clerics form a special elite corps and, because of their powers as sacramental ministers, they are superior to the laity and should be treated as such. Priests were given special privileges in society and this inevitably led to corruption and abuse.[148] The distorted notion of the power and standing of clerics is not new. As the well-known Catholic writer Russell Shaw says:

> Yet the clericalist mind-set does fundamentally distort, disrupt, and poison the Christian lives of members of the church, clergy and laity alike, and weakens the church in her mission to the world. Clericalism is not the cause of every problem in the church, but it causes many and is a factor in many more. Time and again ... it plays a role in the debilitating controversies that today afflict the Catholic community in the United States and other countries.[149]

Following the Second Vatican Council, many clergy and Catholic laity hoped that the hold of clericalism would wane, especially in light of the council's emphasis on the role of lay members in church life. Yet recent studies indicate that the present generation of young priests see themselves as essentially different from the laity and as men set apart by

God.[150] It appears from this and other indicators that Catholic clericalism is not only alive, but at times malignant.

The clericalism of the past and its present-day expressions have a common goal—the retention of the power, prestige, and image of the members of the elite, especially the bishops. Currently it manifests itself as not admitting any weaknesses on the part of the clergy, suppressing scandals, and silencing victims of clergy abuse. Yet despite promises to the contrary, the Catholic hierarchy, supported by significant numbers of the laity, want clericalism to stay. Commenting on the situation, the theologian and psychologist Donald Cozzens, a priest of the diocese of Cleveland, Ohio, had this to say:

> Until we take to heart the understanding of the church as fundamentally the baptized communion of Jesus' disciples ... the church itself, even after promising transparency and accountability as the American bishops did in the wake of the clergy sex abuse scandal, will continue to practice denial, dissimulation and deception. These characteristics flow, quite naturally, from an understanding of the church as a society made up of unequals.

The Impact on Victims of Sexual Abuse

The popular belief in the exalted role of the priest carries the potential for much good if it is used rightly, for the benefit of all, and is accompanied by a conviction of respect for those served by priests. Experience demonstrates, however, that this belief and its supporting theology can result in great harm to believers. Victims of clergy sexual abuse regularly assert they were paralyzed and numb when the abuse occurred because of their disbelief that so sublime a personage would stoop to harm them. For many Catholics, any and all expressions of sexuality outside of marriage were considered mortal sins, carrying the potential for eternal damnation. The emotional and psychological turmoil triggered by abuse at the hands of a cleric is difficult to describe or even imagine. The priest represented the divine presence to many victims. The priest was the enforcer of the church's stringent moral code and he was also the source of relief from the sins committed against this moral code.

Catholics are taught from the outset that all willful expressions of sexuality in thought, word, deed, or desire are mortally sinful outside of marriage. As a result, the confusion is compounded when the abuser is a priest. The youthful Catholic often believes the priest can do no wrong, therefore the sinfulness of any sexual actions must be attributed to the victims. Therefore, it has been common for victims to express feelings of great guilt for leading a priest into sin and blaming themselves for the abuse.

The impact on Catholic victims is unique and, in the opinion of some experts, particularly devastating precisely because the abuser is a priest. Catholic victims, brought up in a church dominated by clerics, believe the teachings that priests take the place of Christ. In the minds and emotions of the victims the priest is much more than a pastor or minister. He is a very special father figure and the earthly representative of God himself. Many victims experience a kind of toxic transference, and experience in their sexual abuse a form of spiritual death. Dr. Leslie Lothstein of the Institute for the Living graphically describes the uniqueness of clerical abuse:

> The difference is that the role of the priest
> puts the priest in close connection with Jesus

and with God. And what you hear from the victims—and I've heard this from priests who have been victims—is that they feel that their soul has been murdered. It's soul murder, soul murder, and they can never get over the guilt and shame of what their responsible role was—why was I chosen, how did this happen to me, and can I ever be reconnected with god?[151]

Victims describe the spiritual impact of abuse by a priest in many ways but the common denominator is spiritual devastation and, as Lothstein and Leonard Shengold put it so well, *soul murder*. For many, the aftermath is a lifetime of painful loss and acute emptiness. These victims were almost universally devout, believing, and, in many cases, religiously naive Catholics. Some describe the abuse as a ripping away of their souls; others are filled with an anger that roars to life whenever they see a priest or some other reminder of their abuse. Victims regularly report panic attacks when in or near a church, nausea and violent anxiety upon seeing or hearing a priest, and even anger at God for having somehow violated and abandoned them.

In most cases of Catholic clergy sexual abuse, the victim is devout, believes in church teaching without question, and is the product of a practicing Catholic family. They have been taught from their earliest years not to question, doubt, or criticize the word of the priests and bishops for fear of incurring divine wrath. The church teaching, imparted by the clerics and other official representatives, is fortified by the parents who themselves have been raised to treat the church officials with a mixture of fear, awe, and respect. They validate the official teaching and encourage their children to defer to clerics by their words but especially by their attitudes of servility and fear.

This stratified ecclesial society with its projection of the superior authority of the clergy can easily prevent Catholics from ever achieving a mature degree of participation in the church. In short, Catholic adults are expected to be docile and obedient and to accept as true all utterances of the priests, bishops, and popes. Though St. Paul urged the Christians in Corinth to "stop thinking like children" (I Cor. 14:20-21), Christian leaders have promoted the opposite attitude.

This serious lack of religious maturity has had disastrous results for the victims of clergy sexual abuse as well as for their families. As many victims develop past the age of their abuse, they remain trapped in a cocoon of fear that prevents them from disclosing the abuse. Parents and other family members often fall prey to the deceptive manipulations of clerics to whom they report their children's abuse. Their religious immaturity and childish reaction in their communications with clerics fill them with the fear that disclosure will result in a serious sin on their part. Far too many people fear to question the clerics who enjoin their silence by a variety of means ranging from convincing—but fake—solicitude to intimidation and even threats. The clerical system can persuade and intimidate them into believing that the clerical leaders always have the last word and that their word is correct. Such Catholics are taught that to disagree with, disbelieve, or dispute the word of a priest or bishop is a sign of weak faith and probably a sin. They are unable to distinguish between their justifiable anger at clerics, especially abusive clerics, and their faith in God. The seeds of this confusion are planted by the church's own teaching and nurtured by the clerical elite.

The impact on victims of clergy sexual abuse is fourfold:

1. *Seduction and grooming.* It is considered a great honor when the priest singles out the son or daughter of a

devout family for particular attention. Parents have generally been completely unsuspecting of the attention paid to a young son or daughter, and have even unwittingly enabled the abuse by allowing and encouraging overnight trips, helping at the rectory, and accompanying the priests beyond the ordinary altar service. This process is commonly referred to as "courtship" or "grooming." Eventually the cleric makes the first sexual move and the young victim is, more often than not, paralyzed, or stunned into disbelief.

2. *Moral confusion.* Victims reared in an atmosphere that accepted the traditional church teaching on sexuality were convinced of and could not question the doctrine that any form of sexual expression, be it thought, word, or especially deed, is mortally sinful. Furthermore they were taught that homosexuality is unnatural, homosexual people "fundamentally disordered," and all sexual expressions of it were particularly sinful. In the face of this, the priest—the personification of this stringent sexual morality and one who is theoretically devoid of any potential for sexual temptation—is the very one leading the male victim into a forbidden sexual act. The victim, male or female, is now caught in a powerful dilemma. He or she has been groomed and led along to a place of significant trust. Now, something forbidden has happened. Confusion, guilt, and shame set in after the shock begins to wear off. The guilt is especially toxic if the young victim has experienced pleasurable sexual feelings. This plunges the victim into deeper confusion. The clerical world has also taught the victim that the only acceptable relief from the guilt of sin is confession and absolution given by the priest. But the very source of relief from sin is also the efficient cause of

the sin, so the victim is immobilized and the guilt, shame, and trauma only intensify.

3. *Non-resistance to prolonged abuse.* By far, most sexual abuse is not limited to an isolated act. Perpetrators often claim it only happened once, but subsequent investigation generally discovers patterns of abuse over days, weeks, and sometimes years. Observers often wonder, and rightly so, how some victims remain in such "relationships." Many victims have later reported that they felt trapped and increasingly powerless as the abuse continued. Some reported being conscious of a bond with the abuser, which of course further confused the issue by increasing ambivalence and guilt. Uninformed critics have frequently claimed that in such cases the victim was a willing participant and even the aggressor. The pathological dynamic of the relationship suggests that such ideas are far from the truth and constitute only defensive, wishful thinking by those incapable of accepting the reality of a clerical scandal.

4. *Failure to report.* The existence of the trauma bond also explains why so many victims failed to report abuse after it started and even for months or years after it had ended. They did not report because they *could not* report. Apart from the fear and shame that often arose from sexual abuse, victims had to deal with the entire Catholic institution that loomed before them. Many believed their abusers when they convinced them that no one would believe them. Still others succumbed to implied or direct intimidation and threats from church authorities. The clerical elite, incapable of seeing a victim's report of sexual abuse as anything more than a threat to the church's security, often responded in a predictable manner: The victim would be turned into

a potential victimizer and made to feel guilty for contemplating an action that would embarrass a priest.

The inability to resist prolonged abuse is best explained by the psychological phenomenon known as the *trauma bond*. Dr. William Foote, a psychologist from Arizona and a medical expert on clergy sexual abuse, has explored the relationship or bond created between a clerical sexual abuser and his victim. The term "traumatic bond" was first used by Dr. David Dutton, a Canadian psychologist who had done extensive research on domestic violence and child abuse. According to Dr. Foote, Dutton describes traumatic bonding as: "the development of strong emotional ties between two persons, with one person intermittently harassing, beating, threatening, abusing, or intimidating the other." Dr. Dutton notes that this phenomenon is based on the existence of a power imbalance wherein the maltreated person perceives him or herself to be subjugated to and dominated by the other.[152]

Catholic victims, conditioned by their religious indoctrination, look on the clerical sex abuser with a mixture of awe and fear. The cleric's attitude of superiority and power elicit a certain degree of emotional security in the victim. These strong feelings of security and awe at the clerical state often impede victims from recognizing the seductive patterns the abuser is using to court them. Victims are so constrained by this awe, fear, and wonder that they cannot extricate themselves from abusers: They are victims of *religious duress.*

In many ways *religious duress* is similar to the notion of *reverential fear,* a well-established category in religious literature. This is a fear that is induced not from an unjust force from without, but from the respect, awe, or reverence one has for a legitimate authority figure. A victim of sexual abuse experiences such a fear of causing the displeasure or even the wrath of the authority figure that his or her free will is significantly impeded. Child or adolescent victims are especially vulnerable to a priest-abuser. First, the priest is an adult with automatic power over the victim. He is also a priest with vast spiritual authority. Moreover, the aura of secrecy surrounding the abuse often creates a special relationship that entraps the victim.

The trauma bond becomes stronger and even more pathological as the relationship continues. It is often affirmed, in the victim's view, by the church's apparent approval of the priest's behavior. The clerical world, unwilling or unable to proactively confront clergy sexual abuse, appears to the victim to be unconcerned. The victim feels trapped until either the abuser ends the relationship or some other event from without causes it to terminate. In some instances the abuse had grown so insufferable to the victims that they were able to break the bond and flee.

Summary. The reality of religious duress and the abject fear it causes is not subjective to some few individuals who may be predisposed to it due to other emotional or psychological issues. This reality is objective and found across a broad spectrum of Catholic people regardless of educational or familial background, economic or cultural status, or age. The emotional and psychological reaction to the institutional church and to some or all clerics is the result of a systematic pattern of religious indoctrination. This indoctrination is grounded in established teachings and beliefs held by the official church. When these beliefs—epitomized in the belief that priests are sacred personages who stand in the place of God—become interwoven with the natural fear and wonder of the unknown, the result can be a fear so grave that it impedes the normal evaluative thought processes and constrains the will from choosing to act in circumstances that would benefit the individual. The fear that arises from the threat of displeasure of religious officials carries over to a fear of displeasing God and this fear can be overpowering and immobilizing.

Chapter 9

The Ownership of Church Property: A Primer

There is no question that the Catholic Church in America can be accurately described as wealthy. It has extensive equity investments, assets, vast land holdings, buildings, and institutions—all designated "Catholic." But who owns the property? That question has been the subject of debate over the centuries and the answer is still not clear. In 2005, Raymond Burke, the Archbishop of St. Louis, Missouri, and St. Stanislaus Kostka parish remained at loggerheads over $9 million in assets under the control of the parish board. In 1891 a former archbishop, Peter Kenrick, transferred parish property to a parish-run corporation with a lay board of directors. According to civil laws the money belongs to the parish, but the archbishop insists that according to canon law the funds should be turned over to him. Other controversies about church property are brewing around the country in the aftermath of the financial costs of the sex abuse crisis.

Catholic Church property belongs, according to canon law, to the juridic person that lawfully acquired it (Canon 1256). A physical person such as a bishop or a parish pastor cannot lawfully (according to canon law) *own* church property; however physical persons are the *administrators* of church property.

A *juridic person* is the canonical equivalent of a civil law corporation, though not precisely equal to it in nature. The

1917 term was *moral person.* In the 1983 code, a juridic person is an entity that is the subject of law, rights, and obligations. For example, a diocese is a juridic person.

An *administrator* is a canonical office that confers specific powers—including the power to alienate or change ecclesiastical property—on the incumbent.

Church property, known in the code as *ecclesiastical* property, is any property or goods owned by a juridic person. It includes land, buildings and their contents, and sacred vessels. It consists of anything that has value.

The main juridic persons under consideration here are: the Holy See, which is the office of the pope, dioceses, parishes, and religious communities. With regard to religious communities, the main juridic persons are provinces and local communities.

Juridic persons come into existence by a decree, either explicit or implicit, issued by the church authority competent to do so. Only the pope can create a diocese and only a bishop can create a parish.

In the United States, dioceses are created from the territory of other dioceses and usually follow state or county lines and divisions as boundaries.

A diocese is never created without the simultaneous appointment of its bishop.

A crucial concept in understanding the tenure and control of church property is the relationship of the diocesan bishop to the juridic person of the diocese. The diocese and bishop are one. In fact, the ring given a bishop at the time of his ordination symbolizes his "marriage" to his diocese.

The pope, as the incumbent of the Holy See, is the supreme authority of the entire Catholic Church. However, the Holy See does not own the church property of all Catholic entities subordinate to it. Because the pope has universal jurisdiction over the entire church, he has *eminent domain* over church property that belongs to subordinate bodies. This means that although the pope cannot claim ownership of local churches, he has the jurisdiction or power to sell them (Canon 1273).

The means whereby church property is held depends on the regulations of the *Code of Canon Law*, the nature of the property in question, and the civil laws and customs of the place where the property is located. Church property is held by a variety of civil law means throughout the United States.

In the United States, church property has mainly been held over the past two centuries in three ways: Parish Corporation, Corporation Sole, and in Fee Simple. In 1911 the Vatican, through the Congregation for the Council (now defunct) issued norms for the U.S. bishops on the acceptable means of civilly holding church property. In this document, the Parish Corporation was deemed most acceptable to the Vatican in that it was considered most compatible with canon law; Corporation Sole was considered tolerable with some provisions; and Fee Simple was to be abandoned.

This 1911 document is no longer valid. It remained in force only until the promulgation of the 1917 code but was probably brought back into force by the Vatican after that code was published. However, there is no Vatican decree granting this document force after the 1983 code came into being. Hence it is no longer in force.

Authority over church property rests with the administrators who are given a variety of powers in the code concerning administration. One of the primary acts of power is the alienation of church property. Alienation is the sale, gift, long-term loan, or mortgage, or any action that weakens or eliminates control over the property by the juridic person that holds dominion or ownership.

There are specific norms in canon law for alienation. An administrator of church property (bishop or a pastor) cannot simply sell or otherwise alienate any church property under his authority. Depending on the nature of the property and its value, he is required to seek certain permissions. Basically, a bishop cannot alienate any church property whose value exceeds $5 million without the explicit permission of the Holy See through the Vatican Congregation for the Bishops.

In 1968, John J. McGrath, a Catholic priest with degrees in civil and canon law, published a small book titled *Catholic Institutions in the United States: Canonical and Civil Law Status* (Catholic University of America Press, 1968). Fr. McGrath's primary argument can be summed up in his own words: "If anyone owns the assets of the charitable or educational institution, it is the general public. Failure to appreciate this fact has led to the mistaken idea that the property of the institution is the property of the sponsoring body."

Consequently, ownership of schools, hospitals, parish, and diocesan properties, according to McGrath belongs to those who donated them (or their descendants) and not to the sponsoring bodies such as the papacy, a diocese, or religious order.

Fr. McGrath was primarily concerned with the ownership of educational and health care institutions, which he claimed did not actually constitute church property. This part of his theory was attacked by Adam Maida (now Cardinal Maida, Archbishop of Detroit) in an address to the Catholic Lawyers Association in 1973.[153]

The Vatican also responded negatively to the McGrath thesis.

By analogy, if the McGrath Theory is applied to dioceses and parishes, each entity would be required to have a board of directors or trustees, and 51 percent of the membership of those boards would be required to be laypeople in order to reflect the fundamental premise of the thesis. This is essentially the same arrangement as the nineteenth century trustee arrangement that the Vatican had already condemned. Under this arrangement, each parish would be owned by its trustees "in Fee Simple." Thus the church authorities effectively would cede control over parish properties to the laity.

In order to retain control over church properties in the United States, all forms of civil tenure somehow involved the diocesan bishop. In their book *Church Property, Church Finances and Church Related Corporations,* Cardinal Maida and Nicholas Cafardi stated that the Corporation Sole was the preferable civil law means for dioceses to hold church property (p. 129). Thus, each diocesan parish would be a corporation with one member, the diocesan bishop. In other methods of incorporation, the bishop would be an ex-officio member with other members chosen from the diocesan consultors and often including the pastor in parishes.

While it is not precisely true to say that the diocesan bishop or the diocese, as a separate juridic entity, owns the church property of each parish, it is true that the bishop, as the sole agent of the diocese, has administrative control over each parish. Were a bishop to create separate corporations for each parish with a board totally distinct from the diocesan administration, significant problems would arise if a parish community, through its board, were to challenge his decision to close a parish, or if itself were to close a parish or otherwise dispose of significant parish holdings.

The details of the property transfers being initiated by Bishops Robert Vasa of Baker, Oregon and Robert Brom of San Diego, California, or the bankruptcy filings by bishops John Vlazny of Portland, Oregon, Gerald Kicanas of Tucson, Arizona, and William Skylstad of Spokane, Washington, are not clear at this time (February 2005).

If these bishops have totally separated themselves from each parish by setting up completely separate corporations, then it is possible that they have acted in a manner that is analogous to that followed in the nineteenth-century church but that was subsequently condemned by the Vatican.

In order to understand the ownership of church property in the United States, it would be essential at this time to have answers to the following questions:

1. How is each diocese incorporated in its own state?
2. How is each parish incorporated?
3. What is the make-up of membership of any diocesan or parish board?
4. Who holds the civil title or ownership to all properties and other holdings of the diocese that are not attached to or affiliated with parishes?
5. Is the bishop conveying properties, securities, or other holdings from diocesan ownership to parish ownership?
6. Is the bishop, or any of the individual entities such as parishes and schools, establishing any other forms of corporate structures to hold church properties?
7. What is the nature of all securities held by the diocese and each parish? Are any funds, bonds, or stocks being set up for a specific purpose such as development, pension, or special disaster? This question is important because money as such is not considered church property, *but* any funds or securities and the like that are set up for a specific purpose become church property and subject to all the canonical regulations concerning the administration of church property.
8. Does a diocese have properties in other dioceses and under what title are these held?
9. Does a diocese or any entity that is part of or related to a diocese have cash or securities of any kind in accounts located in banks or institutions that are outside the territory of the diocese or outside the United States?

Chapter 10
Ecclesiastical Shell Game

There is more to the bankruptcy filings by the dioceses of Portland, Tucson, and Spokane than meets the average eye. Church officials justify the filings on the grounds that the demands of the victims of clerical sexual abuse will bring financial devastation to their dioceses. With the help of high-priced public relations firms, they are attempting to create the impression that the church has been brought to its financial knees by a succession of ever-increasing demands by adult sex-abuse victims and their lawyers.

Church officials claim their good-faith offers of generous settlements have been rejected, leaving them no choice but to file for bankruptcy. They obviously hope to turn public opinion against the clergy-abuse victims. Yet by trying to portray the victims and their attorneys as money-grubbers, diocesan officials are denying the reality that the vast majority of victims have shown over and over again that it's not the money they're after, but justice. Most only resorted to the civil courts because the church authorities repeatedly failed them.

The claims of impending financial ruin would be taken more seriously if dioceses—not just Portland, Tucson, and Spokane, but any—had a history of producing complete and accurate financial reports. But none do. The bankruptcy processes are showing the dioceses' financial pictures to be complex and the machinations used to protect their holdings more and more arcane and anything but "church-like." More to the point, the whole truth about costs needs to be exposed. The church's attorneys are not working *pro bono*, nor are they working on a contingency basis as are many of the victims' lawyers. The church's lawyers are commanding hefty fees, and some find that it is in their interest to prolong negotiations and mediations even when it is clear that an alleged priest is guilty.

Dioceses that claim bankruptcy should first disclose how much they have paid attorneys to wage long and complex battles that often end in settlements with victims. The people of God, the lay faithful, end up paying what the insurance carriers won't cover. But the most painful outcomes are not monetary. They involve a further loss of faith in the institutional church and even more pain for victims.

Most outrageous is the fact that many dioceses and archdioceses and the USCCB as well, have contracted with expensive public relations firms to help spin the entire mess that the exposure of widespread abuse unleashed. Los Angeles, for example, uses Michael Sitrick and Associates, the same firm that represented Enron, Charles Keating of Savings and Loan notoriety, and the tobacco industry to manage its image. There is something askew when a diocese needs to spend the people's hard-earned dollars on public relations firms to create an image of honesty and pastoral integrity. Many see these efforts as the bandage on an abscess—it covers but does not cure.

One oft-repeated mantra is that many claims are "old cases" brought by adults who could have come forward years ago, but did not. The advice is that they should now, therefore, put their abuse behind them and move on. Many claims have related to years or even decades-old incidents of sexual abuse. Many victims are living painfully traumatic lives filled with a myriad of emotionally and spiritually destructive experiences. Many people don't know or refuse to accept that sexual abuse—especially Catholic clergy sexual abuse—is particularly destructive. Well-demonstrated facts prove that the effects of the abuse do not simply go away. Rather, if unchecked by appropriate intervention or counseling, the impact of violation not only continues to fill the victim with pain, but spreads its devastating effects to all aspects of life. Victims did not come forward for many years because they *could not* come forward. Many were imprisoned by a web of unreasonable guilt, denial, fear, and shame. Many were paralyzed by the belief that to reveal clerical sex abuse would invoke God's wrath for harming a priest. The revelations of the past decade and the public support for adult survivors of childhood abuse have enabled some victims to emerge from the shadows and begin a healing process. A significant part of this healing involves justice.

Contrary to the impression some bishops are trying to create, filing for bankruptcy is *not* a last-ditch survival effort on the part of the church. It is a sophisticated way of avoiding more painful revelations about internal corruption and a potential for limiting victims' compensation. Bankruptcy might start off as, among other things, a public relations strategy by church institutions, but will end up re-victimizing victims and pushing the church even further into the black hole of mistrust and disrespect. Bishop Wilton Gregory, president of the USCCB, said in February 2004 that sexual abuse by priests is "history." The only thing that is now past is the institutional church's power to completely control internal scandal and disruption. Many in the church, especially church leaders, either can't or won't accept the fact that there are far more victims than the recent John Jay church-sponsored surveys counted. The claims of victims who will come forward in great numbers are real.

What effect will the bankruptcy process have? *Delay.* First it will obscure the system of abuse in the church.

Second, all victims involved in the court process will suffer through endless delays brought on by a variety of hardball tactics used by church lawyers. The bankruptcy filings have effectively built more delays into resolving claims and bringing closure to victims.

In view of the flood of misinformation about sex abuse propagated by the church over the past twenty years, Catholics and the general public have a right to know what has really happened to allow thousands of priests to abuse and tens of thousands of minors to be violated. It seems the true story of clergy abuse continues to be minimized and denied and will be revealed only when the civil judicial systems force it out. Full disclosure will never come from the institutional church. Even the bishop's own Review Boards demonstrate many bishops' reluctance to be candid. Without grand jury investigations and trials, the possibility of the whole truth about clergy abuse being exposed remains remote.

Some dioceses propose a fund from which to pay out claims to present victims. A process is set up to evaluate each claim and its relative merits with a view to deciding how much compensation should be adequate. This could work fairly well depending on the sensitivity and compassion of those charged with creating and managing the process. Or it could turn into a painful travesty that devalues victims and causes even more trauma.

One of the more devious aspects of the bankruptcy filings is the resultant denial of future compensation for past victims of sex abuse who are not yet ready to go public. This is how it works: The diocese would set up a fund for all currently known victims and publicly invite anyone else who had been sexually abused by a cleric or religious to come forward and make a claim. A cut-off date would be set beyond which no claims would be entertained. Such "drop dead" dates have already been part of the Tucson and

Portland bankruptcies. They ignore the fact that sex abuse of minors by priests is still an ongoing reality embedded in the system behind the secret codes.

This is especially problematic because it ignores the reality of the debilitating psychological and emotional effects of sexual abuse on its victims. As David Clohessy, the president of the Survivors Network of Those Abused by Priests (SNAP), said so poignantly in 2005, "It's as if Jesus announced that after a certain date he'd simply do no more healing, so get in line now or miss the chance."

Victims of clergy sex abuse deserve every possible opportunity to begin the long and painful healing process of which financial compensation is only one small part. The prospect of a domino effect of diocesan bankruptcies will surely cause irreparable harm to the church and to the victims. Public relations programs will attempt to portray the dioceses as religious entities trying to preserve their financial resources to keep their many beneficial programs afloat. In reality, the church will be just another corporation obsessed with its own financial security.

Epilogue

Lost and Found: Speaking to History

Where sin abounded, grace did much more abound.

—Romans 5:20

It is better that scandals arise than that truth be silenced.

—St. Gregory the Great

Chapter 11

Loss of Faith: In the Wake of Betrayal

Men who abuse minors are called "Slayers of the Soul." According to Leonard Shengold, M.D., author of *Soul Murder* (Yale University Press, 1989), to abuse or neglect a child, or to deprive a child of a separate identity and joy in life, is to commit soul murder. Dr. Leslie Lothstein described his clinical observation of priest victims with the same terms (Cf. Ch. 8). Children desperately need to maintain a mental image of a loving and rescuing parent. However, torture and deprivation under conditions of complete dependency elicit a terrifying combination of helplessness and rage. These are feelings that the child must suppress in order to survive. The child, therefore, denies or justifies what has happened, deadens emotions, identifies with the aggressor, and even carries the guilt that rightfully belongs to the abuser. This dynamic and all of the elements that Dr. Shengold mentions come into play when a priest sexually abuses a child. Sexual abuse does not simply harm, it kills a part of a child.

Some victims of abuse can eventually work through, to acceptable degrees, the psychological trauma of abuse. They sometimes can free themselves from addictions, sustain adequate relationships, and maintain employment, but an important part of their life experience is gone forever and cannot be revived.

Clinicians who interview and treat victims of clerical sexual abuse discover that one of the most common consequences of abuse by a Catholic priest is the complete loss of comfort, support, and spiritual sustenance. That loss includes a sense of meaning of life that they had experienced and were entitled to get from their religious faith. Those who do not understand the nature and depth of this deprivation think that the victim can merely "forget about it," "move on," or "find another religion." Some victims cannot. A part of them is dead—their ability to have a religious faith is gone.

Three analogous situations can help one understand the depth of a victim's dilemma. First, *the loss of a child*: The death of a child is the one loss that is absolute in experience. A parent can never fully recover from this loss. Certainly, life must go on, but there is nothing that can substitute for the lost child. The parent cannot and will never forget. The impact of this loss is reinforced by the fact that it is "unnatural" for children to precede their parents in death.

Second, *the loss of an integral part of one's body*: A person who loses a limb or one or other of his or her senses can compensate, substitute, and learn to live with the consequences, but every accommodation is just that, an adjustment, and not a revival. A part of that person is gone, dead, and will never come back.

Third, *the loss of belonging and of patriotism*: A man who is betrayed and, as a result, loses citizenship and a sense of patriotism for his country is not healed by aligning himself with another country. It is one thing to find a better place by choice, quite another to be ripped from one's origins.

Those who doubt that some men and women can suffer the deprivation of their faith as acutely as the loss of a child, the loss of a limb, or the loss of citizenship have never had the experience of treating victims of sexual abuse by clergy.

People who have been grounded since childhood in one faith, in which their self-worth, acceptance, spiritual identity, and salvation were vested, cannot simply forget that faith and join another. Victims betrayed and abused by a priest can "go on" with their lives, but the part that is missing cannot be restored. Something is dead; something has been truly killed.

Chapter 12

Healing Steps: Forgiving the Hierarchy

Forgiveness is rarely easy. It is not easy for a victim of a crime to say as Jesus said to the Roman soldiers who crucified him: "Father, forgive them, for they know not what they do." Yet that is what every Christian is called to do, even victims of the most cruel emotional abuse that any person could suffer. What makes it especially difficult for victims of clerical sexual abuse to forgive the perpetrators of these crimes is the incontrovertible fact that so many of these victims have had not only their lives destroyed—they have lost an innocence that will never be recovered in this life—but their faith—the one source of strength that might support their quest for forgiveness—has also been taken away. In some cases, sadly, forgiveness may be impossible. There are, however, certain steps that people who seek inner peace by forgiving a perpetrator can take. There is no guarantee that these steps will work for everybody, but they will work in most cases and are certainly worth a try.

First of all, it is necessary to accept the fact that life is not fair. Physical, intellectual, emotional, environmental, and even spiritual gifts and limitations are bestowed with a mysterious haphazardness. Life endows more benefits on some more than others for no special reason. Fate dispossesses others of advantages with an equal caprice. Some people grow up in homes, neighborhoods, and circumstances that are nourishing and supportive; others endure unspeakable hardship and neglect. Some enjoy good health; others are afflicted with pain, suffering, and loss. Life gives each person some good things and deprives them of others. They cannot control these endowments or events. No one can change his or her inheritance from life. They simply have to stop resisting reality. If they can forgive life, they will probably find more things to be thankful for than any of them realized. Therefore, forgive life! (In religious terms, this means accepting the will of God.)

Learning to Be Able to Forgive Self

They must also learn to forgive themselves. Who has not made misjudgments and taken missteps? "Human nature is so faulty," Flannery O'Connor said, "that it can resist any amount of grace and most of the time it does." Even the most blessed person, if honest, will have had thoughts, words, and actions to regret—everybody has made lamentable and reprehensible choices. If they can bring themselves to forgive themselves—and they should repent and forgive themselves for any guilt that is rightfully theirs—they will come to understand what it is to forgive another. "Forgive as we have been forgiven." That is the gold standard, and it applies to forgivers in need of forgiveness. It is important for people to be grounded in an honest sense of their own guilt, when warranted, and self-forgiveness, because abuse—sexual violation and betrayal by the trusted—distorts the realities of their justifiable guilt and self-recrimination. The guilt, the shame, the loss of dignity that rightfully belongs to the abuser for his behavior, is thrust into the soul of the innocent victim. This venom poisons the soul of the victim, sometimes even to death. The cancer of this unmerited guilt has to be excised because it is foreign, false, and cannot be incorporated into a system of honest responsibility. The self-distortion that results from sexual abuse by one who advertises himself as holy and sexually safe is almost unbearable. The burden becomes incomprehensible when an institution that calls itself the Body of Christ vilifies or heaps opprobrium on the victim, and colludes to hide its part in the process of abuse rather than heal the virus at its source—which is itself.

Are all burdened by the abuse of the clergy? Yes. Are all confused by the part the church hierarchy has played in the drama of hypocrisy that is called the crisis of sexual abuse? Certainly! Forgiveness of self and others is a process of isolating responsibilities and realities.

Jesus never softened his condemnation of anyone who would "scandalize one of these little ones." A millstone should be strung around his neck and he be thrown into the sea. That millstone does not belong to the victim. That is the burden of the abuser and his supporters. He must resolve that by himself with his God.

There is a Christian model. The center of the Christian mystery and Christian life is the act of redemptive forgiveness on the cross that is reenacted daily in the Mass. Inexhaustible and infinite forgiveness is available to anyone who avails him or herself of it. Sublime in mystery and simple in theory, it is unspeakably complex in human application.

The value of this forgiveness was the sacrifice of life: love unto death. The price for this forgiveness was truth. Jesus was crucified for love because he told the truth. People can only enter into redemptive forgiveness by struggling for radical truth within themselves and in their church. Each day at Mass they endeavor to express radical truth: *mea culpa, mea culpa, mea maxima culpa.*

Sacramental confession exists for people to explore the deeper truth about themselves because their daily struggles sometime fail. Ritual forgiveness is perhaps easier to comprehend and utilize when people are reconciling their own faults than when they are facing the morass of corruption in the ministry and the church that holds the power to administer reconciliation.

How can people understand? How can they compute the sexual violation—the rape—by a priest or bishop who says Mass daily and who absolves sinners in confession? How can people endure the betrayal that was executed in the name of religion, in the guise of ministry?

People are not Christs, but some are followers of Christ, and therefore have a right to expect their church, their bishops, and their priests, to bring them closer to Christ's example and aid them in their Christian striving. They are disappointed and disillusioned by the number of priests and bishops who violate their commitment to celibacy. Despite the widespread betrayal, however, they need to struggle like Christ for truth and love. They need to enter into the process whereby they decipher what it means both to forgive and be forgiven. But they must humbly realize that, just as Christ's infinite forgiveness has not and cannot reform those who refuse to respond, neither can the individual or collective power of their forgiveness reform our church. But they can make a dent. They are making a difference. In the meantime, they feel isolated because the familiar religious supports are no longer available or trustworthy. However they have each other to explore the practical ways back to reconciliation and reform. Christ's truth and love is their guide. In Christ they will succeed.

No Shortage of Good Company

Victims need to realize they are not alone. It may not be of immediate consolation to victims of abuse to know the extent of the abuse problem in the Catholic Church in the United States. But a review of some facts will extend some comfort. Facts of the abuse should also challenge all Catholics who care about the church.

The John Jay study commissioned by the American bishops said that between 3 and 6 percent of Catholic priests abuse minors. They also cautioned that the figures they reported could not accurately determine the exact dimensions of the problem because of underreporting. The bishop of the diocese of San Diego acknowledged that sixty-six priests were reported for abuse. He, using only his own judgement, dismissed twenty-two of the reports as "unreliable." The diocese, however, now has 150 civil law cases pending against it. Documents to be produced in court will provide a more factual account. The Boston Archdiocese admitted that 7.6 percent of its priests abused minors during the same period covered by the John Jay study (1950–2002). Because of further revelations, that percentage is now approaching 10 percent. New Hampshire reported 8.2 percent of its priests were abusers. Twenty-four percent of the priests serving in the diocese of Tucson, Arizona, in 1986 were sexual abusers. Fifty-six of 710 priests in the Los Angeles Archdiocese in 1991 were sexual abusers. That figure includes two bishops. Los Angeles is a jurisdiction that admitted records of allegations of abuse against 244 of its priests between 1930 and 2003.

Over 50 percent of the parishes of the Los Angeles archdiocese have had an abuser serving them. Forty-five percent of the parishes in the St. Paul-Minneapolis archdiocese have had sexual abusers on their staffs. Boston had the same. Studies of the number of priest abusers belonging to religious orders have not been completed, but preliminary estimates suggest figures over 10 percent. All available figures do not include the abuse of vulnerable adults. And knowledgeable experts in the field of child abuse state that the number of victims who have come forward so far should be multiplied by a factor of ten.

Organizations such as Voice of the Faithful can play an important role in assembling accurate data. Precise data supports victims, the integrity of the priesthood, and the good of all. It should be remembered that the same proportion of bishops as priests violate celibacy. Many bishops are in no position to make celibacy credible. The church has resisted cooperation with and even defied legitimate civil authorities striving to determine the parameters of the problem of clergy abuse. So far, reports from grand juries have produced the most reliable pictures of the dynamics of abuse and the conspiracies people engaged in to cover it up. That picture is dire indeed.

In order to forgive, victims don't have to forget. In fact, remembering is essential to the healing process. Covering an abscess, shielding it from light and air, fosters festering and decay. The church cannot heal if she forgets her past. The church is creating a huge moral chancre by working to forget its part in the dynamic of abuse, and pretending clerical abuse is "history." Clerical abuse truly has a long and inglorious history extending back almost as far as church records exist.[154] Attempting to keep the history of clerical abuse secret has contributed to the current crisis. Absolution for a perpetrator of sexual abuse asking for forgiveness involves a process in which he must remember, not ignore, the abuse. First, he must acknowledge the full extent of his violations; then he must take complete and full responsibility for his actions or negligence and their consequences; he must compensate adequately for the abuse and the harm done; and finally, he must effectively and positively determine that he will not repeat the behavior for which he wants forgiveness.

The cost of being forgiven is truth—plain, simple, unvarnished truth based on fact. Nothing less than truth and reformation will do for the priests or bishops who have taken sexual advantage of a boy, girl, or vulnerable adult. Nothing less than reformation is required from bishops and priests who have countenanced abuse, covered up abuse, neglected to respond to reasonable indications of abuse, excused or protected abusing clergy. All of these men ignored the "scandal" thrown in the paths of the little ones. They are guilty of scandal.

Where have the 90 percent of priests been who have not abused minors sexually? Had they no suspicions? Had they heard no rumors? How many fellow priests and bishops disregarded complaints and reports? After all, even a "suspicion of abuse or neglect" noted by a physician or therapist is enough to trigger an investigation by civil authorities.

A review of thousands of pages of depositions by priests, church officials, and bishops reveals such a pattern of arrogance, evasion, and mendacity, that several Catholic lawyers have said: "I never could have imagined that bishops could lie like this." Several Catholic victims' lawyers have entered therapy to help them come to grips with the personal trauma they have suffered because of revelations about their church that they have been forced to face.

Many bishops stand up to say they are "sorry for the pain that victims have suffered." Well intended but hollow apologies will not heal. They have no shortage of excuses: "We didn't know! Psychiatrists misled us! We were only following our lawyers' advice!" What bishop does not, and did not know that sex between a minor and a priest is a serious violation of celibacy? What bishop does not know that sex (by anyone) with a minor or vulnerable adult is illegal? No one needs a psychiatrist or a lawyer to instruct him of these basic facts.

The fact that such activity is sinful does not offer forgiveness as a convenient cover-up. Forgiveness is not an excuse for secrecy and "forgetting" reality.

Few bishops have sought forgiveness for their neglect, their blindness to the real harm done to victims, their collusion in covering for abusing priests, their preference for preserving image over the protection of their flock, and their unwillingness to assure the celibate practice of their priests. The hierarchy of the U.S. Catholic Church has yet to produce a bishop or priest with a fraction of the moral leadership that the late Archbishop Oscar Romero exercised in El Salvador.

The price of forgiveness is reformation. There are no cut-rate, half measures that can merit forgiveness or ensure healing and health. It's either reform or wither away! The process of forgiving a transgression or violation is really an easier process than being forgiven. Forgiving another means freeing oneself of the bonds of resentment, grudge, hate, and retaliation. It means standing up for the truth. Resentment, grudge, hate, and retaliation are burdens. Once people free themselves from these weights—it's like carrying a ten-pound brick in each hand—they can heal. They must be dropped; they do nobody any good.

Freeing themselves—forgiving *another*—does not mean people must roll over and die or become toadies of an abusive system or institution. To remember in freedom allows them to mobilize their energies to heal others and themselves.

Cultivate Anger but Control Emotion

Next, anger should be cultivated. Anger is a normal consequence of being betrayed, molested, victimized, deceived, or persecuted (as Christ was) by religious authority. Anger provides the energy necessary for survival. Anger is not an evil word, although it has been vilified in the clergy-dominated culture where docility and subservience are extolled above self-assertion and independence (and even reason). "Anger," St. Augustine said, "is the beginning of courage."

If Jesus Christ is a model of forgiveness, he is also a model of anger. Christ expressed his anger directly and forcefully. He cast the money changers out of the temple and he railed against hypocritical religious authorities. "Whitewashed vaults that look clean on the outside, but their insides are filled with rot and dead men's bones," he called them in plain talk, untempered with gentleness. Jesus preached justice based on fact and truth. It takes courage to speak truth to power and corrupt power makes for a formidable enemy.

The sexual abuse crisis continues to expose the unimagined hypocrisy of the Catholic Church in matters sexual and financial. There is no other way to say it. There is no gentle way to realize that the church, as measured by the yardstick of hypocrisy, is every bit as corrupt sexually and financially as it was at the time of the Protestant Reformation. Without anger no one is capable of responding to such a harsh reality; they need the courage and tenacity that the cultivation of just anger generates.

Whereas anger is justified and a necessary component of a healthy response to abuse, as an emotion it must be controlled. To see clearly and rationally one has to move beyond feeling.

After all, the misguided, unbridled, malignant, and malicious sexual emotions of abusing clergy are at the core of the problem of abuse. Abusers might try to disguise and justify their feelings as love. But whatever the host of emotions, intentions, or rationalizations that lead a priest or bishop to sexually abuse, the behavior remains destructive, irrational, and indefensible. There is no rational defense of abuse by one who portrays himself as "celibate" (sexually inviolate) for the Kingdom, and who poses as somone worthy of trust and obedience.

It is also clear that the hierarchy, in order to protect image and property, has responded emotionally to the revelations of abusing bishops and priests. The history of the current response to celibate violations remains for the most part reactionary. It was not always that way. There are well-documented periods in church history when the church exercised strong leadership to combat celibate violations by its clergy.

But now, any rational moral action on the part of the hierarchy to the sexual abuse crisis has been forced by the rational analysis of the press, law enforcement, lawyers, victims, and lay groups who have focused on the facts. Facts, not emotion, are required to solve the epic challenge confronting the church. The late Pope John Paul II's assessment of the resources people can bring to bear on problem solving should be taken to heart: "It always has been the conviction of the church," he said, "that God gave man the ability to arrive, with the light of his reason, at an understanding of the fundamental truths about his life and his destiny and, concretely, at the norms of correct action."

Now is not the time for recrimination, drama, weeping, gnashing of teeth, grand gestures, or emotional diatribes. Now is the time for facts and reason to guide thinking and decisions about sex and faith.

Victims also need to overcome fear. "Let not your heart be troubled," Jesus said, "nor let it be afraid. If you believe in God believe also in me." These are not merely words of consolation. They are a testimony about where security really lies. Security does not reside in popes, bishops, or priests, no matter how holy. Real security is in Jesus Christ and him crucified.

Theologian Romano Guardini used to say: "The church is the cross on which Christ is crucified daily." It is tempting for the hierarchy to attempt measures to mitigate the sting of clerical celibate failure by confessing, "We are a church of sinners." However, when the bishops are taken at their word they become incensed, defensive, offensive, and retaliatory. They say it, but they can't apply it themselves. That's when the faithful become the church.

Catholics today happen to live at a time when singularly holy popes have sustained the throne in Rome. That, of course, has not always been the case. Much of the history of the Roman Catholic Church reads like a cheap paperback novel. Popes have been lechers, murderers, and pedophiles, hardly the qualities required of the Vicar of Christ. People's faith in Jesus Christ is not dependent on the sanctity or the sins of the priests and bishops. But the moral qualities of bishops and priests do have profound effects. Pope Pius X said that more souls are lost because of miscreant priests than from any other source.

It is understandable that some who have been sexually and administratively abused (raped) by the church hierarchy can no longer tolerate any association with the institution. The loss of the religion of one's birthright is a severe deprivation. To have one's faith ripped from one's soul by the betrayal of those trusted leaves scars on the soul that only Jesus, not religion, can transform to badges of moral honor. Jesus does not abandon. He is faithful. Not all priests and bishops are. Not all the successors of the apostles are credible.

People must pray that a sufficient number of clergy can rise to the moral and spiritual challenge facing the church today. It will take clergy who are what they claim to be—celibate for the Kingdom.

Charity is the real essence of Christianity. But theologian Yves Congar, O.P. once said: "In the Catholic Church it has often seemed that the sin of the flesh was the only sin, and obedience the only virtue." There are reasons for this overshadowing of charity: Sex and obedience are intimately connected at the core of the Catholic Church. Pope John Paul II has pointedly declared that celibacy is essential to the priestly vocation.

Social Contract Broken

There is a social contract between priest and people, with celibacy at its core. Priests promise to give up all human sexual involvement in exchange for the trust, respect, belief, support, obedience, and allegiance of the faithful. The faithful, for their part, receive comfort, forgiveness, and salvation.[155]

That contract has been seriously violated by a sufficient number of bishops and priests to bring the church to an epic confrontation. Through their violations, bishops have relinquished all moral credibility in every matter of human sexuality. Sexual abuse of minors is merely the poster issue for the crisis. The crisis is about non-celibate (sexual) behavior of priests and bishops and their disregard for the rational judgements of married Christians in regard to human sexuality.

The hierarchy has concentrated on the selection of candidates for the priesthood as if a bad influence invading seminaries and the priesthood were causing the sexual crisis. Much evidence shows that clerical candidates are subjected to sex in seminaries and from sexually active priests, even spiritual directors. Corruption of the priesthood is not coming from outside forces; it is specious to blame candidates or culture. Corruption of the priesthood is generated and perpetuated within the clerical system. Corruption does not seep up from the bottom. Corruption is raining down from the top.

Hence, the current crisis will not be solved easily. If celibacy is central to the priesthood as the pope declares, then the church must first acknowledge that it does not take training for celibacy seriously. At one time a man had to memorize the entire New Testament to qualify for ordination to the episcopacy. Now, at least a three-year sequence in biblical studies is required for priestly ordination. If celibacy is so important to the priesthood, why would anything less than a three-year, six semester study sequence not be considered as an inadequate preparation for it? Critics say there is nothing to teach or learn, or that seminaries are now doing an adequate job. Facts speak otherwise.

There are voices saying that the sexual crisis is of recent origin, caused by Vatican II and stimulated by the sexual revolution of the 1960s and 1970s. Even the Vatican once implied that it was simply an "American" problem. This book describes the long-standing and widespread prevalence of celibacy violations, including clergy sex with minors, and proves otherwise. Written accounts and concerns go back to the year 309 CE and continue with remarkable frequency up to the present time.

The sexual crisis of the present time is not a new phenomenon. Sadly, past realities are being reincarnated in the American church today. Integrity and credibility are sorely lacking. As corruption of the priesthood becomes ever more evident, and the credibility of the hierarchy is ever more compromised, the social contract with the laity becomes strained to the breaking point. It is not a problem of politics or public relations and cannot be cured by either. The demise of obedience to church leadership is not the cause of the crisis in the church, it is a result of clerical malfeasance. Respect, trust, and obedience can no longer be expected from the laity. But, with genuine charity on all sides, this crisis provides an opportunity to revivify the pastoral care of the church and a chance to rededicate the priesthood to celibate integrity and the hierarchy to honesty and accountability. What else is a reformation all about? Charity will win out in the end.

Finally, victims should act as the church they are. In 1517, the church could claim that a "functional diocese had no need for lay interference." Legislation from that time defines the five functions of a diocesan priest in order of importance: First the priest was to preserve his image; his behavior should not provide cause for scandal about the priesthood or the church. Second, a priest's most important function was to protect the income of the church. Third, a priest was the protector of the "sacred," the church building, its vessels, and vestments. Fourth, a priest had the *cura animarum* or duty to hear confessions, distribute communion, administer the last rites, and to instruct his flock. And fifth, a "priest functioned as an agent of the bishop, transmitting and receiving information concerning the desired diocesan order."[156]

Is it not remarkable how operational this outline of clerical functions is in today's church? As effective as those priorities of functions may have been at one time, their breakdown and inadequacies are brutally apparent now. The church needs to reevaluate its pastoral priorities. And the church does need the involvement of the laity.

Recently, time after time, bishop after bishop has reduced himself to an image preserver, or income supervisor, or property protector, an administrator above all and before any consideration of the care of souls. Bishops have become CEOs and CFOs not in addition to, but rather instead of, pastors.

Public relations have been a principal and primary response of the hierarchy to the abuse crisis. Slogans—Restoring Trust—rather than substantial moral leadership, have occupied bishops' efforts. At an estimated cost of $50,000 a month, public relations have reportedly cost the Los Angeles diocese over a half million dollars already. The USCCB reportedly has public relations campaigns costing millions. Whatever genuine progress has been made to meet the sex abuse crisis has been made as a result of lay pressure.

One courageous, completely honest bishop who would lift his head above the crowd would be worth more than all the PR campaigns put together. Of course all Christians know what it would cost: Another crucifixion!

Honesty the Best Policy

The isolation from solid common-sense lay involvement has resulted in continuing harm not just to the violated minors and faithful, but to the bishops themselves who continue to shoot themselves in the foot. Cases of sexual abuse in Dallas could have been settled with several victims of Fr. Rudy Kos in 1995 for a few hundred thousand dollars and some consolation from the bishop. Instead, church authorities chose the corporate route mentioned earlier. A jury in 1997, appalled by hearing what the Dallas Archdiocese knew and did, awarded the plaintiffs $119.6 million in compensation and they finally settled for $32.5 million. The bishop of Dallas still reigns. A young man violated by Msgr. Michael Harris cost Los Angeles and Orange Diocese $5.2 million. The victim had simply requested $300,000 to pay for therapy and the chance to continue his education. The unwillingness of the church to be open, accountable, and clean its own house, is costing it dearly, financially and spiritually. The church has admitted that the crisis has already cost $800 million dollars. That figure does not, of course, include all the collateral costs.

The latest church maneuver to protect its "assets" is to file for bankruptcy, a tactic that demonstrates where exactly the bishops' treasures lie. Not in truth and openness! The bishops' security and hope lie in property and power. Many people will be unjustly harmed by this political end run. But as the saying goes, "The church turns to politics when it fails to produce enough saints" (François Mauriac). The Archdiocese of Portland and the dioceses of Spokane, Washington, and Tucson, Arizona have already filed for bankruptcy and others will follow.

Perhaps some good for the reformation of the church can be retrieved in the end from bankruptcy procedures. Already the U.S. Department of Justice is involved in the cases. The cold eye of a bankruptcy judge may sort out the actual financial dealings of these churches and give the faithful the honest accounting they deserve. (For instance, some bishops claim that compensation to victims hinders a diocese from continuing its works of charity, when in truth only 8 percent of the money spent on Catholic charities is diocesan funding. The rest is garnered from public funds.)

Bankruptcy proceedings will reveal the amount that the dioceses in question have spent on legal fees, and if these expenditures far exceed the expenses of plaintiffs' lawyers and compensation to victims, in addition to the amount of money spent on public relations. Moreover, the moral bankruptcy of the hierarchy has put an end to the silence and subservience of the laity. The laity should now focus an analytical eye on the dynamics of that demise.

It is clear that the bishops cannot reform themselves or adequately regulate sexual behavior in the ministry.[157] They will never be able to achieve the integrity demanded by their office without the pressure, support, and supervision of the laity, who are the church. This is not a contest, but an invitation to cooperation.

Those who are "The Church" must demand the accountability and the transparency to which the pope and some bishops have pledged themselves. The laity need to review all the documentation that records the path taken into this abyss. There is no other way to repair current pitfalls and build a better path to the forgiveness and healing that is only possible in Jesus Christ.[158]

Finally, victims should examine themselves periodically to see if they are making progress. Here are a few tips: Demand the truth from yourself and those you wish to relate to, especially religious figures. Deal constructively with reality, no matter how harsh. Be willing to change. Personal healing is not possible without it. Work toward freeing yourself from symptoms, tensions, and anxieties that are produced by violations and betrayal by religious powers. Find satisfaction in forgiveness, both giving and receiving it. Establish satisfying relationships of mutual satisfaction and helpfulness, free of the traumas and scars of the past. Direct your instinctive angry energy into creative and constructive action. Expand your capacity to love. Love is more powerful than any violation, personal or institutional. Charity does really heal. Perfect charity heals perfectly.

Chapter 13

Talking with the Bishops: Challenge for a New Century

When Pope John Paul II died in 2005, a number of things happened for the very first time: the news went around the world via e-mail from the Vatican at the speed of light; between two and five million people assembled in Rome within days of his death; some one thousand political dignitaries of all stripes from every part of the globe turned up for his funeral six days later; and millions more in every corner of the world watched his obsequies on television, as they happened live in St. Peter's Square.

Neither news, nor so many people have ever traveled so fast. None of this could have happened without modern means of communication. Before there were telephones, automobiles, jet planes, or even steamboats, there were couriers, horses, and sailing ships. Then it took many months to get a message from Rome to the New World and—provided it got there—many more months to get a reply back.

According to Catholic theology, the government of the church is a divinely instituted hierarchy with all authority emanating from God, flowing through the pope, the bishop of Rome, to the bishops. Bishops let limited amounts of power trickle down to priests, where it evaporates like an *arroyo* in a desert. The faithful—the vast majority of the people of God—get nothing. As Pope Pius X said in a 1906 encyclical letter:

> This church is in essence an unequal society
> ... right and authority ... reside only in the
> pastoral body ... as to the multitude ... its
> sole duty is that of allowing itself to be led
> and of following its pastors as a docile flock.

What was dogma in theory, however, did not become a possibility until travel at the speed of sound and communications at the speed of light were invented. Much as the popes—especially the great "centralizer" Pius IX (d. 1878)—longed for the power to control every nook and cranny of the church, they never succeeded. The mind control that the Vatican wields over the church in our day is a comparatively recent phenomenon and would not have been possible without the means of communication to enforce it.

The Catholic Church, however, has not yet learned the true meaning or the actual value of communication. Catholic Church communication is still, and almost exclusively, a one-way street—exercised through directives, edicts, propaganda, and public relations. Stuck in its hierarchical, top-down mode, it speaks but does not listen, and rules with little regard for the heartfelt opinions of the people.

The Second Vatican Council brought a glimmer of hope for greater dialogue by recognizing the whole church as the "People of God." It held out the promise of granting more power to local synods of bishops, and encouraging the laity to play a more active part in church affairs. But the glimmer died, as the papacy of John Paul II either lost interest in or felt threatened by the surge of uncontrollable enthusiasm that the council generated.

Pope John Paul II, during his twenty-seven-year reign, tolerated a campaign by Vatican bureaucrats and led a revolt by Rome against bishops and people who showed a willingness and an ability to manage their own affairs. Local synods and national conferences of bishops were stifled—stripped of their powers before they got a chance to exercise them. Cardinals and bishops were appointed not on account of their holiness, scholarship, or leadership abilities, but on the basis of their conformity to tradition, doctrinal orthodoxy, and their willingness to be led. Leaders such as these expect nothing more—or less—of their followers.

John Paul was much loved by the masses, but his flock was not moved by his moral judgments, especially in regards to human sexuality. Many well-educated bishops and laypeople are looking forward to a new century in which Rome listens to the people and treats them as "one in Christ." How the church deals with the problems exposed by the child abuse crisis will depend to a large extent on how the church of the future resolves its communication problem.

Presently, the concentration of power in the ranks of the hierarchy and the denial of any authority to the laity continue to undermine the quality of the communication between these groups. Bishops—convinced that their status is God-given—instinctively tend to reject all criticism as an attack, if not on their person, even more reprehensibly, on their office. Rather than respond to the substance of a criticism—or even an honest question—bishops often react defensively, as though in shock at being asked to publicly account for their behavior: That's not the way things are supposed to work! Fundamental issues get lost when a bishop perceives questions as a threat to his authority. His attitude is reenforced by the church's own political structures, which reserve all authentic power to bishops and reduce the role of collegiate or corporate bodies to mere consultation.

The clergy sex abuse phenomenon, however, has changed the way Catholics talk with bishops. Accustomed to controlling every situation, bishops have reluctantly been confronted with the fact that their competence has limits. Since the canonical structures of the church provide no basis or avenues for communication based on the concept of the equality of participants, the aggrieved have sought relief in the civil courts of the United States (and several other countries). For the first time in recent history, the bishops have been faced with an earthly moral force equal to, and in many ways surpassing, their own. Their response has often been defensive and angry; in some cases, they, reactively, have even belittled abuse survivors rather than evaluate their own responsibility and culpability.

The frustration and anger engendered in tens of thousands of sex abuse victims—as well as millions of laity—over the revelations of the extent of clergy abuse and its cover-up has changed the way a significant segment of the Catholic and non-Catholic population interacts with bishops. As the facts of sexual abuse by clergy unfolded in the media and in the courts, trust and respect for bishops eroded and the traditional acceptance of the status of the episcopacy within the church faltered.

Communication between bishops and victims is very often challenging, confrontational, and driven by anger, distrust, and cynicism. Those directly involved with the sex abuse phenomenon—including victims, their loved ones, their supporters, the media, and attorneys—have been astonished and saddened by the arrogance, dishonesty, and lack of compassion manifested by many bishops. Some bishops now recognize that they have lost the trust and respect of multitudes. Nonetheless, the fundamental attitude of superiority still permeates the bulk of episcopal conversations about significant issues facing the Catholic Church.

Anger and mistrust have prevented meaningful dialogue. Many bishops are so obsessed with what they fear might be a challenge to their authority that they are unable to consider the reasons for the anger. The horror of the sexual abuse of countless children, minors, and vulnerable adults has been overshadowed for many bishops by what they perceive as an affront to their dignity, a rejection of their authority, and disrespect for their persons and their office. In fact, most of the anger experienced by the victims, their supporters, and others seeking reform and change is grounded not just in the enormity of the crimes committed, but in the inability of many bishops to fully grasp the gravity of the situation. People have reason for their anger and lack of respect. As many have said time after time, "They just don't get it. It's all about them."

The welfare of the victims should be the primary concern of the church because these men and women, boys and girls have not only had their bodies and emotions deeply scarred, but their souls devastated (Cf. Chapter 11). Precious little concern for the souls of those faithful—and trusting—Catholics who were raped and brutalized by priests and bishops was apparent from a church whose fundamental and ultimate mission is the "salvation of souls."

The agenda of the victims and survivors has remained constant. First, they want bishops to acknowledge that their abuse is real. They want to be believed. They do not want to be patronized, nor will they be satisfied with hand wringing, profuse apologies, and promises of prayer. They want to be able to believe that the bishops completely understand the horror and trauma they have experienced. In looking for some sign of an honest understanding and sensitive response, too many victims have walked away disappointed and convinced that they were viewed as threats, nuisances, or pitiful, and not as spiritual and emotional casualties of betrayal.

Second, victims have wanted the bishops to do something about the perpetrators. Many began their search for healing with understandable thoughts of revenge. But almost miraculously, most worked through this negativity and sought only assurance that the men who raped their bodies and souls would be provided help, and—most importantly—be restricted from ever being able to hurt another person, young or old, again. In all too many cases, the victims found out to their shock that promises made by bishops were never kept. Perpetrators were recycled. Additional children were wounded.

Third, the victims, Catholics and the public at large, have wanted honest answers from the bishops to some very painful and fundamental questions: Why did they cover up? Why did they allow known child abusers to move from place to place? Why did they ignore victims and not offer any significant pastoral care? Why have they consistently and stubbornly refused to look at their own style of governing to find the answers to such devastating questions?

And finally, why has the church's leadership persisted in defending the tradition that image—*bella figura*—is more important than the spiritual and emotional welfare of the tens of thousands of clergy abuse victims? Even the National Review Board they commissioned and grand jury reports note that these questions have not been answered. The public sees a preponderance of public relations maneuvers covering more equivocation, more diversionary tactics, and more arrogance.

Certainly not every bishop has failed to realize the gravity of the church's present state. In response to victims, some bishops have rejected the high-pressure tactics that their lawyers recommended. Many have found honest compassion in their hearts for victims and empathy for many Catholics who are angry and disappointed because their trust in the priesthood has been betrayed. Yet the body of bishops remain defensive and aloof. The goodwill and efforts of those who truly "get it" are hidden by the intransigence of bishops who continue to focus on themselves, trapped in a narcissistic self-image that serves as a barrier to genuine understanding "getting in" and pastoral compassion "getting out."

The tragic nightmare of clergy abuse has awakened the laity from a spiritual coma induced by clericalism. Some realize that they can be adults in church as well as in their homes, their places of work, and society. The results, however, have been predictable. Men and Women who have spoken up and questioned bishops have been accused of a catalogue of sins—from arrogance, misunderstanding, and disloyalty, to heresy. Some, when asking for discussion and dialogue have been told that there will be none, unless the overriding authority of the hierarchy is first acknowledged, as if *all truth* resides in them. In other words: Dress like a grown-up for the meeting, but act like a docile, obedient, and awe-filled child.

Traditional theology and canon law ensure that communication with bishops on a level playing field is nearly impossible. Without realizing the possibility of equality in dialogue, the church will never *really* be the body of Christ. Its leaders will never be recognized as true pastors, but as mere bureaucrats in medieval garb. Catholic laymen and -women need to acknowledge the irrational fears that caused them to bow in deference before "father" and even more profoundly to "His Excellency." Fears and constrictions must be met head on. Acknowledge religion-induced fears; move past them. Too much is at stake for the future of religion and humankind to allow dialogue to be crushed by fearful subservience or irrational rage.

The laity need to forge a new set of rules for communicating with the hierarchs. Heretofore, there have been two basic behavior patterns: one from the pre-abuse-crisis days and another borne of the scandal. Formerly, Catholics lived the "reality" of the church as a stratified society. The laity deferred to the bishops and accepted their assessments, conclusions, and action plans without question. This was almost always true in direct dealings with bishops. When out of earshot, however, a meta-pattern emerged—even among some priests: Some people would quietly express disagreement and disappointment, or even anger at bishops and their actions. Yet few laypeople—or clergy—would take the risk to confront or forthrightly question his or her bishop. That simply wasn't done. Bishops were, after all, the divinely appointed successors of the apostles.

Along with the sex abuse scandal came a new way of communicating that was direct, but too often angry and "in-your-face" confrontational. But the media and the courts forced bishops to face the issues of clergy abusing minors. The bishops could no longer retreat to the security of their chancery offices. They no longer could enjoy the illusion that the clamor would dissipate in time and everything would return to "normal." The trust, deference, and respect for authority that had been seared into Catholic souls quickly evaporated and were replaced by anger and disdain.

Irrational anger, of course, will never persuade the bishops of the validity and urgency of the survivors' complaints. However, the angry encounters with bishops, including the vociferous demonstrations that have taken place at chanceries and cathedrals, have had an impact. Although many bishops seem to give the impression of being above the fray and immune from the angry emotional confrontations, these challenges have, in fact, shocked many bishops into the realization that they can no longer presume homage and preferential treatment.

Confrontation tends to either harden or blur both sides of a conversation. Some bishops won't allow the laity-led Voice of the Faithful (VOTF) to meet on church property, accusing them of having "agendas," being disloyal and "anti-Catholic," "fostering dissent," or, worst of all, "failing to respect the bishops." The Survivor's Network of Those Abused by Priests (SNAP) and some VOTF chapters have been vilified, not because their message is heretical or dissenting, but because their anger and confrontational tactics (and truth) are more than the bishops can handle.

What is being lost in all of this is the path to mutual understanding. The victims and many laypeople believe the bishops not only will not, but cannot get it. The bishops, for their part, seem convinced that the victims and their supporters, in their anger, will never be able to see and accept the hierarchy's side, nor the honest and sincere concern many of its members have for victims and for the prevention of further abuse. The goal is not to beat one or the other side into submission. It is to arrive at a sufficient degree of mutual respect that allows bishops and laypeople to listen to one another rather than talk at, or past, one another.

The time for confrontation that is predominantly angry and irrational is past. In many cases anger and rage have been justified. Yet such expressions have been only transitional. Persistence in that mode of communication will only tempt bishops to become rigidified in their attitudes toward all victims and survivors of clergy abuse. Bishops will not be open to laypeople who have had what they perceive to be the temerity to question them.

The time for dialogue on a level playing field is at hand. There is much to talk about and many hard questions yet to be answered. Name calling and verbal abuse are as much a barrier to finding answers as is the infantile deference that has enabled clericalism to flourish and control. Fear does not create an atmosphere for dialogue. Bishops who refuse to include laypeople and survivors on every level of discussion and decision making with regard to the clergy abuse scandal must be invited in a rational and respectful manner to explain their reasoning for such exclusion.

Those bishops who think that VOTF, SNAP, Call to Action (CTA), Future Church, or other lay reform groups have hidden agendas and are dissenters, heretics, or anti-Catholic need to be educated. At the same time, laypeople need to listen to bishops explain the reasons for their misgivings and accusations and talk about the sources of their information. Bishops who refuse to reveal the names of verified sex abusers or who have secretly reassigned known offenders must be encouraged to explain their dilemmas to the people of God.

Pope John Paul II, at the beginning of his papacy said, "Be not afraid." In the twenty-first century, there is no longer room for fear, secrecy, or arrogance in any faction of the church. Far too much is at stake. Far too many souls have been devastated by the perpetuation of communication dominated by those elements. Now is the time for dialogue. It is reasonable to investigate the tension between the spirit of Vatican II and the traditional clerical mistrust of the laity.

In promoting dialogue it is important to understand the context from which the opposition between bishops and laypeople arises. Theology and tradition teaches that the church is founded on Christ and the apostles—the predecessors of the bishops. As a consequence, bishops are essential components of the institutional structure of the church. Their power to teach, legislate, administer, sanctify, and judge is believed to be the divinely instituted means whereby God communicates with mortals. Consequently, any question or communication that is perceived as a challenge to bishops is interpreted as much more than a personal attack or manifestation of disrespect. Such interactions are often regarded as provocations and expressions of disbelief in an essential tenet of faith.

At the same time, victims and others who object to the bishops' autocratic exercise of authority do not consider such disputes an affront to any doctrinal issue. Rather, they judge them as honest reactions to the reality of misused or abusive authority. The bishops see themselves as divinely appointed leaders, and their critics see them as flawed administrators.

However, episcopal power is not the real issue. Betrayal of trust, violation of the pastoral contract, soul murder, rape, sexual assault, character assassination, slander, and financial mismanagement in the name of religion are some of the abuses that people are up in arms about. These issues will not go away nor will they be rectified unless drastic attitudinal changes take place, primarily on the part of the church's leadership.

Building bridges and opening lines of genuine communication between bishops and laypeople is a noble goal for members of the Christian community. It will never happen without integrity and trust on all sides. Trust will not happen until secrecy and fear, so deeply ingrained in Catholic tradition, is eradicated. Laypeople should not have to fear frank and direct exchanges of ideas with bishops or other church leaders. This is the first essential step in the search for truth and accountability. Banishing the fear and inhibition that lurks in the background of religious indoctrination is the beginning of authentic Christian empowerment. Searching for plausible answers does not equal disrespect, nor is it a sign of dissent. It is, in fact, a sign that one has accepted the sometimes painful and daunting responsibility of adult membership in the body of Christ.

Talking together begins with dialogue. Dialogue cannot tolerate submission. Laypeople have been nurtured in an ecclesiastical culture that made trusting dialogue impossible. The duplicity of church officials exposed by the sex abuse scandal led to the subsequent erosion of confidence and respect for clerics and especially bishops. This will be reversed only when both sides move beyond roles and see one another as Christians. This may be more difficult for bishops for whom the question of sexual abuse unleashes the whole sexual agenda facing the church including their own celibacy, but Catholic laymen and -women should not shirk their duty to learn new modes of interaction with the hierarchy.

Progress toward a productive relationship between bishops and laity depends on dialogue. Concern for the victims of sex abuse and the clergy who have betrayed their church demands that difficult issues be raised. If the sexual abuse crisis has taught us anything, it is that free, open, unrestricted dialogue is absolutely essential for the reformation of the church—that includes all of us.

Angry confrontations and authoritarian protestations are not productive. Talking together in the context of mutual respect and recognition of each other as equals in Christ—brought together by a shared concern for the suffering of the most vulnerable among us—is the task of a new century.

The long, sad history of sexual abuse by clergy has been written. Now the church—priests and people—have a chance to write a different record—one of mutual concern and effective protection of the vulnerable, and support for the trustworthiness and integrity of the clergy.

The sexual abuse crisis is not isolated from the questions of the celibate practice of all clergy and the moral questions that involve marriage and all human sexual behaviors. These are the main, yet unspoken, reasons why sexual abuse has been such an inflammatory and dangerous issue for the hierarchy. One foundation of their power and control rests on the celibacy of the clergy. That area of religious ideal and personal practice has heretofore been shrouded in secrecy and taboo, certainly for the laity. That is no longer the situation. For the first time, certainly since the Protestant Reformation, the sexual life and adjustment of bishops and priests is open for discussion by laypeople. This is the task of the new century: Clergy and laypeople need to talk together about sexuality and how it affects them all.

Chronology of the Paper Trail

The sexual abuse of children in the Roman Catholic Church is not a modern scandal. Records indicate that it is an age-old problem—almost as old as the church itself.

Going as far back as the Council of Elvira in 309 CE, official documents reveal a church preoccupied with regulating the sex lives of its clergy. Very often, the behavior the church was attempting to control was the sex lives of its legitimately married clergy. Sometimes that preoccupation involved behavior that was simply at odds with the church's arbitrary, yet mandatory, law of celibacy, which de facto rules out all sexual activity for clergy. At other times—and far too frequently—it involved clerical behavior that was not just immoral, but reprehensible and criminal.

Regardless of how objectionable and criminal the sexual abuse of children was regarded, it has been a recurring and widespread problem within the ranks of the clergy for the best part of two thousand years. To make matters worse, the church has for a long time—but especially in more recent times—engaged in a widespread conspiracy not only to deny the existence of sexual abuse but, often deliberately, to provide cover for its perpetrators.

Many people, Catholics included, have been shocked to rediscover within the last decades just how prevalent clerical misbehavior is. Abuse, however, really is not a new phenomenon. Sexual activity by popes, bishops, and priests—members of a ruling hierarchy bound to celibacy—has triggered every reform the church has been forced to undergo. The rape and sodomy of children is woven into the tradition of clerical history. And it has been amply recorded in documents and literature.

Popes, bishops, and priests have known for centuries that the sexual abuse of children is a problem. The church may have legislated against it, but the fact remains that the hierarchy has consistently failed to protect the youngest and most vulnerable members of its flock from sexual abuse by predatory clergy. Roman documents, papal encyclicals, and council resolutions down through the ages expose the persistence of violations of celibacy and criminal sexual activity with children and others.

Failures in the discipline of celibacy should come as no surprise: they are predictable. The power of a professedly celibate and all-male minority to define the morality of love and to control the sex lives of the lay majority provides a climate where the sexual abuse of children by some bishops, priests, and religious can flourish and be covered up.

The never-ending flow of legislation emanating from official quarters proves beyond a shadow of a doubt that from its earliest days the church has been trying to contain the abuse of minors by members of the clergy and cover up the resulting scandal. This chronology should be read against the backdrop of the crisis caused by clerical sexual abuse in the United States and the hierarchy's ongoing repudiation of any suggestion that it confess to prior knowledge of widespread failure in the discipline of clerical celibacy.

I. Apostolic Period: 1st–6th Centuries

60   *Didache*—an early Christian manual on morals and church practice.

220   Writings of Julius Paulus (Cf. Text)

309   Council of Elvira

438   Theodosian Code—a collection of general constitutions of the church.

530   Digest of Justinian (Vol. IV)—a comprehensive set of passages from juristic text books and commentaries.

533   Institutes of Justinian—a revised and modified edition of earlier institute.

II. Early Medieval Period: 7th–11th Centuries[159]

600   Penitential of St. Columban
650   Penitential of Cummean
690   Penitential of St. Theodore, Archbishop of Canterbury
700   Penitential of St. Bede—prolific writer, "Father of English History."
906   *Libri Duo* of Abbot Regino of Prum
1012   *Decretum* of Bishop Burchard of Worms—a collection of canon law.
1051   *Book of Gomorrah* of St. Peter Damian

III. Late Medieval Period: 12th–15th Centuries

1139   Lateran Council II
1140   *Decretum Gratiani* of Gratian—"The Father of Canon Law."
1179   Lateran Council III
1215   Lateran Council IV
1234   *Decretals of Gregory IX*—compiled by St. Raymond of Penafort, canon lawyer.
1449   Council of Basle. (1431–1449)
       First editions of *Corpus Iuris Canonici*—an extensive collection of previous canons and decrees that would remain the source of church law until 1917.

IV. Early Modern Period: 16th–19th Centuries

1514   *Supernae Dispositionis,* Papal Constitution, Leo X. (May 5, 1514)

1563   Council of Trent. (1545–1563)

1561   *Cum sicut nuper* of Pope Pius IV. (April 16, 1561)

1566   *Cum primum* of Pope Pius V. (April 1, 1566)

1568   *Horrendum* of Pope Pius V. (August 30, 1568)

1622   *Universi dominici gregis* of Pope Gregory XV. (August 30, 1622)

1726   *Lavellana,* Sacred Congregation for the Council. (July, 6 1726)

1741   *Sacramentum poenitentiae* of Pope Benedict XIV. (June 1, 1741)

1742   *Etsi pastorales* of Pope Benedict XIV. (May 26, 1742)

1745   *Apostolicae muneris* of Pope Benedict XIV. (February 8, 1745)

1775   *Ad Cochinchia,* S.C. of Propaganda Fidei. (August 26, 1775)

1866   *Instruction,* Holy Office. (February 22, 1866)

1869   *Apostolicae Sedis* of Pope Pius IX. (October 20, 1869)

1890   *Instruction,* Holy Office. (July 20, 1890)

V. Modern Period: 20th–21st Centuries

1917   *Code of Canon Law,* promulgated. (September 15, 1917)

1922   *De Modo Procedendi in Causis Sollicitationis,* Holy Office Instructions on how solicitation in the confessional were to be resolved. (June 9, 1922)[160]

1961   *Careful Selection and Training of Candidates for the States of Perfection and Sacred Orders,* Congregation for Religious. (February 2, 1961)

1962   *Instructio de Modo Procedendi in Causis Sollicitationis,* Holy Office. (March 16, 1962)

1965   Vatican Council II. (1962–1965)

1971   *The Role of the Church in the Causation, Treatment and Prevention of the Crisis in the Priesthood,* Conrad Baars, M.D. and Anna Terruwe, M.D. (Cf. Bibliography)

1972   *The Catholic Priest in the United States: Psychological Investigations,* Eugene Kennedy, Ph.D. and Victor Heckler, Ph.D. (Cf. Bibliography)

1975   *Humana Persona, Declaration on Sexual Ethics,* Congregation for the Doctrine of the Faith. (December 29, 1975)

1983   *Code of Canon Law (revised)*

1985   *The Problem of Sexual Molestation by Roman Catholic Clergy: Meeting the Problem in a Comprehensive and Responsible Manner (The Manual)* by Thomas Doyle, Ray Mouton, Michael Peterson. Published for the first time in this volume. (May 15, 1985)

1986   *Letter on Pastoral Care of Homosexual Persons,* Congregation for the Doctrine of the Faith. (October 1, 1986)

1988   Statement from the General Counsel of the U.S. Conference of Catholic Bishops. (February 1988)

1990   The Report of the Archdiocesan Commission of Enquiry Into the Sexual Abuse by Members of the Clergy—3 Vols. St. John's Newfoundland, Canada— (June 1990)

1992   Apostolic Constitution, *Fidei Depositum.* (October 11, 1992)

1993   *Letter of Pope John Paul II to U.S. Bishops*

1994   *Restoring Trust, Vol. I,* U.S. Conference of Catholic Bishops

1995   *Restoring Trust, Vol. II,* U.S. Conference of Catholic Bishops

1996   *Restoring Trust, Vol III,* U.S. Conference of Catholic Bishops

2001   *Sacramentorum Sanctitatis Tutela,* Pope John Paul II. (April 30, 2001)

2001   *De Delictis Gravioribus,* Congregation for the Doctrine of the Faith. (May 18, 2001)

2002   *A Report of the Investigation of the Diocese of Manchester,* New Hampshire, Office of the Attorney General. (March 3, 2002)

2002   U.S. Cardinals called to the Vatican. (April 22–25, 2002)

2002   *Suffolk County Supreme Court Special Grand Jury Report Regarding the diocese of Rockville Center, New York.* (May 6, 2002)

2002   *Charter for the Protection of Children and Young People,* USCCB. (June, 2002)

2002   *Essential Norms for Diocesan/Eparchial Policies Dealing with Sexual Abuse of Minors by Priests or Deacons,* U.S. Conference of Catholic Bishops, Approved by the Vatican. (December 8, 2002)

2003   *The Sexual Abuse of Children in the Roman Catholic Archdiocese of Boston,* (Office of the Attorney General Commonwealth of Massachusetts. (July 23, 2003)

2004   *A Report on the Crisis in the Catholic Church in the United States* by the National Review Board. (February 27, 2004)

2004   The John Jay College of Criminal Justice *Report of Clergy Sexual Abuse of Minors by Catholic Clergy.* (February 27, 2004)

2005   There were twelve Grand Jury Investigations of clergy sexual abuse of minors by Roman Catholic bishops and priests in various jurisdictions throughout the United States, but reports from those investigations were not available at the time of publication.

Correspondence

Fitzgerald Letters

Letter 1. Sept. 12, 1952

Pro Christi Sacerdote
Via Coeli: Monastery of the Servants of the Paraclete
Office of the Servant General
Jemez Springs, New Mexico
Sept. 12, 1952

His Excellency
The Most Rev. Robert J. Dwyer, Ph.D.
Bishop of Reno
129 Court Street
Reno, Nevada

Most Reverend and Dear Bishop:
It is rather a coincidence that Your Excellency's letter should have arrived on the very day that Edmund Boyle left Via Coeli and, in view of your inquiry from Arizona, we would be inclined to seek secular activity. His record here was one of conformity to the rule and cooperation yet with no marked indication of fervor or potential zeal. We find it quite common, almost universal with the handful of men we have seen in the last five years who have been under similar charges—we find it quite universal that they seem to be lacking in appreciation of the serious situation. As a class they expect to bound back like tennis balls on to the court of priestly activity. I myself would be inclined to favor laicization for any priest, upon objective evidence, for tampering with the virtue of the young, my argument being, from this point onward the charity of the

Mystical Body should take precedence over the charity of the individual and when a man has so far fallen away from the purpose of the priesthood, the very best that should be offered him is his Mass in the seclusion of a monastery. Moreover, in practice, real conversions will be found to be extremely rare. Many bishops believe men are never free from the approximate danger once they have begun. Hence, leaving them on duty or wandering from diocese to diocese is contributing to scandal or at least to the approximate danger of scandal. If Edmund Boyle returns here or if we learn of his whereabouts we will notify Your Excellency at once. Finally, I must in justice state again that while here he conformed to the community schedule. Does not his case, dear Bishop, emphasize the wisdom of not accepting for the priesthood men with physical blemishes (his eye condition) and men with insanity in their family background?

I consider it a special grace to have been present at Your Excellency's consecration and felt both your and Bishop Hunt's words were very much to the point. Count on our prayers. Father Woeber sends kindest personal regards. He speaks often of Your Excellency's graciousness to him on the occasion of his visit some time ago in Salt Lake City.
I have the honor to be Your Excellency,
Cordially in Spiritu Christi,

(signed)
Fr. Gerald s.P.
Servant General.

Via Coeli is Under the Authority of the Archbishop of Santa Fe

Letter 2. May 7, 1963

Pro Christi Sacerdote
Via Coeli: Monastery of the Servants of the Paraclete
Office of the Servant General
Jemez Springs, New Mexico
May 7, 1963

His Excellency
The Most Reverend Vincent J. Hynes, JCD
Bishop of Norwich
274 Broadway
Norwich, Conn.

Most Reverend and Dear Bishop:
Thank you for your good letter of May 3. It is good because it clarifies and gives a definite idea of what we are facing into. It may seem contradictory on my part, in that I frequently argue with Bishops and Superiors that a priest should have his Mass. However there are exceptions and I am very much of the opinion that when a padre has fallen into the classification of this young man, he needs a very solid jolt to attempt (if this be possible) to achieve the realization of the gravity of his offence. Personally I would want to spend the rest of my life on my knees asking God's Mercy for I know of no more terrible threat than the words of Our Lord: those who tamper with the innocence of the innocents—"it were better that they had never been born."

What I am personally afraid of is that these men have the equivalent of that which the Scriptures put in the form: "I will harden their hearts lest they be converted." Actually of course we believe the hardness comes out of the heart itself but I am afraid to let this type of man go immediately back to the altar after having violated the living altar of the human soul.

If, therefore, dear Bishop, you feel that you can go along with these sentiments, I would suggest that you write a letter to the part concerned saying: "after consultation with the Council and considering the gravity of this offence which has strong civil and even stronger divine retributive sanctions, I then leave you under suspension for a minimum period of six months["]. After six months you yourself can write to me expressing sentiments of sorrow and horror and the Paraclete Fathers confirm their impression of your realization of the seriousness of your offence, I will consider then a lifting of the suspension a divinis." The reason for asking you to do this, dear Bishop, is because if the severity of the penance is known to originate with us it will initiate a personal resentment against us which would nullify the purpose we have in mind—the ultimate rebuilding and regilding of a consecrated soul.
Most cordially in Spiritu

(signed)
Fr. Gerald of the Holy Spirit
Very Reverend Gerald Fitzgerald, s.P.
Servant General

Via Coeli is Under the Authority of the Archbishop of Santa Fe

Letter 3. From the Bishop of Norwich, Conn.

The Very Reverend Gerald M.C. Fitzgerald, s. P.
Via Coeli
Jemez Springs, New Mexico
Dec. 19, 1963

Dear Father Fitzgerald:
This is in reply to your kind letter of December 2, 1963 about Father Bernard Bissonnette which I received after my return from Rome. Father Bissonnette's serious faults are common knowledge among all the clergy and well known also to many of the laity of our diocese. Since our diocese is so compact it would be impossible for me to give him an assignment here where his past faults would be unknown. I therefore do not see how I can ever accept him back in this diocese.

Since my return from Rome I have learned from the priests of the diocese who were with him in the Seminary that he had this moral fault even as a seminarian. Fellow seminarians reported it to the Superior, but evidently it was never reported to my predecessor. I am sure that if it had been he would never have been ordained.

If Father Bissonnette can find a benevolent bishop, I would have no objection, but in conscience I could not give him a recommendation.

If he cannot resume active work in a diocese, he would have only two alternatives: to stay indefinitely at Via Coeli, if you can keep him, or to request the Holy See to reduce him to the lay state.

I am grateful for the help you have been to our diocese and our priests. With best wishes for a Happy Christmas, I am,
Sincerely yours in Christ,

Vincent J. Hines
Bishop of Norwich.

Letter 4. From the Bishop of Duluth, Minn.

Bishop's Residence
2215 East Second Street
Duluth 12, Minnesota
January 12, 1966

TO ANY CATHOLIC BISHOP WHO MAY BE INTEREST-
ED IN ACCEPTING THE SERVICE OF THE REVEREND
BERNARD BISSONNETTE.
Your Excellency:
This is to introduce Father Bissonnette, a priest of the Diocese
of Norwich. Because of Father Bissonnette's conduct, Bishop
Hines felt constrained to send him to "Via Coeli" at Jemez
Springs, New Mexico. He was later transferred to a branch of
"Via Coeli"—"Our Lady of the Snows" at Nevis, Minnesota.

From time to time I have given guest priests at these two
institutions a chance to rehabilitate themselves in the Diocese
of Duluth. Unfortunately, all of these former ventures turned
out quite miserably.

In a relatively small diocese where the "grape vine" is
rather effective these instances made pastors rather "gun shy"
with regard to further experiments.

Last June I accepted Father Bissonnette for service in the
Diocese of Duluth at Nashwauk, Minnesota. Father Dolsina,
the pastor, is a very zealous priest—one of the best pastors in
the diocese. It is quite possible that Father Dolsina is too much
of a perfectionist to deal with a problem priest.

As you will see from the psychologist's and psychiatrists
(sic) report, which Father Bissonnette will present to you in a
sealed envelope, there is a rather strange combination of sub-
servience to authority and of resentment toward authority. In
talking to Father Bissonnette I get the impression that he is not
aware of his resentments though they reveal themselves in a

certain aggressiveness that makes him a bit difficult to deal with. He does not take hints. It has to be "laid on the line."

A very considerable tension developed in Father Dolsina's life. I wrote Father Bissonnette a rather sharp letter. Thereafter, up to the time I left for the Council I heard no more from Father Dolsina. There was no evidence of the recurrence of the psychosexual problem. But apparently the tension in the pastor increased. While I was at the Council the Vicar General sent Father Bissonnette to Father Patrick Corbett, the pastor of St. James Church in Duluth. Actually, Father Corbett does not need a second assistant.

There has been very little to do for Father Bissonnette outside of hearing confessions and offering Masses. When a priest, especially one with a serious problem, is not kept busy, the big problem is apt to reassert itself. So far it has not appeared.

You will notice that the recommendation of both the psychologist and psychiatrist is to have Father Bissonnette teach in a High School. The reasons are given.

We have only one Catholic High School in the Diocese of Duluth besides the girls' academy. I conferred with the principal of our Catholic High School about using Father Bissonnette as a teacher. All the faculty assignments are filled. It might be possible to juggle the schedule so that Father Bissonnette could teach Latin. That process, however, would be so artificial that the faculty members would recognize it. Just how this might show in the attitude of the faculty members toward him, I do not know. But there is a risk that might depress Father Bissonnette.

If I send Father Bissonnette to another pastor I fear that Father would begin with two strikes on him. The priests in this Diocese already know that he has had two appointments within seven months.

I do think that the gained control of his psychosexual problem is a matter of notable success. Apparently this is not yet a fixed pattern of his life—i.e., the problem. In the past he has

had his failures but apparently this is not as yet an overpower-
ing drive in his life with which he cannot cope in reasonably
favorable circumstance. This opinion is born (sic) out in the
report of the psychologist and the psychiatrist.

No evidence has come to my attention that in the past
seven months that there is any indication of a relapse in this
matter. To me this is an evidence of considerable achievement
that I may not overlook.

I would be glad to give Father Bissonette another appoint-
ment but I have nothing to offer him that would follow the
guidelines of the psychologist and the psychiatrist. I am con-
cerned that Father Bissonnette be given a chance to reestablish
himself. I do think this is possible. It is frightening to abandon
a priest who is struggling earnestly, and with some evidence of
success, to gain the necessary control over himself.

I shall be grateful for any consideration you can give to my
plea.
Sincerely in Christ,

(signed)
Francis J. Schenk
Bishop of Duluth

Letter 5. Sent to Archbishop Pilarczyk, President of the Bishop's Conference, after the first LinkUp convocation in 1992

The Rev. Thomas P. Doyle, O.P., J.C.D.
Box 485, 227 N. Elm Street
Bunker Hill, Indiana 46914
October 22, 1992

The Most Reverend Daniel Pilarczyk,
President, NCCB/USCC,
100 East 8th Street,
Cincinnati, Ohio 45202

Dear Archbishop Pilarczyk,
This past weekend, October 16–18, an organization called VOCAL held its first conference in Arlington Heights, Ill, a suburb of Chicago. VOCAL stands for Victims of Clergy Abuse Linkup and is an organization of and for the victims of sexual abuse by the clergy. Its membership includes victims, their families and supporters. Although it is nondenominational, the vast majority of the membership is Catholic.

Although the conference was well publicized and open to anyone, it is unfortunate that no member of the hierarchy was present nor any member of any diocesan administration, including the archdiocese of Chicago. There were only five priests in attendance. I say unfortunate, because in light of statements made by some bishops, including Cardinal Bernardin about the seriousness of the problem and the need to not only learn more about it but extend sensitivity to victims, this would have been an ideal opportunity to hear first-hand what hundreds of people have experienced through this terrible problem.

I found the conference very enlightening and would like to share with you some observations on the weekend. Besides myself as one of the featured speakers, other main speakers included the founder, Jeanne Miller, the mother of a victim, Jason Berry, author of the book Lead Us Not Into Temptation, *Dr. (sic) AW Richard Sipe, Dr. James Cavanaugh, director of the Isaac Ray Center, Chicago, Jeffrey Anderson, attorney, Rev. Marie Fortune and Fr. Andrew Greeley. The conference was attended by several hundred people from throughout the United States and Canada. I am enclosing a copy of the program. There was also extensive press coverage, both newspaper and television, from throughout the United States.*

Many people told their stories both publicly and privately. All were shocking and some were outright disgusting. There was a general feeling of anger among those in attendance. The anger was directed, naturally, at the clergy who had abused people. This was secondary however, because the brunt of the anger was directed toward the hierarchy and other church administrators to whom victims and their families had turned for help.

The purpose of the conference was to present an opportunity for victims to gather together for mutual support and assistance. The primary purpose, however, was to explore ways of convincing the authorities of the institutional church ... the bishops ... that this is indeed a serious problem that needs to be addressed not with rhetoric but with responsible action.

Those in attendance, including the speakers, expressed a great deal of anger and frustration with the Bishops' Conference and with individual bishops for their collective inaction to this issue. There were many, many stories from victims and their families of attempts to get action from their bishops. These attempts were met with lies, denial, harassment, lack of action and in some cases, even lawsuits for defamation of character of the accused priest. I even heard stories of people who approached dioceses with set policies and procedures who discovered that these procedures were on paper only.

The NCCB has stated its concern for this issue but has basically done nothing save a couple of statements issued by the general counsel. Frankly, the people directly involved with the problem of sexual abuse by priests do not hold out any hope that the conference will ever do anything effective. As one speaker put it so well, "concern for the victims of sex abuse by priests is not on the agenda of politically correct items for the bishops." The statements from the conference to the effect that this is a local problem and not within the competence of the NCCB have little meaning in light of the fact that the conference has issued pastoral statements and letters on everything from nuclear arms to migrant workers.

Many bishops have spoken eloquently of their concern for this grave problem but very few have backed up their words with effective and consistent action. This is not simply my opinion but the experience of hundreds of victims and their families. Had there been responsible action in the face of complaints, the millions of dollars paid out and the many lawsuits could well have been avoided.

The general feeling of frustration is coupled with the conviction that it is useless to wait for the church's leadership to do anything. Hundreds of people have been harmed beyond description by the fact of sexual abuse by priests and the shabby treatment accorded by the church leadership. Many have not lost their faith in God but have certainly lost their faith in the institutional church.

Eight years have passed since this issue became a public matter, with the infamous case of Gilbert Gauthé in Lafayette. I have been directly involved since that time, hoping that the church as an institution would do something. It has done little if anything and I for one have given up hope that there ever will be any action.

I am writing simply to share some information on the conference as well as the feelings and opinions of hundreds of people involved in the issue.

Sincerely in Christ,

(Signed)
Thomas P. Doyle, O.P., J.C.D.

Letter 6. Archbishop Pilarczyk's response to Fr. Doyle

The Reverend Thomas P. Doyle, O.P., J.C.D.
Box 485
227 N. Elm Street
Bunker Hill, IN 46914
November 18, 1992

Dear Fr. Doyle:
I am responding to your letter of October 22 reflecting upon the recent conference conduct by the Victims of Clergy Abuse Linkup (VOCAL). I understand that there is a great deal of anger, some of which may be justified, about the way that some diocesan bishops may have responded to the question of sexual abuse committed by Catholic priests. Your concern seems to be that the NCCB systematically ignores the problem and that individual bishops have shown little inclination to deal in a realistic way with this difficult and traumatic situation. We bishops have heard again in our recent meeting the pain and the anxiety of the victims of abuse, heard a report by Cardinal Mahony on his meeting with victims, and responded in a tangible way.

In 1985 the President of the NCCB, Bishop Malone, received a copy of the report that you prepared with Fr. Peterson and Mr. Mouton commenting on what you saw at the time as a growing crisis of some proportion for the Catholic Church in this country. You assumed, at the time and subsequently, that the bishops were both unaware of the situation and unresponsive. Although there may be some disagreement about the specific way in which the NCCB responded to the matter, the fact remains that your report presented no new issue (of which the NCCB was unaware) or presented information that required some materially different response. You know, from your canonical training, that the NCCB does not have the power to bind individual Bishops in matter of priestly discipline. We can only suggest and advise. In these cases, our staff consistently advised dioceses on how best to handle the situation relating to the sexual abuse of children by clergy. Those principles are laid out in my public statement after the June, 1992, Bishops' meeting in South Bend, Ind. A copy of that statement (enclosed) reaffirms what has been our view all along: this is a tragedy of immense proportion for all institutions in this society which are concerned with the welfare of children. The problem of the sexual abuse of children is no more extensive in Catholic institutions than in any other institutions in our culture. The best way to respond to this situation is to deal with it openly and effectively, by those closest (not farthest) from the pastoral situation in the parish and diocese.

We bishops have been greatly pained by the problem of sexual abuse of children, whether committed by clergy or anyone else. As shown in our recent meeting, it has never been our intention either to hide the problem or to walk away from the problem. Nonetheless, in the face of sometime conflicting advice about how best to deal with it from a series of well-meaning advisers and critics, some of us may have not moved quickly enough or openly enough, as others would have liked, in dealing with this situation. Consequently, ill motives have been attributed to us that are both unfair and untrue.

Finally, we know that the victims of sexual abuse, whether committed by clergy or anyone else, *need an opportunity to express themselves to each other, to professionals, and to society at large. We have much to learn as a society from* listening to *these stories and hearing this pain relayed sometimes 20, 30, or 40 or more years after the fact. We hope, however, that the victims are willing also to hear our pain. People need to recognize that their bishops and others who administer this Church are as hurt and angry as they are that this tragedy could have happened.*

I hope that, as you reflect on these words, you will recognize that the Conference has attempted to deal responsibly with this tragedy. It has attempted to do so by bringing together leaders and experts, by helping those who must deal with this situation to do so with the best available information and advice. We have helped dioceses draft policies and to put them into effect. We have undertaken training. Most of all, we encourage each other's best pastoral instincts—to reach out to prevent abuse, heal pain, and reconcile division. Rather than look to the past and lament what more might or could have been done, it is best to look to the future and invest our energy and resources to break the cycle of abuse.

I would like to hope that we can count on your expertise and cooperation in dealing with this problem.
Sincerely,

(Signed)
Most Reverend Daniel E. Pilarczyk
President, NCCB/USCC
Archbishop of Cincinnati

(Note: Despite the final sentence of Archbishop Pilarczyk's letter, no member of the U.S. hierarchy or his staff has ever contacted Fr. Doyle or Mr. Mouton.)

Endnotes

1. *Entretiens ecclesisastiques,* in *Oeuvres complètes,* Paris: Migne, vol. 1, p. 698.

1a. Decree on the Bishops' Pastoral Office in the Church.

2. Joyce Salisbury, "The Latin doctors of the church on sexuality," *Journal of Medieval History* 12 (1986), 280–282 and Peter Brown, *The Body and Society: Men, Women and Sexual Renunciation in Early Christianity* (New York: Columbia University Press, 1988), pp. 341–365.

3. Peter Brown, *The Body and Society,* pp. 366–386.

4. Jerome, "Against Jovinian," in *Patrologiae Latinae* 23, p. 293.

5. Jacqueline Murray, "Hiding behind the Universal Man: Male Sexuality in the Middle Ages," in Vern Bullough and James Brundage, editors, *Handbook of Medieval Sexuality* (New York: Garland Publishing, 1996), p. 126.

6. James A, Brundage, *Sex, Law and Marriage in the Middle Ages* (Brookfield, Vt.: Ashgate Publishing, 1993), p. 2. (Hereinafter cited as "Brundage, *Sex, Law and Marriage.*")

7. John Rist, *Stoic Philosophy* (Cambridge: Cambridge University Press, 1969), p. 103.

8. Brundage, *Sex, Law and Marriage,* p. 9.

9. Jean Leclercq, *Monks on Marriage: A Twelfth Century View* (New York: Seabury Press, 1982), pp. 1–9.

10. John Noonan, "Marital Affection in the Canonists," in *Studia Gratiana XII* (Bologna, 1967), pp. 479-510.

11. Pastoral Constitution, "The Church in the Modern World," December 7, 1965, par. 48–51 in Austin Flannery, *Vatican Council II: The Conciliar and Post-Conciliar Documents* (Northport, N.Y.: Costello Publishing, 1975 and 1992), pp. 950–954.

12. Canon 277 (1983 Code of Canon Law) and Canon 132 (1917 Code of Canon Law).

13. F. L. Cross and E. A. Livingstone, *The Oxford Dictionary of the Christian Church,* 2nd ed. (Oxford: Oxford University Press, 1974), 259. Also, J. Lynch, "Marriage and Celibacy of the Clergy, the Discipline of the Western Church: An Historical Synopsis," *Jurist* (1972), pp. 14–38, 189–212.

14. "Presbyterorum ordinis," December 7, 1965, art. 16 in Austin Flannery, editor, *Vatican Council II: The Conciliar and Post Conciliar Documents,* Vol. 1 (Northport, N.Y.: Costello Publishing, 1975), pp. 892–894.

15. David Rice, *Shattered Vows: Priests Who Leave* (Tarrytown: N.Y.: Triumph Books, 1990), pp. 6–7.

16. "Encyclical Letter on Priestly Celibacy," June 24, 1967 in Flannery, *Vatican Council II,* Vol II, 1982, p. 285.

17. John Paul II, "Letter to Priests, *Novo incipiente nostro,*" April 6, 1979 in Flannery, pp. 354–359.

18. Priest groups from the Minneapolis-St. Paul, Chicago, Milwaukee, Pittsburgh, and New Ulm dioceses have issued public letters. See Rosalind Bentley, "Twin Cities' Priests Seek Optional Celibacy" in *Minneapolis Star-Tribune,* December 12, 2003. See also Laurie Goodstein, "Celibacy Issues Flares Again Within Ranks of U.S. Priesthood," *New York Times,* Sept. 5, 2003.

19. Among those who have made their views public are: Cardinal Godfried Danneels of Belgium, Bishop Muskens of Breda, The Netherlands, and Father Timothy Radcliffe, former Master General of the Dominican Order.

20. See Cross and Livingstone, op. cit., p. 401.

21. Brundage, *Law, Sex and Christian Society in Medieval Europe* (Chicago: University of Chicago Press, 1987), p. 69. (Hereinafter "Brundage, *Law, Sex and Christian Society.*")

22. Ibid., p. 71.

23. Samuel Laeuchli, *Power and Sexuality: The Emergence of Canon Law at the Council of Elvira* (Philadelphia: Temple University Press, *1972*), p. 134.

24. Brundage, *Law, Sex and Christian Society,* p. 150.

25. *Digest of Justinian* XLVIII, v. 6, 1.

26. Ibid., XLVII, 11, 2 in Theodor Mommsen and Paul Kreuger, editors, *The Digest of Justinian,* 4 Volumes (Philadelphia: University of Pennsylvania, 1985), 816. The *Digest* was originally published on December 15, 530. It is a collection of texts, opinions, and interpolations on a wide variety of issues in Roman law. The Mommsen-Kreuger edition was first published in 1878.

27. *Institutes of Justinian,* Lib. IV, Tit. XVIII, 4. In Thomas Collett-Sanders, translator, *The Institutes of Justinian* (London:

Longmans Green, 192), p. 505. The *Institutes*, published on November 21, 533, were intended as a manual for law students.

28. *Codex Theodosianus*, IX, VII, 3 (December 16, 342).

29. Ibid., IX, VII, 6 (August 6, 390) in Clyde Pharr, editor and translator, *The Theodosian Code* (New York: Greenwood Press, 1952), p. 232.

30. See Derrick S. Bailey, *Homosexuality and the Western Christian Tradition* (London: Longmans, Green and Company, 1955), p. 76.

31. See Vern Bullough and James Brundage, *Sexual Practices and the Medieval Church* (Buffalo: Prometheus Books, 1982), 60. The authors cite a canon from the *Penitential of Columban* (600 CE) that prescribed a ten-year penance for clerics who committed sodomy.

32. Derrick Bailey, p. 78.

33. John Boswell, *Christianity, Social Tolerance and Homosexuality* (Chicago: University of Chicago Press, 1980), p. 42.

34. Warren Johansson and William Percy, "Homosexuality," in *Handbook of Medieval Sexuality*, Vern Bullough and James Brundage, editors (New York, Garland Publishing, 1996), p. 159. "The type predominating in medieval society [age asymmetrical] need not have been the same during all centuries or in all areas, but fifteenth century evidence from Florence and Venice, far more detailed than for any previous medieval society, indicates that the classic age-asymmetrical variant remained normative."

35. Pierre J. Payer, *Sex and the Penitentials* (Toronto: University of Toronto Press, 1984), pp. 40–44.

36. John MacNeill and Helena Gamer, *Medieval Handbooks of Penance* (New York: Columbia University Press, 1938), p. 226.

37. Vern Bullough, *Sexual Practices in the Medieval Church* (Buffalo, N.Y.: Prometheus Books, 1982), p. 59.

38. Johansson and Percy, op. cit., pp.168–69.

39. Ibid., See also John Boswell, op. cit., p. 187, "There is in fact a considerable body of evidence to suggest that homosexual relations were especially associated with the clergy. Some Christian authors have rather defensively rejected this idea but with little supporting documentation."

40. Johansson and Percy, op. cit., p. 175.

41. Pierre J. Payer, "Introduction" to *The Book of Gomorrah* (Waterloo, Ontario: Wilfred Laurier University Press, 1982), p. 5.

"The Book of Gomorrah stands out as a carefully planned and eloquently executed discussion of the subject reflecting both a legalistic concern with correct ecclesiastical censure and a passionate pastoral concern for those caught up in the behavior."

42. Ibid., 13. See also Paul J. Isely, "Child Sexual Abuse and the Catholic Church: An Historical and Contemporary Review," in *Pastoral Psychology* 45 (1997): p. 281.

43. Vern Bullough, *Sexual Practices and the Medieval Church*, p. 61.

44. Pope Victor II (1055–57), Pope Stephen IX (1057–58), Pope Nicholas II (1059–61).

45. Brundage, *Law, Sex and Christian Society*, pp. 212–213.

46. Pierre Payer, *The Book of Gomorrah*, p. 61. The citation is from the *Regula Fructuosi* and the English translation from C. W. Barlow, *Rule for the Monastery of Compludo* in *Fathers of the Church*, p. 63 (Washington, D.C.: Catholic University of America Press, 1969), p. 169.

47. Ibid., p. 214.

48. See D. 27, 28, 31, 32, 82, 84 in *Decretum Magistri Gratiani*, editio Lipsiensis Secunda, editor, A. L. Richter (Graz, Friedberg: 1879, 1959). The manner of citing Gratian is unique. The citations here noted refer to the first part of the *Decretum*, and each number refers to a section known as a *distinctio*.

49. Brundage, *Law, Sex and Christian Society*, p. 252.

50. John Lynch, "Marriage and Celibacy of the Clergy: The Discipline of the Western Church: An Historico-Canonical Synopsis," *Jurist* 32 (1972): pp. 199–200.

51. Brundage, *Law, Sex and Christian Society*, p. 252.

52. *Decretum*, c. 12–14, C. XXXII, q. 7 in Richter, Vol. I, pp. 1143–1144.

53. *Decretum*, D. 1, de pen., c. 15 in Richter, Vol I, p. 1161.

54. Brundage, *Law, Sex and Christian Society*, pp. 314–315.

55. *Corpus Iuris Canonici*, editio Lipsiensis Secunda, editor E. Friedberg, Graz, *Akademische Druck*, 1959. The *Corpus* consists of Gratian's work, the *Decretals of Gregory IX*, and several other collections of papal decrees. It was compiled and published by John Chapuis in 1500.

56. James A. Brundage, op. cit., pp. 403–404.

57. Fourth Lateran Council, Canon 15 in H. J. Schroeder, editor, *Disciplinary Decrees of the General Councils* (St. Louis, B. Herder Book Co., 1937), 256. Interestingly enough the following Canon condemns clerical drunkenness. Clerics guilty of drunkenness are to be suspended from office and source of income.

58. Canon 11, Third Lateran Council, 1179, in Schroeder, p. 224.

59. See note 46, the excerpt from the *Rule of the Monastery of Compludo.*

60. John Boswell, *Christianity, Social Tolerance and Homosexuality* (Chicago: University of Chicago Press, 1980), p. 188.

61. Michael Goodich, "Sodomy in Ecclesiastical Law and Theory," *Journal of Homosexuality* 14 (1976): p. 427.

62. Brundage, *Law, Sex and Christian Society*, p. 416.

63. Richard Fraher, "Preventing Crime in the High Middle Ages: The Medieval Lawyers Search for Deterrence," in James Sweeney and Stanley Chodorow, editors, *Popes, Teachers and Canon Law in the Middle Ages* (Ithaca, N.Y.: Cornell University Press, 1989): p. 215.

64. Richard Fraher, p. 220.

65. See Richard Sherr, "A Canon, A Choirboy and Homosexuality in Late 16th Century Italy: A Case Study," in *Journal of Homosexuality* 21 (1991): pp. 1–22. This is an interesting story of a priest accused of sodomizing a thirteen-year-old choirboy in the town of Loreto. The priest was tried by the church court, defrocked, and then turned over to civil authorities who sentenced him to death by decapitation. The victim was whipped and banned from the papal states.

66. Ibid., p. 231.

67. Cross and Livingstone, op. cit., pp. 705–706.

68. Brundage, *Law, Sex and Christian Society*, 533. See also Guido Ruggiero, "Sexual criminality in the early Renaissance: Venice, 1338–1358," in *Journal of Social History* 8 (1974–75): pp. 22–23 and Michael Goodich, "Sodomy in ecclesiastical law and theory," *Journal of Homosexuality* 2 (1976): pp. 427–429.

69. Cf. Peter Heath, "English parish clergy on the eve of the Reformation," *Studies in Social History* (London: Routledge and Kegan, 1969), pp. 104–108, 118–119; E.P.H. Hair, *Before the Bawdy Court: Selections from Church Court and other records*

relating to the correction of moral offenses in England, Scotland and New England; 1300–1800 (Elek. 1972), p. 90.

70. Elizabeth Abbott, *A History of Celibacy* (Cambridge: DaCapo Press, 1999), p. 108, p. 113 and John Lynch, "Marriage and Celibacy of the Clergy: The Discipline of the Western Church: An Historico-Canonical Synopsis," *Jurist* 32–2 (1972): p. 207.

71. Elizabeth Abbott, op. cit., p. 102.

72. Brundage, *Law, Sex and Christian Society*, p. 551.

73. Ibid., p. 554.

74. Cf. Cross and Livingstone, op. cit., p. 1050. Pope Paul III himself had three sons and a daughter, yet promoted the reform.

75. Brundage, *Law, Sex and Christian Society*, p. 568.

76. Canon 10, Session XXIV in H. J. Schroeder, editor, *The Canons and Decrees of the Council of Trent* (St. Louis: B. Herder, 1941), p. 182.

77. Session XXV, Canon 24 in Schroeder, pp. 247–248.

78. Monastic Orders are the oldest, reaching back to the fourth century. The Benedictines are the predominant monastic community (sixth century). Theoretically, members live their entire lives in the same monastery. Mendicant Orders began in the thirteenth century and, like monastic orders, stressed the common life. They differed in that the members moved from place to place as needs arose. The best-known mendicant orders are the Franciscans, Dominicans, Augustinians, and Carmelites.

79. John Lynch, op. cit., pp. 209–210.

80. Pope Pius V, "*Romani Pontifices*, 1 April 1566, in P. Gasparri, editor, *Codicem Iuris Canonici Fontes*, Vol. 1 (Vatican, Typis Polyglottis, 1926), p. 200 (Hereinafter identified as *Fontes*).

81. Pope Pius V, "*Horrendum*" Papal Constitution, August 30, 1568 in *Fontes*, No. 229.

82. John McHugh and Charles Callen, *Catechism of the Council of Trent for Parish Priests* (South Bend, Ind.: Marian Publications, 1923), p. 261. The Catechism was mandated by the Council of Trent and first published in 1566.

83. See Pierre Payer, *Sex and the Penitentials* (Toronto: University of Toronto Press, 1983), p. 5 and Cross and Livingstone, op. cit., p. 1059.

84. Stephen Haliczar, *Sexuality in the Confessional: A Sacrament Profaned* (Oxford: Oxford University Press, 1996), p. 8.

85. Richard McBrien, editor, *Encyclopedia of Catholicism* (San Francisco: Harper Collins, 1995), p. 345.

86. Stephen Haliczer, *Sexuality in the Confessional*, pp. 168–169.

87. Canon 982, in *The Code of Canon Law: A Text and Commentary*, James Coriden, Thomas Green, Donald Heintschel, editors (New York: Paulist Press, 1985).

88. Canon 1387.

89. *Book of Gomorrah*, chap. VI, pp. 41-42.

90. C. 8, 9, 10, C.XXX, q. 1 in Friedberg, Vol. I, 1099.

91. A spiritual relationship is a canonical entity that arises between a priest and one whom he baptizes. In the canonical tradition that has constituted an impediment to marriage.

92. St. Thomas Aquinas, *Summa Theologiae*, Vol. III, Suppl. Quest. 56, art. 2, reply to obj. 8. in *St. Thomas Aquinas, Summa Theologica* 3 Vols., translated by the English Dominicans (New York: Benziger, 1948), p. 2772.

93. Henry Charles Lea, *A History of the Inquisition in Spain* (New York: MacMillan, 1907), Vol. 2, Book 8, Chapter 6, p. 101.

94. Juan Ortega-Uhink, op. cit., "Decreta et resoluciones (1622–1741)," pp. 52–84.

95. In *Codex Iuris Canonici* (New York: P.J. Kenedy & Sons, 1918), Documentun V, pp. 709–712.

96. Canon 977 (1983 Code): "*The absolution of an accomplice in a sin against the sixth commandment of the Decalogue is invalid, except in danger of death.*" Canon 1378 stipulates that a priest who violates this Canon is automatically excommunicated.

97. Pope Pius IX, *Apostolicae Sedis*, Papal Constitution, October 12, 1869, Par. IV, n. 4, in *Fontes* Vol III, p. 28.

98. Charles Henry Lea, p. 124.

99. Ibid., p. 128.

100. Haliczer, p. 109.

101. Charles Henry Lea, p. 109.

102. Ibid., p. 134.

103. Stephen Haliczer, *Sexuality in the Confessional: A Sacrament Profaned* (New York: Oxford University Press, 1996).

104. Charles Henry Lea, p. 135.

105. *Acta Apostolicae Sedis* or *Acts of the Apostolic See* is the official periodical that contains Vatican legislation. Canon 9 of the

1917 Code states that official publication takes place through the *Acta*.

105a. Canon Law Society of America. Guide to the Implementation of the U.S. Bishops' *Essential Norms for Diocesan/Eparchial Policies Dealing with Allegations of Sexual Abuse of Minors by Priests or Deacons*, 2003.

105b. Cf. Instructio Supremae S. Congregationis S. Officii, *De modo procedendi in causis sollicitationis*, June 9, 1922; and Instructio Supremae Sacrae Congregationis Sancti Officii, *De modo procedendi in causis sollicitationis*, March 16, 1962; No. 73, *De crimine pessimo*.

106. "Sacramentorum Sanctitatis Tutela," May 18, 2001, Congregation for the Doctrine of the Faith, in *Acta Apostolicae Sedis*, 93 (2001), pp. 785–788.

107. It is ironic that six months prior to the promulgation of the 2001 legislation that imposed secrecy, Pope John Paul II stated in an address to the church in Oceania that the Church "*is seeking open and just procedures to respond to complaints in this area, and is unequivocally committed to compassionate and effective care for victims, their families, the whole community and the offenders themselves.*" *Ecclesia in Oceania*, Novvember 22, 2001, par. 49.

108. "Certamente non ci sembra un comportamento pastorale quello di un vescovo o di un superiore che, ricevuta la denuncia, informano del fatto l'autorita giudiziaria civile, per evitare di essere implicati nel processo civile che la vittima potrebbe intraprendere." *La Civilta Cattolica*, quaderno 3646, May 18, 2002, pp. 352–353.

109. Cardinal Maradiaga of Honduras compared U.S. Media coverage to Stalinist persecution of the church (Reuters, June 7, 2002). Cardinal Iniguez of Guadalajara, Mexico, blamed the media for exaggerating the problem (Zenit News Service, June 10, 2002). American Cardinal Avery Dulles stated in an interview with the *Boston Globe*, April 17, 2002: "*I don't think there's any great crisis in the U.S. ... It's really practically no news. To the extent it's a crisis, it's created by the news media. I suppose every individual case is terrible but it is not something peculiar to the Catholic church*". Finally, the Italian Catholic newspaper *Avvenire* (June 7, 2002) severely criticized U.S. attorneys for being partly to blame for the crisis.

110. Jason Berry and Gerald Renner, *Vows of Silence* (New York: The Free Press, 2004), pp. 97–98, citing Eileen Welsome, "Founder Didn't Want Molesters at Paraclete," *Albuquerque Tribune*, April 2, 1993.

111. A.W. Richard Sipe, "Affidavit," Doe v NOSF, District Court of El Paso, Texas, February 9, 2004, No. 19, p. 5.

112. Ibid., No. 22–23, pp. 5-6.

113. From an affidavit of Bishop Bernard Flanagan, Commonwealth of Massachusetts, Mark Barry vs. Roman Catholic Bishop of Worcester and Thomas A. Kane, June 6, 1995: p. 152.

> Q. *At the same time you wrote this letter which was February of '71, a few years after you received the initial complaint of Holley, had there been talk within the priesthood about sexual misconduct among priests?*
>
> A. *By 1971 I think there was, yes.*
>
> Q. *How do you remember that?*
>
> A. *I think by 1971 I had heard of other cases of this type* [sic] *sexual misconduct and knew that they were taking place in other dioceses too.*

114. Cf. Thomas Doyle, "Roman Catholic Clericalism, Religious Duress and Clergy Sexual Abuse." *Pastoral Psychology* 51 (2003).

115. Sacred Congregation for Religious, "Careful Selection and Training of Candidates for the States of Perfection and sacred orders," 2 Feb. 1961 in *Canon Law Digest*, Vol. 5, p. 457.

116. Ibid., Cited in *Canon Law Digest*, Vol. 5, p. 468.

117. Ibid., p. 470.

118. Ibid., p. 471.

119. Conrad Baars, M.D., "*The Role of the Church in the Causation, Treatment and Prevention of the Crisis in the Priesthood.*" Unpublished, 1971.

120. Eugene Kennedy and Victor Heckler, *The Catholic Priest in the United States: Psychological Investigations* (Washington, D.C.: U.S. Catholic Conference, 1972).

121. Ibid., p. 11.

122. A. W. Richard Sipe, *A Secret World: Sexuality and the Search for Celibacy* (New York: Brunner-Mazel, 1990). Figure 13.1, p. 265.

123. A. W. Richard Sipe, *Celibacy in Crisis: a Secret World Revisited* (New York: Brunner-Routledge, 2003).

124. David Rice, op. cit., p. 24.

125. Pope John Paul II, quoted in an address to the Congregation for the Clergy, January, 2004, in Associated Press, January 9 2004: *Legitimate pastors* [referring to priests], *in the exercise of their office, should never be considered as simple executors of decisions stemming from majority opinions coming out of church assemblies. ... The structure of the church cannot be conceived on simply human political models.*

126. *Catechism of the Catholic Church* (New York, Doubleday, 1995), no. 2389, p. 574.

127. Thomas Doyle, F. Ray Mouton, and Michael Peterson, *The Problem of Sexual Molestation by Roman Catholic Clergy: Meeting the Problem in a Comprehensive and Responsible Manner.* 1985 (Private).

128. Cf. Part II, Chapter 3, Thomas Doyle, *A History of the Manual.*

129. Rachel Zoll, "*More than 1300 Priests accused of abuse since 1950*," Associated Press, February 10, 2004.

130. Obtained from various press sources as of 2005: Archbishops Robert Sanchez, Eugene Marino, Rembert Weakland. Bishops Kendrick Williams, James McCarthy, Anthony O'Donnell, Patrick Ziemann, Keith Symons, Joseph Ferrario, Daniel Ryan, Robert Lynch, Paul Dudley, Lawrence Welsh, Joseph Hart , Howard Hubbard, and Thomas Dupre.

131. Vatican City, October 12, 2003, Zenit.Org, "*Media Exaggerated U.S. Scandals, says Cardinal Sodano.*" The scandals have received disproportionate attention from the media, claimed the cardinal, who, as Papal Secretary of State, is the second highest official in the Catholic Church.

132. Pope John Paul II, Message to Irish Bishops, June 26, 1999, found on the Vatican website.

133. This conclusion is based on the author's experience as an expert witness or consultant in civil court cases from 1988 to 2005.

134. Pope Benedict XV, March 12, 1919 wrote in *Canon Law Digest* Vol I, 120: *The law of clerical celibacy cannot be permitted to be in any way brought into question, as the Holy See regards it as the peculiar ornament of the Latin Church, and one of the principal sources of its active vigor.* Pope Paul VI, addressed a Letter to the Bishops at the Second Vatican Council in response to word that

celibacy would be publicly discussed: *It is not opportune to debate publicly this subject which demands the greatest prudence and is of such great importance. And we intend not only to conserve, as far as in Us lies, this long standing, holy and providential law, but even to confirm its observance by calling on Priests of the Latin Church to give due consideration to the causes and reasons which today give great relevance to this very law, thanks to which Priests can center their love entirely on Christ and give themselves wholly and generously to the service of the Church and of souls.* Cf. *Canon Law Digest*, Vol. VI, p. 231.

135. Karl Rahner, editor, *Encyclopedia of Theology: The Concise Sacramentum Mundi* (New York: Seabury Press, 1975), p. 207.

136. Cf. Thomas Doyle, op. cit., pp.205–208.

137. Anthony Padovano, "The American Catholic Church: Assessing the Past, Discerning the Future," in *Call to Action: Spirituality Justice Reprint*, January–February 2004, pp. 5–6.

137a. Moore, Thomas Verner. 1936. "Insanity in Priests and Religious," *The Ecclesiastical Review.* Part 1, 95: pp. 485–98. Part 2, 95: pp. 601–613.

138. Three examples are: "Reflections on the Homosexual Network and the 1985 Clergy Sex Abuse report," by Paul Likoudis, *The Wanderer*, May 30, 2002; "Dr. Judith Reisman Advises Catholic Church," by Karl Maurer (www.freerepublic.com) and "The Sex Abuse Lobby, the Bishops and VOTF," by Fred Martinez, September 22, 2002 (www.newsmax.com). Variations on the themes of these articles have appeared on other websites.

139. Settlement for seven cases and fees and expenses exceeded $5,000,000.00. The average settlement for each case cost more than $700,000. Ten cases remain to be settled.

140. Approximately thirty cases have been reported in the press involving approximately one hundred children. At the rate the cases were settled in the first paragraph, over $400,000,000.00 will be needed just for these cases. As this was being typed on June 8, 1985, the Associated Press reported the arrest of a priest in Florida. At the rate cases are developing, $1,000,000,000 over ten years is a conservative cost projection.

140a. Goffman, Irving, *Asylums: Essays on the Social Situation of Mental Patients & Other Inmates.* New York: Anchor Books, 1961.

140b. Greeley, Andrew, *Sex: The Catholic Experience.* Chicago: Thomas More, 1994.

141. Boyer, Pascal, *Religion Explained,* (New York, Basic Books, 2001), p. 5.

141a. Kierkegaard, S., *Fear and Trembling.* (Princeton University Press, 1941) and *The Concept of Dread,* (Princeton University Press, 1944).

142. Ibid., p. 23.

143. J. Pohle, "Priesthood," in *The Catholic Encyclopedia* (New York: Benziger, 1911), vol. 11.

144. McHugh and Callan, editors. *Catechism of the Council of Trent* (New York, 1923).

145. St. John Vianney. *Catechism on the Priesthood.*

146. Pope John Paul II, Letter to Priests—Holy Thursday, 2004.

147. Canon 207.1, reads: *Among the Christian Faithful by Divine Institution there exist in the church sacred ministers, who are called clerics in law, and other Christian Faithful, who are called laity.*

148. Cf. J. Sanchez, *Anti-clericalism: A Brief History* (Notre Dame, Indiana, Notre Dame University Press, 1972), p. 7.

149. Russell Shaw, *To Hunt, To Shoot, to Entertain* (San Francisco, Ignatius Press, 1993), p. 13.

150. Dean Hoge, *The First Five Years of Priesthood.* (Collegeville, Minn., The Liturgical Press), 2002. P. 27. Hoge found that the majority of priests ordained ten years or less believed that there is an ontological difference bestowed on priests at ordination which sets them apart from laypeople.

151. Katherine DeGiulio, *Interview with Dr. Leslie Lothstein.* National Catholic Reporter Website, August 9, 2002.

152. William Foote, Ph.D. Affidavit, *Does I, II, III vs. Catholic Diocese of El Paso, Father Irving Klister,* October 9, 1998. No. 11.

153. "Canonical and Legal Fallacies of the McGrath Thesis on Reorganization of Church Entities," *The Catholic Lawyer,* Vol. 19, 1973, pp. 275–286.

154. Doyle, T.P., Sipe, A.W.R., and Wall P.J., *Canonical Documents on Clergy Sexual Abuse.* (Chicago: Precept Press, TBP 2006).

155. Shupe, Anson, *Spoils of the Kingdom: Clergy Misconduct and Social Exchange in Religious Life.* (Urbana, Ill., The University of Illinois Press, 2005).

156. Trexler, Richard C., *Synodal Law in Florence and Fiesole, 1306–1518.* (Rome: Vatican Press, 1971).

157. Cf. The already completed Grand Jury Reports from: Rockville Center, Long Island; Boston, Massachusetts; New Hampshire; Phoenix, Arizona.

158. *BishopAccountability.org* is a competent and reliable source of facts and data about the sexual abuse crisis. They process and post the most complete library of documentation so far assembled.

159. Dates for the Apostolic and Early Medieval Period are approximate, and attributions of some works to particular individuals are disputed.

160. The existence of this document is verified in Juan Ortego-Uhink, *De Delicto Sollicitationis* (Washington, D.C.: Catholic University of America Press, 1954). It, like the 1962 document, was not publicized in any way by the Holy See upon its promulgation.

Glossary of Terms

Guide to Ecclesiastical Language

Absolution: the remission of sin that Catholics believe takes place when a priest pronounces the words or formula of absolution after a penitent has confessed his or her sins.

Anathema: from a Greek word meaning "cut off" or "cursed." It is normally used by Rome and councils of the church to condemn a person who embraces a heretical doctrine.

Archbishop: the bishop of an archdiocese and presides with limited influence over a number of neighboring dioceses grouped together as a province. As such he is also called a metropolitan.

Archives: the place where official church documents and historical and confidential records are kept. Each diocese is required to have a Secret Archives (Canon 489) under the direct control of the bishop where particularly sensitive records such as reports of investigations into allegations of sexual abuse of minors are kept. People privy to these investigations and tribunals take an oath never to reveal the contents of these records and a violation of this secrecy incurs automatic excommunication.

Benefice: an endowment attached to an ecclesiastical office in order to free the office holder to conduct his ministry without having to be concerned with raising financial support. Benefits were never common in the United States and they are being phased out worldwide since the Second Vatican Council.

Bishop: a priest who is chosen by the pope and consecrated to govern a particular diocese. Although bishops are subject to the pope, they exercise authority in their own dioceses in their own right. They are regarded as the successors of the apostles and among their chief obligations are the duties to oversee the activities of their priests and protect the spiritual welfare of all the faithful.

Bishopaccountability.org: a World Wide Web depository of documents relating to the sexual abuse of children in the Catholic Church.

Book of Gomorrah: a dramatic and explicit outcry against forbidden clergy sexual activity written by St. Peter Damian around 1051. Peter, an ordained monk who became a bishop and a cardinal, was an ardent church reformer who railed against the sexual immorality of the clergy of his day and the irresponsibility of superiors who neglected to deal with it. He condemned all forms of homosexual behavior, especially sexual contact with young boys.

Cardinals: bishops who are chosen by the pope as advisors on account of their outstanding reputation for doctrine, morals, piety, and prudence to serve as his principal assistants and advisers in the central administration of the church. When a pope dies, the cardinals meet in a conclave to elect a successor. Although not necessarily so, most of the archbishops of the largest and most important dioceses in the United States and elsewhere are also cardinals.

Canon Law: the body of laws governing the Catholic Church. The first official and complete code was promulgated in 1917 and remained in effect until 1983 when, following the Second Vatican Council, a revised code was published. Among the 1,752 canons are laws governing the powers of the hierarchy, the administration of the sacraments, and the legal procedures to be followed when crimes are being investigated, along with the penalties to be imposed on guilty parties.

Cardinal's Oath: When a man, ordinarily a bishop, is created a cardinal he kneels before the pope and makes a vow of fidelity. Included in that oath are the following words: "never to reveal to anyone whatever has been confided in me to keep secret and the revelation of which could cause damage or dishonor to the Holy Church." (Cf. Mental Reservation.)

Catechism: an organized presentation of church teaching on faith and morals in language that is intelligible to the average layperson.

Catholic Church: the worldwide ("catholic" means universal) group of Christians who accept the pope, who is bishop of Rome, as their spiritual leader. Technically, Catholics believe Jesus Christ is "head" of the church and the pope is his vicar on earth. Catholics claim to have a direct line of succession back to the apostles and regard all other groups of Christians as somehow separated from the "one, true church." There are approximately 1.07 billion Catholics in the world and 67.3 million in the United States. In Catholic theology the church is often referred to as "the Mystical Body of Christ," "the Communion of Saints," and "People of God," a term that emphasizes the role of the lay faithful as distinct from the hierarchy.

Council: an assembly of all Catholic bishops called by the pope to discuss important issues.

Celibacy: the state of a person who is not married. All Roman Catholic priests are obliged to make a vow or promise of celibacy, that is, not to marry. This promise includes the commitment to "perfect and perpetual chastity" (Canon 277). Consequently, all Roman Catholic priests are forbidden to engage in any sexual activity. Eastern rite Catholic may marry before ordination, but not after. Religious celibacy is defined as a freely chosen, dynamic state, usually vowed, that involves an honest and sustained attempt to live without direct sexual gratification in order to serve others productively for a spiritual motive.

Censure: a term denoting a variety of church penalties that focus on the reform and reintegration of an offender rather than his punishment.

Chastity: a moral virtue that moderates sexual activity either by eliminating it altogether or keeping it in its proper place. Members of religious orders take a vow of chastity that, of its very nature implies that, because they are celibate, there is no place for sex in their lives. People who are married are expected to remain chaste by not involving themselves in immoral sexual behavior, although they, of course, are not expected to refrain from sex.

Clergy: deacons, priests, and bishops who are ordained for ministry within the Catholic Church. *Diocesan* clergy are subject to a bishop within a particular diocese; *regular* clergy belong to religious institutes such as Benedictines, Franciscans, and Jesuits.

Clericalism: a social atmosphere that regards clerics with exaggerated respect and authority.

Concubinage: the state of a man and woman living together without the benefit of matrimony.

Conference of Bishops: the U.S. Conference of Catholic Bishops (USCCB) was formed in 2001 with the merger of two national conferences—the National Conference of Catholic Bishops (NCCB) and the United States Catholic Conference (USCC)—both of which were organized in 1966 in the wake of the Second Vatican Council. While the conference cannot interfere with each bishop's direct link to Rome, it does speak on behalf of the entire body of bishops and, with the permission of Rome, it can issue directions on minor matters within dioceses, such as some liturgical innovations. Since 1966 the conferences have issued well over one hundred statements addressing internal church, moral, social, and political issues.

Confession: an admission of guilt by a penitent to a priest in the course of the sacrament of penance (now called reconciliation). Priests normally hear confessions in a *confessional* or confession box, a place that is specially reserved for that purpose in a church.

Continence: abstention from sexual activity. Roman Catholic priests and members of religious orders are required by their celibate state to be continent. In the first centuries of Christianity, the church sometimes attempted to enforce continence even on its lawfully married clergy.

Council: a formal gathering of church leaders. An *ecumenical council* is an assembly of all the bishops of the world summoned by the pope; it is the highest authority in the church; a *plenary council* is an assembly of all the bishops of a particular country.

Corpus Iuris Canonici: the Latin title of the *Body of Canon Law*, an important compendium of church laws, decrees, and commentaries that was promulgated in 1234. It was superseded in 1917 when the Code of Canon Law was promulgated.

Deacon: the lowest rank in the order of the hierarchy that governs the Catholic Church. Until recently, the diaconate was reserved for men on their way to the priesthood. Vatican II restored the permanent diaconate for men who may be married before they are ordained, but they may not marry after ordination.

Decretals: papal letters, strictly speaking written in response to a question.

Defrock: a popular term that denotes involuntary laicization by force or decree of papal authority.

Degradation: a church penalty by which a cleric is perpetually deprived of his office, benefice, dignity, and the power conferred on him by ordination. In the Middle Ages degradation was ceremonially imposed by literally stripping the offending cleric of his official garments. In recent times, dismissal with perpetual deprivation of office has taken the place of degradation.

Delict: a free and deliberate violation of a church law to which a specific penalty is attached.

Discastery: a court or judgement hall; also refers to the officials appointed to act as a court and pass judgement. A discastery is a department of the Roman Curia divided into various juridical areas (nine Congregations—i.e., The Congregation for the Doctrine of the Faith; The Congregation for Bishops; Clergy; Evangelization; Catholic Education, etc.) and three Tribunals (the Apostolic Penitentiary, Signatura, and Roman Rota) plus other entities that make up the Papal Household .

Diocese: a group of local Catholics normally living within specific territorial boundaries and led by a bishop. Dioceses are divided into parishes each with its own priest as pastor.

Duress: the existence of force or threats, physical or psychological, not necessarily explicit, that severely inhibit a person from acting freely or compel him to perform an action. Religious duress occurs, for instance, when a minor who has been sexually abused by a priest is threatened never to speak of the crime to another.

Encyclical: a formal letter of instruction from a pope to all bishops and, sometimes, the laity.

Ephebophilia: Although this is not an official psychiatric term it is commonly used to refer to sexual activity of an adult with an adolescent. Other than the age of the minor the criteria for the diagnosis of pedophilia apply to this behavior.

Episcopal: an adjective that describes anything related to a bishop.

Excommunication: an ecclesiastical penalty that bars a Catholic, lay or clerical, from participating in public worship, including the Eucharist, or to perform any official church functions.

Faculties: the authorization or right a priest has to perform certain church functions, such as hearing confessions or preaching. Permission to render these services are granted by a bishop and restricted to a particular area.

Fathers of the Church/Patristic Period: a celebrated group of Christian writers who lived between the end of the first to the end of the eighth century and whose authority in moral and dogmatic theology continues to carry special weight.

Forum, Internal and External: two levels at which judicial matters are handled within the Catholic Church. The *internal forum* pertains to the realm of conscience where the most sensitive information is shared between a person and a priest as in the confession of sins. Information shared in this forum cannot be revealed by the priest who receives it, for any reason. Matters pertaining to the internal forum are never recorded or written down in any way. The *external forum* is the level at which the church exercises its power to govern. Matters handled in the external forum include all investigations into allegations of impropriety, the commission of canonical crimes, and all judicial or administrative processes related to such allegations.

Grace: a free gift from God that enables people to participate in the life of God. Catholic theology sometimes refers to grace as "God's favor." *Sanctifying* grace makes people holy or pleasing to God, *actual* grace enables people to be good and avoid evil.

Grooming: the behavior used to condition a minor for sexual contact. This can include ingratiating oneself with the victim's family, giving special attention, gifts, or even alcohol to the prospective victim. Sexual abuse begins with the grooming process and can be augmented by promises or threats.

Hierarchy: the three-tier ranking of bishops, priests, and deacons, who govern the Catholic Church under the authority of the pope, the Bishop of Rome. The term is also used to denote a local governing body, such as the U.S. hierarchy.

Holy Office: established in 1542 as the "Holy Office of the Inquisition" to deal with churchwide heresy. Pius X (d. 1914) changed its name to the "Congregation of the Holy Office." Pope Paul VI (d. 1978) gave it a more positive twist in 1965 and a new title "Congregation for the Doctrine of the Faith," responsible for promoting and safeguarding sound doctrine and morals.

Homosexual: a term used either to describe the sexual identity of a person whose biological sex urges are directed to his or her same sex or to identify sexual behavior between partners of the same sex.

Incardination: the process whereby every secular priest is affiliated with his diocese.

Inquisition: a special ecclesiastical tribunal established in the thirteenth century to investigate and prosecute heretics, who were then handed over to the civil authorities for punishment. In 1252 Pope Innocent IV licensed torture as a way of forcing heretics to confess. The Spanish Inquisition remained active until 1834.

Interdict: a punishment, or censure, imposed on Catholics who commit particularly serious offences. People under interdict are deprived of the sacraments and forbidden to participate in church services.

Laicization: the process whereby a member of the hierarchy is "reduced" by the Vatican to the ranks of the laity. It can be voluntarily requested by a cleric, or imposed by authority as punishment for an exceptionally serious ecclesiastical crime.

Laity: all members of the Catholic Church who are not ordained or have taken vows to live in a religious institute. They constitute the vast majority of the membership of the church.

Mandatory Celibacy: the Catholic Church requires every priest, at the time of his ordination, to make a promise to his bishop that he will not marry and will keep "perfect and perpetual chastity."

Mental Reservation: a tactic used by a person who is caught between an obligation to keep a secret and a duty to tell the truth. Catholic moral theology allows a person caught in such a dilemma to use misleading words to deceive another so long as a deliberate lie is not told. This is commonly employed in order to avoid a greater harm or to deny information to one judged not to have a right to the truth (Cf. Cardinal's oath).

Minor: in canon law, a minor is a person under sixteen years of age, but, a 2001 notice from the Vatican raised the canonical age for victims of sexual abuse to eighteen.

Military Vicariate: now properly called the Archdiocese for the Military Services (AMS), is an authentic diocese as defined by the Code of Canon Law. It serves active duty military personnel and their families and residents of Veterans Administration facilities. The AMS can assign duties to a priest, known as military chaplains, attached to it, but officially they remain incardinated in their own dioceses or subjects of their own religious institutes.

Monk: a man who has taken vows of poverty, chastity, and obedience to live in a monastery subject to an abbot and a rule such as the Rule of St. Benedict (e.g., Benedictines, Trappists). The term is popularly, but incorrectly, applied to Friars who are members of certain religious orders living in priories (e.g., Franciscans, Dominicans).

Motu Proprio: an instruction, normally concerning an administrative matter, issued by the pope on his own initiative.

NAMBLA: The North American Man/Boy Love Association, is a U.S.-based group that seeks to eliminate age-based restrictions on sexual behavior. Critics say its aim is to legalize the sexual abuse of children.

Papal Nuntio: a person who represents the pope to the church, hierarchy, and civil government of a nation. The Catholic Church and the United States established diplomatic relations in 1984, and the nuntio lives in Washington, D.C. Although each bishop has a direct connection with the pope, much of the business of the church is ordinarily conducted through the nuntiature.

Pedophilia: is a psychiatric designation of an adult who has intense sexual attractions, urges, fantasies (lasting six months) or behaviors involving a prepubescent boy or girl—usually under thirteen years old. The adult must be at least sixteen years old or five years senior to the child.

Pederasty: in early Greece designated a man's love of boys. It often connotes anal intercourse with the boy as the passive partner.

Penance: one of the seven sacraments of the Catholic Church. Penance is sometimes referred to simply as confession but, especially in recent times, it is called the sacrament of reconciliation. It requires the confession of sins to a priest usually in private (with sincere repentance and firm resolve not to repeat the offense) and the recitation by the priest of the formula of absolution. The priest also imposes a penance, such as an obligation to say certain prayers or perform a good deed, as a token of the penitent accepting punishment for the sin committed.

Penitential Books: lists of sins with appropriate punishments that first appeared in the Celtic church in the sixth century. They were used as guides to priests hearing confessions. They are usually ascribed, rightly or wrongly, to important personages or monastic settlements of the period.

Penitentiary: a Catholic priest who has authority to forgive especially serious sins and censures. The Apostolic Penitentiary in Rome is a cardinal with power to issue decisions on questions of conscience and grant absolutions and dispensations that canon law reserves to him alone.

Pontifical Secret: the strictest form of secrecy in church law. It is imposed on everybody who participates in an official investigation into allegations of sexual abuse of minors by a priest.

Anybody who violates it is automatically excommunicated and can be reinstated by none other than the pope in person.

Pope: the *de facto* supreme ruler of the Catholic Church. He is called Bishop of Rome, the Vicar of Jesus Christ, the Successor of St. Peter, and Servant of the Servants of God.

Priest: a man who is ordained to the priesthood and given power and authority to administer the sacraments and serve the needs of the church. All priests are subject either to a bishop (in the case of a diocesan or secular priest) or the religious institute of which they are members.

Religious Institute: a group of men or women with vows of poverty, chastity, and obedience and sharing a common life. The chief divisions of religious institutes are monastic and mendicant orders, societies, and congregations.

Order: an organized group of men in solemn vows of poverty, chastity, and obedience, living a common life and ruled by a superior.

Sacrament: a sacred ceremony that affects what it signifies. For instance, a penitent who confesses sins to a priest is forgiven by reason of the recitation of the formula of absolution.

Scholasticism: a system of inquiry that developed in the universities of Europe in the eleventh century and flourished until the sixteeth. It questioned and applied the rules of logic to ancient and authoritative texts.

Seminary: an undergraduate- or graduate-level school where candidates for the Catholic priesthood are trained.

Servants of the Paraclete: a religious institute of men founded in 1947 to serve and treat priests with problems. They operate a number of treatment centers in the United States and England for priests with substance abuse or psychosexual problems.

Sexual Abuse: any sexual activity between two people that is either illegal or not welcomed by one of the parties. Clergy sexual abuse of a minor involves sexual activity by a cleric—a deacon, priest, or bishop—with a person, male or female, under the age of eighteen.

Sin: an offense against God. Catholics divide sin into *mortal sin,* a grievous offense deserving everlasting punishment in hell unless it is forgiven in the sacrament of penance, and *venial sin,* a less serious offense deserving limited punishment in purgatory. Venial sins can be forgiven without confession.

SNAP: the Survivors Network of Those Abused by Priests is the nation's largest, oldest, and most active support group for women and men wounded by religious authority figures, priests, ministers, bishops, deacons, or nuns.

Sodomy: commonly used to denote sexual activity with anal or oral penetration primarily between men. However, church documents have used the same term to denote sexual relations with animals or any unnatural sexual activity between members of the same or opposite sex.

Solicitation: an invitation to sexual contact in word, gesture, or any indication by a priest to a person who intends to go to confession to him. The violation may be under the pretext of confession, in the place of, or with the promise of confession. Punishment for such behavior by church law should be at least suspension of the priest's faculties and dismissal to the lay state in more serious cases. The church has frequently promulgated documents concerned with this particular violation (Cf. Chronology).

Stuprum: a Latin term denoting any form of sexual defilement that involves force. Often this term is used to denote the corruption of youth.

Suspension: an ecclesiastical penalty that partially or totally restricts a priest's authority to govern the church or his ability to perform the sacraments.

Synod: an assembly of bishops representing their national conferences and others selected by the pope to advise him on important issues affecting the whole church. A *diocesan* synod is an assembly of priests, religious, and laypeople called by a bishop to advise him on matters affecting a local diocese.

Vatican City: a forty-four-acre sovereign state in Rome established in 1929 by the Lateran Treaty with Italy. The pope resides in the Vatican and most of the administration of the Catholic Church is conducted within its boundaries.

Virginity: the state of a person who has vowed perpetual abstinence from sex or the designation of one who has not had sexual intercourse.

Voice of the Faithful: a Boston-based organization founded in the wake of the sexual abuse crisis to promotes greater lay control of the Catholic Church. It aims to support victims of clergy sexual abuse and shape structural changes within the Catholic Church.

Vow: a public promise to perform a meritorious action or conduct a particular style of life. The most common religious connotation applies to the vows of poverty, chastity, and obedience taken by a member of a religious institute.

Bibliography of Selected Sources

Books: General

Abbott, Elizabeth. 1999. *A History of Celibacy*. New York: Scribner.

Allport, Gordon. 1954. *The Individual and His Religion*. New York: The MacMillan Company.

Bailey, Derrick. 1955. *Homosexuality and the Western Christian Tradition*. London: Longmans, Green and Company.

Balboni, Barbara Susan. September 1998. *Through the Lens of the Organizational Culture Perspective: A Descriptive Study of American Catholic Bishops' Understanding of Clergy Sexual Molestation and Abuse of Children and Adolescents*. Ph.D Dissertation. Law, Policy, and Society. Boston: Northeastern University.

Bell, Roy, and Stanley Grenz. 1995. *Betrayal of Trust: Sexual Misconduct in the Pastorate*. Downers Grove, Ill.: Intervarsity Press.

Benyei, Candace Reed. 1998. *Understanding Clergy Misconduct in Religious Systems: Scapegoating, Family Secrets, and the Abuse of Power*. New York: Haworth Pastoral Press.

Berry, Jason. 1992. *Lead Us Not into Temptation*. New York: Doubleday.

Berry, Jason, and Gerald Renner. 2004. *Vows of Silence*. New York: Free Press.

Bishops Committee on Priestly Life and Ministry. 1985. *The Health of American Catholic Priests: A Report and a Study*. Washington, D.C.: United States Catholic Conference.

Booth, Leo. 1991. *When God Becomes a Drug*. New York: Putnam.
_____. 1998. *The God Game: It's Your Move*. Long Beach, Calif.: SCP Press.

Boston Globe. Investigative Staff. 2002. *Betrayal: The Crisis in the Catholic Church.* Boston, New York, London: Little Brown and Company.

Brown, Joanne Carlson, and Carole Bohn. 1989. *Christianity, Patriarchy and Abuse.* Cleveland: Pilgrim Press.

Burkett, Elinor, and Frank Bruni. 1994. *A Gospel of Shame.* New York: Viking Press.

Carnes, Patrick. 1984. *The Sexual Addiction.* Minneapolis: CompCare Publications.

_____. 1997. *Sexual Anorexia.* Center City, Minn.: Hazelden.

_____. 1997. *The Betrayal Bond.* Deerfield Beach, Fla.: Health Communications.

Carroll, James. 2002. *Toward a New Catholic Church.* Boston: Houghton Mifflin Company.

Chirban, John T., ed. 1994. *Clergy Sexual Misconduct: Orthodox Christian Perspectives.* Brookline, Mass.: Hellenic College Press.

Coldrey, Barry. 1994. *The Scheme: The Christian Brothers and Childcare in Western Australia.* Melbourne: Argyle-Pacific.

_____. 2000. *Religious Life without Integrity.* Melbourne: Tamanirak Press.

Collins, Paul. 1997. *Papal Power.* London: Harper Collins.

Committee on the Liturgy. August 10, 2000. *The 2000 Revision of the Institutio Generalis Missalis Romani.* Washington, D.C.: U.S. Catholic Conference.

Congar, Yves. 1957. *Lay People in the Church: A Study for a Theology of the Laity.* Westminster Md.: Newman Press.

Congregation for Catholic Education. April 11, 1974. *A Guide to Formation in Priestly Celibacy.* Washington, D.C.: U.S. Catholic Conference.

Cozzens, Donald. 2000. *The Changing Face of the Priesthood.* Collegeville, Minn.: Liturgical Press.

_____. 2002. *Sacred Silence: Denial and Crisis in the Church.* Collegeville, Minn.: Liturgical Press.

Crewdson, John. 1988. *By Silence Betrayed: Sexual Abuse of Children in America.* Boston: Little, Brown and Company.

Crosby, Michael. 1991. *The Dysfunctional Church: Addiction and Codependency in the Family of Catholicism*. Notre Dame University: Ave Maria Press.

DeBlassie, Paul. 1992. *Toxic Christianity*. New York: Crossroads.

Dinter, Paul. 2003. *The Other Side of the Altar*. New York: Farrar, Strauss and Giroux.

Eberley, Ron. 2002. *The Unnatural Law of Celibacy*. New York: Continuum.

Faulkner, Mary. 2003. *Supreme Authority: Understanding Power in the Catholic Church*. Sussex: Alpha Press.

Fichter, Joseph, S.J. 1965. *Priest and People*. New York: Sheed and Ward.

_____. 1968. *America's Forgotten Priests*. New York: Harper and Row.

_____. 1974. *The Organization Man in the Church*. Cambridge, Mass.: Schenkman.

_____. 1982. *The Rehabilitation of Clergy Alcoholics*. New York: Human Sciences Press.

Flynn, Kathryn. 2003. *Sexual Abuse of Women by Members of the Clergy*. Jefferson, N.C.: Mcfarland and Company.

Fortune, Marie. 1989. *Is Nothing Sacred*. San Francisco: Harper.

Frawley, Mary Gail, and Jody Messler. 1994. *Treating the Adult Survivor of Childhood Sexual Abuse*. New York: Basic Books.

Frawley O'Dea, Mary Gail, and Virginia Goldner, eds. 2004. *Studies in Gender and Sexuality*. Special Issue: *The Sexual Abuse Crisis in the Catholic Church*. Volume 5, Numbers 1 and 2. Hillsdale, N.J.: The Analytic Press.

Friberg, Nils, and Mark Laaser. 1998. *Before the Fall. Preventing Pastoral Sexual Abuse*. Collegeville, Minn.: The Liturgical Press.

Gardner, Richard. *Sex Abuse Hysteria*. Cresskill, N.J.: Creative Therapeutics.

Gerdes, Louise, ed. 2003. *Child Sexual Abuse in the Catholic Church*. San Diego: Greenhaven Press.

Gibson, David. 2003. *The Coming Catholic Church*. San Francisco: Harper.

Gonsiorek, John. 1990. *Male Sexual Abuse.* Thousand Oaks, Calif.: Sage Publications.

_____. 1995. *Breach of Trust.* Thousand Oaks, Calif.: Sage Publications.

Grace, Sonja. 1999. *Garlands from Ashes: Healing from Clergy Abuse.* Wanganui, Australia: Garlands.

Gramick, Jeannine, ed. 1989. *Homosexuality in the Priesthood and the Religious Life.* New York: Crossroads.

Granfield, Patrick. 1987. *The Limits of the Papacy.* New York: Crossroads Books.

Hall, Douglas T., and Benjamin Schneider. 1973. *Organizational Climates and Careers: The Work Lives of Priests.* New York: Seminar Press.

Harris, Jerry, and Melody Milam. 1997. *Serpents in the Manger: Overcoming Abusive Christianity.* New York: Barricade Books.

Harris, M. 1990. *Unholy Order: Tragedy at Mount Cashel.* Ontario: Viking Press.

Henton, Darcy, and David McCann. 1995. *Boys Don't Cry.* Toronto: Stewart.

Hopkins, Nancy, and Mark Laaser. 1995. *Restoring the Soul of a Church.* Collegeville, Minn.: The Liturgical Press.

Horst, Elisabeth. 1998. *Recovering the Lost Self: Shame Healing for Victims of Clergy Sexual Abuse.* Collegeville, Minn.: The Liturgical Press.

_____. 2000. *Questions and Answers about Clergy Sexual Misconduct.* Collegeville, Minn.: Liturgical Press.

Horton, Anne, and Judith Williamson. 1988. *Abuse and Religion: When Praying Isn't Enough.* New York: Lexington.

Hough, Joseph, and Barbara Wheeler, eds. 1988. *Beyond Clericalism.* Atlanta: Scholars Press.

Hughes, Everett C., Salley Whelan Cassidy, and John D. Donovan. 1972. *An Evaluation of the Catholic Priest in the United States: Sociological Investigations.* Washington, D.C.: U.S. Catholic Conference.

Inglis, Tom. 1998. *Moral Monopoly: The Rise and Fall of the Catholic Church in Modern Ireland.* Dublin: University of Dublin Press.

Jenkins, Philip. 1996. *Pedophiles and Priests*. New York: Oxford University Press.

_____. 1998. *Moral Panic: Changing Concepts of the Child Molester in Modern America*. New Haven: Yale University Press.

Johnson, David, and Jeff Van Vonderen. 1991. *The Subtle Power of Spiritual Abuse*. Minneapolis: Bethany Press.

Jordan, Mark. 1997. *The Invention of Sodomy in Christian Theology*. Chicago: The University of Chicago Press.

Karlen, Arlo. 1971. *Sexuality and Homosexuality*. New York: W.W. Norton & Co.

Kempe, Ruth. 1984. *The Common Secret: Sexual Abuse of Children and Adolescents*. New York: W.H. Freeman.

Kennedy, Eugene. 2001. *The Unhealed Wound: The Church and Human Sexuality*. New York: St. Martin's Press.

Kennedy, Eugene. 1988. *Tomorrow's Catholics: Yesterday's Church. The Two Cultures of American Catholicism*. Ligouri, Mo.: Triumph Books.

Kennedy, Eugene. 1972. *The Catholic Priest in the United States: Psychological Investigations*. Washington, D.C.: U.S. Catholic Conference.

King, K. 1988. *Images of the Feminine in Gnosticism*. Philadelphia: Trinity Press International.

Kung, Hans. 2001. *The Catholic Church: A Short History*. New York: The Modern Library.

Kurtz, Lester R. 1986. *The Politics of Heresy: The Modernist Crisis in Roman Catholicism*. Berkeley: University of California Press.

Laghi, Pio. 1998. *Vocations to the Priesthood*. Vatican City.

Levine, Judith. 2002. *Harmful to Minors: The Perils of Protecting Children from Sex*. Minneapolis: University of Minnesota Press.

Lobinger, Fritz. 1998. *Like His Brothers and Sisters: Ordaining Community Leaders*. New York: Crossroads.

Louden, Stephen, and Leslie Francis. 2003. *The Naked Parish Priest*. New York: Continuum.

Manning, Joanna. 2002. *Take Back the Truth: Confronting Papal Power and the Religious Right.* New York: Crossroads Publishing.

McKenzie, John. 1966. *Authority in the Church.* New York: Sheed and Ward.

Money, John. 1986. *Love Maps.* New York: Irvington Publishers, Inc.

Neenan, Benedict. 2000. *Thomas Verner Moore.* Paulist Press, Mahwah, N.J.

O'Conaill, Sean. 1999. *Scattering the Proud.* Dublin: The Columbia Press.

Phillips, Donald. 2002. *Unto Us a Child: Abuse and Deception in the Catholic Church.* Irving, Tex.: Tapestry Press,.

Plante, Thomas, ed. 2004. *Sin Against the Innocents: Sexual Abuse by Priests and the Role of the Catholic Church.* Westport, Conn.: Praeger.

_____. 1999. *Bless Me Father for I Have Sinned: Perspectives on Sexual Abuse Committed by Roman Catholic Priests.* Westport, Conn.: Praeger.

Poling, James Newton. 1991. *The Abuse of Power. A Theological Problem.* Nashville: Abingdon Press.

Porter, Muriel. 2003. *Sex, Power and the Clergy.* Victoria, Australia: Hardie Grant Books.

Raphael, Marty. 1996. *Spiritual Vampires.* Santa Fe: The Message Company.

Rose, Michael. 2002. *Goodbye Good Men.* Washington, D.C.: Regnery Publishing, Inc.

Rossetti, Stephen. 1990. *Slayer of the Soul.* Mystic, Conn.: Twenty-Third Publications.

_____. 1996. *A Tragic Grace.* Collegeville, Minn.: The Liturgical Press.

Rudy, Kathy. 1997. *Sex and the Church: Gender, Homosexuality and the Transformation of Christian Ethics.* Boston: Beacon Press.

Rutter, Peter, M.D. 1989. *Sex in the Forbidden Zone.* New York: Fawcett Columbine.

Sanchez, Jose. 1972. *Anticlericalism: A Brief History.* Notre Dame: University of Notre Dame Press.

Schillebeeckx, Edward. 1971. *World and Church.* New York: Sheed and Ward.

Schoenherr, Richard A. 2002. *Goodbye Father: The Celibate Male Priesthood and the Future of the Catholic Church.* Oxford: Oxford University Press.

Sennott, Charles. 1992. *Broken Covenant.* New York: Simon & Schuster.

Shupe, Anson. 1995. *In the Name of All That's Holy.* London: Praeger.

_____. 1998. *Wolves within the Fold.* New Brunswick, Conn.: Rutgers University Press.

_____. 2000. *Bad Pastors: Clergy Misconduct in Modern America.* New York: University Press.

Sipe, A.W. Richard. 1990. *A Secret World: Sexuality and the Search for Celibacy.* New York: Brunner-Mazel.

_____. 1995. *Sex, Priests and Power.* New York: Brunner-Mazel.

_____. 1996. *Celibacy.* Ligouri, Mo.: Triumph Press.

_____. 2003. *Celibacy in Crisis: A Secret World Revisited.* New York: Brunner-Routledge.

Sobo, Elisa, and Sandra Bell, eds. 2001. *Celibacy, Culture and Society.* Madison: University of Wisconsin Press.

Steinfels, Peter. 2003. *A People Adrift.* New York: Simon and Schuster.

Stiles, Hilary. 1987. *The Assault on Innocence.* Albuquerque: B & K Publishers.

Sullivan, Francis, S.J. 2001. *From Apostles to Bishops. The Development of the Episcopacy in the Early Church.* New York: The Newman Press.

Thigpen, Thomas, ed. 2002. *Shaken by Scandals: Catholics Speak Out about Priests' Sexual Abuse.* Atlanta: Charis Books.

Vatican. August 13, 1997. *Instruction on Certain Questions Regarding the Collaboration of the Non-Ordained Faithful in the Sacred Ministry of the Priest.* Vatican City: Libreria Editrice Vaticana.

Wagner, Richard. 1981. *Gay Catholic Priests: A Study of Cognitive and Dissonance.* San Francisco: Specific Press.

Weigel, George. 2002. *The Courage to Be Catholic.* New York: Basic Books.

Wills, Garry. 2000. *Papal Sin.* New York: Doubleday.

Wolf, James. 1989. *Gay Priests.* San Francisco: Harper and Row.

Articles: General

Abraham, W. Nicholas. 1994. "The Significance of Religious Messages in Sexual Addiction." *Sexual Addiction and Compulsivity: The Journal of Treatment and Prevention* 1: 159–184.

Altobelli, Dr. Tom. May 1–2, 2003. "Institutional Processes for Dealing with Allegations of Child Sexual Abuse." Paper Presented at Australian Institute of Criminology, Adelaide, NSW.

Ames, M. Ashley, and David Houston. 1990. "Legal, Social and Biological Definitions of Pedophilia." *Archives of Sexual Behavior* 19: 333–342.

Anderson, Jeffrey. September 18, 2000. "Gods and Monsters: It's Time for the Catholic Church to Reform Its Sexual Abuse Policies." *California Law Business.*

Arnold, John H. 1996. "Clergy Sexual Malpractice." *University of Florida Journal of Law and Public Policy* 25.

Baars, Conrad, M.D. 1971. "The Role of the Church in the Causation, Treatment and Prevention of the Crisis in the Priesthood." Private.

Ballotta, Karen Ann. Fall 1994. "Losing Its Soul: How the Cipolla Case Limits the Catholic Church's Ability to Discipline Sexually Abusive Priests." *Emory Law Journal:* 1431.

Beal, John. 1992. "Doing What One Can: Canon Law and Clerical Sexual Misconduct." *Jurist* 52: 592–633.

Bell, Gregory. October 1992. "The Sexual Abuse of Children: A Violation of Trust." Unpublished paper presented in Milwaukee at the 1992 SCA Convention.

Benson, Gordon. 1994. "Sexual Behavior by Male Clergy with Adult Female Counselees: Systemic and Situational

Themes." *Sexual Addiction and Compulsivity: The Journal of Treatment and Prevention* 1: 103–118.

Berthelot du Chesney, C. 1967. "Anticlericalism." *New Catholic Encyclopedia* Vol. I. New York: 618–620.

Blanchard, Gerald T. 1991. "Sexually Abusive Clergymen: A Conceptual Framework for Intervention and Recovery." *Pastoral Psychology* 39: 237–245.

Byrnes, Timothy. 1993. "The Politics of the American Catholic Hierarchy." *Political Science Quarterly* 108.3: 497–514.

Cafardi, Nicholas. 1993. "Stones Instead of Bread: Sexually Abusive Priests in Ministry." *Studia Canonica* 27: 145–172.

Capps, Donald. 1992. "Religion and Child Abuse: Perfect Together." *Journal for the Scientific Study of Religion* 31.1: 1–14.

Cholij, Roman M.T. 1987. "The *Lex Continentiae* and the Impediment of Orders." *Studia Canonica* 21: 391–418.

Chopko, Mark, and Brent Stinski. 1992. "Restoring Trust and Faith: Human Rights Abuses Do Happen." *Human Rights* 19: 22–26.

Cimbolic, Peter. 1992. "The Identification and Treatment of Sexual Disorders and the Priesthood." *Jurist* 52: 598–614.

Clark, Donald. 14 April 1993. "Sexual Abuse in Church: The Law Steps In." *Christian Century* 110/12: 396–398.

Connors, Canice. May 1992. "Priests and Pedophilia: A Silence that Needs Breaking." *America* 9: 400–401.

Cooper-White, Pamela. February 20, 1991. "Soul-Stealing. Power Relations in Pastoral Sexual Abuse." *The Christian Century*.

Coville, W. J. 1968. "Basic issues in the development and administration of a psychological assessment program for the religious life." In Coville, W. J., D'Arcy, P. F., McCarthy, T. N. and Rooney, J. J. (Eds.) *Assessment of candidates for the religious life: Basic psychological issues and procedures.* Washington, D.C.: Center for Applied Research in the Apostolate.

Cruz, Eduardo. 1991. "Comment: When the Shepherd Preys on the Flock: Clergy Sexual Exploitation and the Search for Solutions." *Florida State University Law Review* 19: 499–524.

Cullinane, Bishop Peter. 1997. "Clericalism: Avoidable Damage to the Church." *Australasian Catholic Review.*

D'Avack, Pietro Agostino. 1953. "L'Omosessualita nell diritto canonico." *Ulisse* 7.

Deibel, David. 1998. "Saving Grace: Defending Priests Accused of Sexual Misconduct." *San Francisco Attorney* 24: 14–17.

Doerr, Edd. Sept–Oct. 1993. "The Political Power of the Catholic Church." *The Humanist*: 16.

Doyle, Thomas. January and February, 1987. "The Clergy in Court: Clergy Malpractice." *The Priest.*

_____. July and August, 1990. "The Clergy in Court: Recent Developments." *The Priest.*

_____. 1990. "The Rights of Priests Accused of Sexual Misconduct." *Studia Canonica* 24.

_____. 1994. "Healing the Pain." *The Blue Book. Annual Proceedings of the National Catholic Council on Alcohol and Drug Related Problems.*

_____. Dec. 2002/Jan. 2003. "Abrogation of Trust in the Catholic Church." *Association of Humanistic Psychology Journal.*

_____. 2003. "Roman Catholic Clericalism, Religious Duress and Clergy Sexual Abuse." *Pastoral Psychology* 51.

Dreese, John J. 22 April 1994. "The Other Victims of Priest Pedophilia." *Commonweal*: 11.13.

Ellens, J. Harold. 1997. "Homosexuality in Biblical Perspective." *Pastoral Psychology* 46: 35–53.

Fain, Constance Frisby. 1991. "Clergy Malpractice: Liability for Negligent Counseling and Sexual Misconduct." *Mississippi College Law Review* 12: 97–141.

Fedje, Jill. 1990. "Liability for Sexual Abuse: The Anomalous Immunity of Churches." *Law and Inequality* 9: 133–161.

Fenton, Zanita. 2001. "Faith in Justice: Fiduciaries, Malpractice & Sexual Abuse by Clergy." *Michigan Journal of Gender and Law* 45 (8 Mich. J. Gender & L 45).

Ferme, Brian. 2002. "Graviora Delicta: the apostolic letter M.P., sacramentorum sanctitatis tutela." In Suchecki, Zbignew, editor, *Il Processo Penale Canonico.* Rome. Lateran University Press 365–382.

Fichter, Joseph, S.J. 1963. "Anticlericalism in the American
   Catholic Culture" *The Critic* 21: 11–15.
Flynn, Frederick. 1953. "Clericalism, Anticlericalism."
   Commonweal 56: 43–47.
Fischer, Kenneth E. 1989. "Respondeat Superior Redux: May a
   Diocesan Bishop Be Vicariously Liable for the Intentional
   Torts of His Priests." *Studia Canonica* 23: 119–149.
Fortune, Marie. 2000. "Spare us the false shepherds." *Siecus
   Report* 28: 14–18.
Francis, P.C., and N.R. Turner. 1995. "Sexual Misconduct within the
   Christian Church: Who Are the Perpetrators and Those
   They Victimize?" *Counseling and Values* 39: 218–227.
Gaboury, Dennis. 1993. "Child Sexual Abuse in the Roman
   Catholic Church. The Victims' Perspective."
   Unpublished paper. Baltimore.
Garrity, Robert M. 1993. "Spiritual and Canonical Values in
   Mandatory Celibacy." *Studia Canonica* 27: 217–260.
Graziano, Sue Ganske. 1991. "Clergy Malpractice." *Whittier Law
   Review* 12: 349–355.
Griffin, Bertram. 1991. "The reassignment of a cleric who has
   been professionally evaluated and treated for sexual mis-
   conduct with minors: canonical considerations." *Jurist*
   51: 326–339.
Hamilton, Marci. Spring 2002. "Religion, the Rule of Law, and
   the Good of the Whole: A View from the Clergy." *The
   Journal of Law and Politics* Vol. XVIII, No 2: 387–443.
Hamm, John Patrick. 1995. "In Defense of the Church." *University
   of Louisville Journal of Family Law* 33: 705–721.
Haywood, Thomas, Kravitz, Howard, and Wasyliw, Orest. 1996.
   "Cycle of abuse and psychopathology in cleric and noncleric molesters of children and adolescents." *Child
   Abuse and Neglect* 20: 1233–1244.
_____. 1996. "Psychological aspects of sexual functioning
   among cleric and noncleric alleged sex offenders." *Child
   Abuse and Neglect* 20: 527–537.
Hill, Alexander D. 1990. "A current church-state battleground:
   requiring clergy to report child abuse." *Journal of Church
   and State* 32: 795–811.

Irons, Richard, M.D. and Laaser, Mark, Ph.D. 1994. "The Abduction of Fidelity: Sexual Exploitation by Clergy-Experience with Inpatient Assessment." *Sexual Addiction and Compulsivity* 1: 119–129.

Isley, P.J. 1997. "Child Sexual Abuse and the Catholic Church: An Historical and Contemporary Review." *Pastoral Psychology* 45: 277–299.

Isley, Paul J., and Peter Isley. 1990. "The Sexual Abuse of male Children by Church Personnel: Intervention and Prevention." *Pastoral Psychology* 39: 85–99.

Jukes, John. 2002. "Canonical Considerations of the Motu Proprio *Sacramentorum sanctitatis tutela*." *Canon Law Society Newsletter*. England. Canon Law Society of Great Britain and Ireland. 129: 26–33.

Kaiser, Hilary. 1996. "Clergy Sex Abuse in U.S. Mainline Churches." *American Studies International* 34: 30–43.

Laasser, M. 1991. "Sexual Addiction and Clergy." *Pastoral Psychology* 39: 213–235.

LeGoff, Jacques. 1984. "L'amour et la sexualite." *L'histoire* 63: 52–59.

Loftus, John Allen. December 1, 1990. "A Question of Disillusionment: Sexual Abuse among the Clergy." *America*.

Loftus, J., and R. Carmago, 1993. "Treating the Clergy." *Annals Of Sex Research* 6: 287–303.

McIntyre, John P., S.J. 1995. "Optional Priestly Celibacy." *Studia Canonica* 29: 103–154.

McLaughlin, Barbara. 1994. "Devastated spirituality: the impact of clergy sexual abuse on the survivor's relationship with God and the church." *Sexual Addiction and Compulsivity: The Journal of Treatment and Prevention* 1: 145–158.

McMenamin, Robert. 1985. "Clergy Malpractice." *Cases and Comment* 90.

Mirkin, Harris. 1999. "The Pattern of Sexual Politics: Feminism, Homosexuality and Pedophilia." *Journal of Homosexuality* 37.

Mitchell, Mary Hart. 1987. "Must Clergy Tell? Child Abuse Reporting Requirement versus Clergy Privilege." *Minnesota Law Review* 71: 723–825.

Moore, Thomas Verner. 1936. "Insanity in priests and religious: I The rate of insanity in priests and religious." *American Ecclesiastical Review* 95: 485–498.

_____. 1936. "Insanity in priests and religious: II The detection of pre-psychotics who apply for admission to the priesthood or religious communities." *American Ecclesiastical Review* 95: 601–613.

Morey, Anne-Janine. Oct. 5, 1988. "Blaming Women for the Sexually Abusive Male Pastor." *The Christian Century.*

Morrisey, Francis. 1992. "Procedure to Be Followed in Cases of Alleged Sexual Misconduct by a Priest." *Studia Canonica* 26: 39–74.

Morrisey, Francis, O.M.I. 2001. "Addressing the Issue of Clergy Abuse." *Studia Canonica* 35: 403–420.

O'Brien, Raymond. 1988. "Pedophilia: the legal predicament of clergy." *The Journal of Contemporary Health Law and Policy* 4: 91–154.

O'Reilly, J.T. and J.M. Strasser. 1994. "Clergy Sexual Misconduct: Confronting the Difficult Constitutional and Institutional Liability Claims." *St. Thomas Law Review* 7: 31–73.

Paulson, Jerome. 1988. "The Clinical and Canonical Considerations in Cases of Pedophilia." *Studia Canonica* 22: 77–124.

Perciaccante, Marianne. Fall 1996. "The Courts and Canon Law." *Cornell Journal of Law and Public Policy* (6 Cornell J.L. & Pub Pol'y 171).

Plante, T. G. 1996. "Catholic priests who sexually abuse minors: why do we hear so much yet know so little." *Pastoral Psychology* 44: 305–10.

Plante, Thomas, Manuel Gerdenio, and Curtis Bryant. 1996. "Personality and Cognitive Functioning Among Hospitalized Sexual Offending Roman Catholic Priests." *Pastoral Psychology* 45: 129–139.

Provost, James. 1995. "Offenses against the Sixth Commandment: Towards a Canonical Analysis of Canon 1395." *Jurist* 55: 632–663.

_____. 1992. "Some canonical considerations relative to clerical sexual misconduct." *Jurist* 52: 615–641.

Quade, Vicki and Ellen Simon. 1992. "Unholy wars: human rights interview." *Human Rights* 19: 18–23.

Rigali, Norbert. 1994. "Church Responses to Pedophilia." *Theological Studies* 55: 124–139.

Rossi, Mary Ann. 1993. "The Legitimation of the Abuse of Women in Christianity." *Feminist Theology* 4: 57–63.

Ruether, Rosemary. 1974. "Misogynism and Virginal Feminism in the Fathers of the Church." In Ruether, R., editor, *Religion and Sexism.* (New York: Simon and Schuster).

Russell, Dawn. 1992. "Paedophilia: The Criminal Responsibility of Canada's Churches." *Dalhousie Law Journal* 15: 380–427.

Ruzicka, M.F. 1997. "Predictor variables in clergy pedophiles." *Psychological Reports* 81: 589–590.

Schoenherr, Richard A. 7 Apr 1995. "Numbers Don't Lie: A Priesthood in Irreversible Decline." *Commonweal:* 11–14.

Schoenherr, Richard A. and Lawrence Young. 1990. "Quitting the Clergy: Resignations in the Roman Catholic Priesthood." *Journal for the Scientific Study of Religion* 29-4: 463–481.

Serritella, James. 1990. "Issues Related to Clergy/Church Misconduct." *Covenant Publications.*

Sheer, R. 1991. "A canon, a choirboy and homosexuality in late sixteenth century Italy: a case study." *Journal of Homosexuality* 21: 1–22.

Sipe, A.W. Richard. 1994. "The Problem of Sexual Trauma and Addiction in the Catholic Church." *Sexual Addiction and Compulsivity: The Journal of Treatment and Prevention* 1: 130–137.

Stauffer, Ian, R, and Christian B. Hyde. 1993. "The sins of the fathers: vicarious liability of churches." *Ottawa Law Review* 24: 561–577.

Stecher, Reinhold, Bishop of Innsbruck. "Thoughts on the Decree on Lay Ministers."

Steinhauser, Karen. 1993. "Legal Issues in Sexual Abuse and Domestic Violence." *Pastoral Psychology* 41: 321–336.

Taylor, Charles. 1960. "Clericalism." *Cross Currents* 10: 327–336.

The Humanist. Sept–Oct 1993 "Vatican Interests versus Public Interest." pp. 33–37.

Tuohey, John. 1995. "The correct interpretation of Canon 1395: the use of the Sixth commandment in the moral tradition from Trent to the present day." *Jurist* 55: 592–631.

Vaughan, Richard, S.J. 1997. "Adult Effects of Childhood Sexual Abuse." *Human Development* 18: 38–42.

Versaldi, G. 2002. "Aspetti psicologici degli abusi sessuali perpetrati da chierici." *Periodica* 91: 29–48.

Villiers, Janice. 1996. "Clergy Malpractice Revisited: Liability for Sexual Misconduct in the Counseling Relationship." *Denver University Law Review* 1,3.

Wallace, Jennifer. 1994. "Case Comments: Tort Law—Fiduciary theory imposes higher duty and direct liability on church for clergy sexual misconduct—Tenantry v. Diocese of Colorado." *Suffolk University Law Review* 28: 331–342.

Warberg, Brent, Gene Abel, Candice Osborn. 1996. "Cognitive-Behavioral Treatment for Professional Sexual Misconduct Among Clergy." *Pastoral Psychology* 45: 49–63.

Whittuck, C.A. 1910. "Clericalism and Anticlericalism." *Encyclopedia of Religion and Ethics* III: 690–695. Edinburgh.

Wilkinson, Allen P. 1990. "Clergy malpractice: cloaked by the cloth?" *Trial* 26: 36–40.

Wolf, Ann. 1994. "Sexual Abuse Issues: An Annotated Bibliography." *Theology Digest* 41.4: 331–344.

Yanguas, Aurelius. 1946. "De Crimine Pessimo et De Competentia S. Officii Relate Ad Illud." *Revista Espanola de Derecho Canonico* 1: 427–439.

Young, John L. and Ezra Griffith. 1995. "Regulating pastoral counseling practice: the problem of sexual misconduct." *The Bulletin of the American Academy of Psychiatry and Law* 23: 421–432.

Historical Studies: Books

Bailey, Derrick S. 1955. *Homosexuality and the Western Christian Tradition*. London: Longmans, Green and Company.

Barstow, Anne Llewellyn. 1982. *Married Priests and the Reforming Papacy*. New York: Edwin Mellen.

Bloch, R. Howard. 1991. *Medieval Misogyny and the Invention of Western Romantic Love*. Chicago: The University of Chicago Press.

Boswell, John. 1980. *Christianity, Social Tolerance and Homosexuality: Gay People in Western Europe from the Beginning of the Christian Era to the Fourteenth Century*. Chicago: University of Chicago Press.

_____. 1994. *Same Sex Unions in Premodern Europe*. New York: Villiard Books.

Brooke, Rosalind and Christopher. 1984. *Popular Religion in the Middle Ages: Western Europe, 1000–1300*. London: Thames and Hudson.

Brown, Peter. 1982. *Society and the Holy in Late Antiquity*. Berkeley: University of California Press.

_____. 1988. *The Body and Society: Men, Women and Sexual Renunciation in Early Christianity*. New York: Columbia University Press.

Brundage, James. 1987. *Law, Sex and Christian Society in Medieval Europe*. Chicago: University of Chicago Press.

_____. 1993. *Sex, Law and Marriage in the Middle Ages*. Aldershot, Hampshire, GB: Variorum.

Bullough, Vern. 1976. *Sexual Variance in Society and History*. Chicago: University of Chicago Press.

_____. 1982. *Sexual Practices in the Medieval Church*. Buffalo, N.Y.: Prometheus Books.

Bullough, Vern and James Brundage, editors. 1996. *Handbook of Medieval Sexuality*. New York: Garland Press.

Chodorow, Stanley. 1972. *Christian Political Theory and Church Politics in the Mid-Twefth Century: The Ecclesiology of Gratian's Decretum*. Berkeley: University of California Press.

Chodorow, Stanley, editor. 1979. *The Other Side of Western Civilization* (2nd Edition), Vol.1, *The Ancient World of the Reformation*. New York: Harcourt, Brace, Jovanovich.

Cholij, Roman. 1988. *Clerical Celibacy in East and West*. Leominster: Fowler Wright Books.

Cochini, Charles. 1981. *Origines Apostolique du Celibat Sacerdotal.* Paris.

Collett-Sanders, Thomas. 1922. *The Institutes of Justinian.* London: Longmans Green.

D'Agostino, Peter. 2004. *Rome in America: Transnational Catholic Ideology from the Risorgimento to Fascism.* Chapel Hill: University of North Carolina Press.

Damien, St. Peter. 1982. *The Book of Gomorrah: An Eleventh Century Treatise against Clerical Homosexual Practices.* Translated with notes by Pierre Payer. Waterloo, Ont.: Wilfred Laurier University Press.

Didache. In Lightfoot, J.B. and Harmer, J.R., editors. 1984. *The Apostolic Fathers.* Grand Rapids: Baker House.

Dinshaw, Carolyn. 1999. *Getting Medieval: Sexualities and Communities, Pre- and Postmodern.* Durham: Duke University Press.

Dortel-Claudot, M. 1973. "Le prêtre et le mariage. Evolution de la legislation canonique des origine au XIIe siécle." *Annee Canonique* 17: 319–344.

Duby, Georges. Bray, Barbara, translator. 1983. *The Knight, the Lady and the Priest.* New York: Pantheon Books.

Dykema, Peter and Heiko Oberman. 1995. *Anticlericalism in Late Medieval and Early Modern Europe.* Koln: E.J. Brill.

Fox, Robin Lane. 1987. *Pagans and Christians.* New York: Alfred A. Knopf.

Frassetto, Michael, editor. 1998. *Mediaeval Purity and Piety.* New York: Garland Publishing.

Freeman, Charles. 2002. *The Closing of the Western Mind: The Rise of Faith and the Fall of Reason.* London: Pimlico.

Gasparri, Pietro, editor. 1926–1939. *Codicis Iuris Canonici Fontes.* 9 Volumes. Vatican City: Typis Polyglottis.

Goodich, Michael. 1979. *The Unmentionable Vice.* Santa Barbara: Ross-Erikson Publishers.

Gryson, Roger. 1968. *Les Origines du Celibat Ecclesiastique du Premier au Septième Siécle.* Gembloux: Editions Duculot.

Guest, Tanis. 1998. *The Pagan Middle Ages.* Rochester, N.Y.: Boydell Press.

Haliczer, Stephen. 1996. *Sexuality in the Confessional.* New York: Oxford University Press.

Halperin, William. 1939. *Italy and the Vatican at War.* Chicago: University of Chicago Press.

Halperin, William. 1970 (first published in 1937). *The Separation of Church and State in Italian Thought from Cavour to Mussolini.* New York: Octagon Books.

Hamilton, Bernard. 1986. *Religion in the Medieval West.* London: Edward Arnold.

Ingram, Martin. 1987. *Church Courts, Sex and Marriage in England, 1570–1640.* Cambridge: Cambridge University Press.

Keisel, Elizabeth. 1997. *Courtly Desire and Medieval Homophobia.* New Haven: Yale University Press.

Laeuchli, Samuel. 1972. *Power and Sexuality: The Emergence of Canon Law at the Synod of Elvira.* Philadelphia: Temple University Press.

Lea, Henry Charles. 1884. *A History of Sacerdotal Celibacy in the Christian Church.* London.

_____. 1907. *A History of the Inquisition in Spain.* New York: MacMillan.

Leclercq, Jean. 1979. *Monks and Love in Twelfth Century France: Psycho-Historical Essays.* Oxford: Clarendon Press.

Lewy, Gunther. 1964. *The Catholic Church in Nazi Germany.* New York.

Liebreich, Karen. 2004. *Fallen Order.* London: Atlantic Books.

Lochrie, Karma, Peggy McCracken, and James Schultz, editors. 1997. *Constructing Medieval Sexuality.* Minneapolis: University of Minnesota Press.

Longworth, T. Clifton. 1936. *The Devil a Monk Would Be: A Survey of Sex and Celibacy in Religion.* London.

MacNeil, John, and Gamer Helena. 1938. *Medieval Handbooks of Penance.* New York: Columbia University Press.

McGinn, Thomas A.J. 1998. *Prostitution, Sexuality and the Law in Ancient Rome.* New York: Oxford University Press.

Mitchell, Timothy. 1998. *Betrayal of the Innocents: Desire, Power and the Catholic Church in Spain.* Philadelphia: University of Pennsylvania Press.

Mommsen, Theodor, and Paul Kreuger, editors. Alan Watson, translator. 1985. *The Digest of Justinian.* 4 Volumes. Philadelphia: University of Pennsylvania Press.

Murray, Jacqueline, and Konrad Eisenbicher. 1996. *Desire and Discipline: Sex and Sexuality in the Premodern West.* Toronto: University of Toronto Press.

Murstein, Bernard L. 1974. *Love, Sex and Marriage Through the Ages.* New York: Springer Publishing.

Noble, David. 1992. *A World without Women: The Christian Clerical Culture of Western Science.* Oxford: Oxford University Press.

Ortega-Uhink, Juan, 1954. *De Delicto Sollicitationis.* Washington, D.C.: Catholic University of America Press.

Payer, Pierre. 1984. *Sex and the Penitentials.* Toronto: University of Toronto Press.

_____. 1993. *The Bridling of Desire.* University of Toronto Press.

Peters, Edward. 1988. *Inquisition.* New York: The Free Press.

Pharr, Clyde, translator. 1952. *The Theodosian Code and Novels.* New York: Greenwood Press.

Powell, James., ed. 1963. *Innocent III: Vicar of Christ or Lord of the World?* Boston: Heath and Company.

Quinn, P.A. 1989. *Better Than the Sons of Kings.* New York: Peter Lang Publishing.

Rocke, Michael. 1990. *Male Homosexuality and Its Regulation in Medieval Florence.* 2 vols. Binghampton, N.Y.: SUNY.

Rousselle, Aline. 1988. *Porneia: On Desire and the Body in Antiquity.* Translated by Felicia Pheasant. Oxford: Basil Blackwell.

Ruggiero, Guido. 1985. *The Boundaries of Eros: Crime and Sexuality in Renaissance Venice.* New York: Oxford University Press.

Ryan, J. J. 1956. *Saint Peter Damian and His Canonical Sources. A Preliminary Study in the Antecedents of the Gregorian Reform.* Toronto: University of Toronto Press.

Salisbury, Joyce E. 1990. *Medieval Sexuality: A Research Guide.* New York: Garland.

Shaw, Russell. 1993. *To Hunt, to Shoot, to Entertain.* San Francisco: Ignatius Press.

Sweeney, James Ross, and Stanley Chodorow. 1989. *Popes, Teachers and Canon Law in the Middle Ages.* Ithaca: Cornell University Press.

Ullmann, Walter. 1962. *The Growth of Papal Government in the Middle Ages: A Study in the Ideological Relation of Clerical to Lay Power.* 2nd ed. London: Metheun.

Weisner-Hanks, Merry. 2000. *Christianity and Sexuality in the Early Modern World.* London: Routledge.

Westermarck, Edward. 1939. *Christianity and Morals.* London: Trench, Trubner.

Historical Studies: Articles

Baldwin, John W. 1965. "A campaign to Reduce Clerical Celibacy at the Turn of the Twelfth and Thirteenth Centuries," in *Etudes d'histoire du Droit Canonique Dediées a Gabriel le Bras.* 2 vols. Paris: Sirey.

Callam, D. 1980. "Clerical continence in the fourth century. Three papal decretals." *Theological Studies* 41: 3–50.

Dalpiaz, V. 1933. "De abusu matrimonii et de crimine sollicitationis." *Apollinaris* 6: 244–249.

Gaudemet, Jean. 1982. "Le celibat ecclesiastique: le droit et la pratique du XIe au XIIe siecle." *Zeitschrift der Savigny-Stiftung Fuer Rechtsgeschichte,* ka 68.

Goodich, Michael. 1976. "Sodomy in ecclesiastical law and theory." *Journal of Homosexuality* 1, no. 4: 427–434.

_____. 1976. "Sodomy in Medieval Secular Law." *Journal of Homosexuality* 1, no. 3: 295–302.

Grabowski, John S. 1995. "Clerical sexual misconduct and early Christian traditions regarding the Sixth Commandment." *Jurist* 55: 527–591.

Helmholz, R. H. 2001. "Discipline of the Clergy: Medieval and Modern." *Ecclesiastical Law Journal* 6. 47–50.

Jason, Peter. "The Courts Christian in Medieval England." *The Catholic Lawyer.* 1997 (37 Catholic Law. 339).

Jochens, Jenny. 1980. "The Church and Sexuality in Medieval Iceland." *Journal of Medieval History* 24: 377–385.

Kamen, Henry. 1983. "Clerical Violence in a Catholic Society: The Hispanic World 1450–1720." in Sheils, W.J., editor, *The Church and War*. London. Basil Blackwell.

Lynch, John E. 1972. "Marriage and Celibacy of the Clergy: The Discipline of the Western Church; An Historical-Canonical Synopsis." *Jurist* 32: 14–38, 189–212.

McLaughlin, T. M. 1941. "The Prohibition of Marriage Against Canons in the Early Twelfth Century." *Medieval Studies* 3: 94–100.

Reed, Albert. 1963. "The Careful Selection and Training of Candidates for the States of Perfection and Sacred Orders." *Jurist* 23: 34–49.

Rocke, Michael. 1988. "Sodomites in Fifteenth Century Tuscany: The Views of Bernardino of Siena." *Journal of Homosexuality* 16: 7–31.

Ruggiero, Guido. 1974–75. "Criminal Sexuality in the early Renaissance: Venice, 1338–1358." *Journal of Social History* 8: 18–37.

Sexual Abuse and Trauma

Bass, Ellen, and Laura Davis. 1988. *Courage to Heal: A Guide for Women Survivors of Sexual Abuse*. New York: Harper and Row.

Blume, Sue. 1991. *Secret Survivors: Uncovering Incest and Its After Effects on Women*. Ballantine Books.

Cameron, Grant. 1994. *What about Me: A Guide for Men Helping Female Partners Deal with Childhood Sexual Abuse*. Creative Bound.

Cameron, Marcia, and Ira Steinman, M.D. 1996. *The Broken Child*. Kensington Publishing Co.

Courtois, Christine. 1988. *Healing the Incest Wound*. New York: W.W. Norton & Company.

Davis, Laura. 1991. *Allies in Healing*. Perennial Books.

Engel, Beverly. 1991. *The Right to Innocence: Healing the Trauma of Childhood Sexual Abuse*. Ivy Books.

Evert, Kathy. 1987. *When You're Ready: A Woman's Healing from Childhood Physical and Sexual Abuse by Her Mother.* Launch Press.

Farmer, Steven. 1990. *Adult Children of Abusive Parents. A Healing Program for Those Who Have Been Sexually or Emotionally Abused.* Ballantine Books.

Forward, Susan. 2002. *Toxic Parents: Overcoming Their Hurtful Legacy and Reclaiming Your Life.* Bantam Publishing.

Gil, Eliana, Ph.D. 1992. *Outgrowing Pain Together.* DTP.

Graber, Ken, M.A. 1991. *Ghosts in the Bedroom: A Guide for Partners of Incest Survivors.* Health Communications.

Grubman-Black, Stephen. 1990. *Broken Boys/Mending Men: Recovery from Childhood Sexual Abuse.* New York: Ivy Books.

Haines, Stacy. 1999. *The Survivor's Guide to Sex: How to Have an Empowered Sex Life after Child Sexual Abuse.* Cleis Press.

Herman, Judith. 1992. *Trauma and Recovery.* New York: Harper Collins.

Hunter, Mic. 1991. *Abused Boys: The Neglected Victims of Sexual Abuse.* Fawcett Books.

Juliann, Mitchell, Ph.D., and Jill Morse. 1997. *Victim to Survivor: Women Survivors of Female Perpetrators.* Taylor and Francis.

Levine, Peter. 1997. *Waking the Tiger.* North Atlantic Books.

Lew, Mike. 1988, 1990. *Victims No Longer: Men Recovering from Incest and Other Sexual Child Abuse.* Harper Collins.

Maltz, Wendy. 2001. *The Sexual Healing Journey: A Guide for Survivors of Sexual Abuse.* Quill.

McLaren, Karla. 1997. *Rebuilding the Garden.* Laughing Tree Press.

O'Hanlon, Bill, and Bob Bertolino. 1998. *Even from a Broken Web.* New York: John Wiley and Sons, Inc.

Rosencrans, Bobbie, and Edith Bauier. 1997. *The Last Secret: Daughters Sexually Abused by Mothers.* Safer Society Press.

Index

U.S. Department of Justice involvement in, 281
victim suffering caused by, 260
Baptism, limbo and, 234–235
Bartemeier, Leo, on percent of clerics abusing minors, 69
Bede, St., 297
Benedict XIV, on soliciting sex in confessional, 44–45, 298
Benefice, 331
Berlin, Fred, 98
Bevilacqua, Anthony, 91–92
Bier, William, on psychological screening of priest candidates, 70
Birth control, morality of, 4
Bishops
  accountability of, in sexual abuse of minors, 332
  anger toward, ineffectiveness of, 290, 294
  as descended from Apostles
    origins of idea, 241, 292
    power derived from, 190, 331
  appointment of, 252, 331
  approaching accused cleric, 151–152
  in attorney provision, 141
  in attorney selection, 112
  authority in diocese, 331
  awareness of psychological dimension to sexual/moral problems of priests, 72
  awareness of sexual abuse by priests
    duration of, 203
    sources of, 203–204
  binding guidelines for evaluating seminary faculties and students, 81
  Catholic education and, 181
  college of, 146
  communication with
    image and, 286–287
    by victims, 286
  Conference of, 334
  in control of media and civil courts, 77
  council of, 333
  credibility of, 278
  criminal neglect by, 121–122, 189
  defensiveness regarding criticism, 285–286, 288
  denial and lies by, 311–312
  in Doyle-Mouton-Peterson Report
    hypothetical responses to clerical sexual misconduct, 108–110
    presumption of good will in, 88

  failure to manage abuse by priests, x, 5, 82–83, 189
    lack of remorse for, 273–274
  files of, right to subpoena, 111
  financial liability of, apart from diocese, 112
  financial responsibility of, to clerics, 139–141
  incardinated clerics and
    communications between, confidentiality of, 220, 222–224
    liability for, 122
    relationship to, 137, 142–144, 181
  investigations by. *See* Investigation of incidents.
  juridic person relationship to, 252
  as keepers of secret archives, 135–137
  lack of attendance at VOCAL conference, 310–311
  on the *Manual,* 60
  married to diocese, 252
  moral abuse prevention by, 181
  power of, 64–65
  priest confession to, inadvisability of, 204, 223
  priests as agents of, 279
  in processing cases in secret Vatican directive, 48–49
  psychosexual immaturity of, 82
  referrals of priests to Paracletes, 74
  refusal to accept priest perpetrator in diocese, 305–306
  religious clerics and, responsibility for, 138–139
  reporting requirements of
    to civil authorities, 111, 225. *See also* Reporting requirements.
    regarding all priests in diocese, 112
    to Vatican, 51
  response to abuse allegations, hypothetical in Doyle-Mouton-Peterson Report, 108–110
  response to victims of abuse, 74–76, 79–80, 83
  rhetoric *versus* responsible action from, 311–312, 314–316
  ring of, 252
  in secret system of dependency, x
  seminarians and, responsibility for, 124, 149–150
  sexual activity of, 61, 271–272
    as reason for inaction, 206

sued for complicity, xi, 112, 203
transferring abusive priests, 77, 132, 186, 189–190, 193, 195, 198, 213, 288, 307–309
understanding of church governmental and judicial system by, 182
visiting clergy and, responsibility for, 124–125, 137–138
Bishops' National Review Board survey, 214
Black Death, 32
Bodily part, loss of, abuse similarity to, 266
Bond with abuser, 247–249, 265
Book of Gomorrah (St. Peter Damian), 20–23, 63, 297, 332
  on soliciting sex in confessional, 41–42
Boyer, Pascal
  on emotional programming in religion, 232
  on origin of religion, 231
Braceland, Francis, on religion interface with psychiatry, 71
Brom, Robert, church property transfer by, 255
Brown, Angela, 80
Burke, Raymond, church assets and, 252
Call to Action, 65–66, 291
Calvin, John, on clerical celibacy, 33
Candidates for priesthood. *See* Priest candidates; Seminarians.
Canon law
  on age of minor, 51, 180
  on applicable penalties, 130–134, 180
  on bishop responsibility
    in Catholic education, 181
    financial, to support clerics, 139–141
    to incardinated clerics, 137, 142–144, 181
    to prevent moral abuse, 181
    to religious clerics, 138–139
    to suspended clerics, 139
    to visiting clerics, 137–138
  on canonical delicts, 129–130
  on canonical nature of bishop-cleric relationship, 142–144
  on celibacy, 180
  on church hierarchy, 144–148
  in clerical abuse of minors, 111–114
  on conducting investigations, 220–222
  definition and history of, 332
  on diocesan hierarchy, 145–146

on diocesan organization and structure, 145–146
on diocesan records, 134–135
in Doyle-Mouton-Peterson Report, 114–116, 127–151
on episcopal conference, 146–147
expert on, to prepare witnesses, 115
on failure to prosecute sexual abuse, 191
on homosexual acts, 180
impact on civil courts, 123
on investigation of complaints, 128–129, 182–186, 206. *See also* Investigation of incidents.
on juridic persons, 147
on jurisdictional power of priests, 239
on laity rights, 187–188
on limits of bishop/superior responsibility, 137–142
on metropolitan and province, 146
on ordination prevention, 201
on pastor supervision of assistant pastors, 183
on priest perpetrators, xi
on recording sexual abuse, 137
on religious clerics, 150–151
on reporting incidents to church authorities, 148–149
on responsibility for seminarians, 149–150
on secret archives, 134–137
self-interest of, 191–193
on stratification between clerics and laity, 240–241
in twelfth century, 5
Canonical entity, Roman Catholic Church in United States as, 115–116
Capital punishment
  for celibacy violations, in Medieval period, 30–32
  passing laws on, 3
  for same-sex corruption of boy, 16
Carardi, Nicholas, 255
Cardinals
  secrecy oath of, 204–205, 332, 338
  selection of, 332
Care of souls, 180
Careful Selection and Training of Candidates for the States of Perfection and Sacred Orders, 298
Case management, uniformity of, 126–127
Catechism of Catholic Church, 332
  on clerical abuse of minors, 59–60

to his bishop, inadvisability of, 204, 223

as reconciliation sacrament, 339

in sexuality as secret system, 208

soliciting sex in, 4–5, 37–47

accuser and witness oath of secrecy in, 49

anonymous accusations of, 49

Benedict XIV on, 44–45, 298

Book of Gomorrah on, 21

canon law on, 129

canonical inquiries regarding, 47

confidentiality in, 49

false denunciation about, 41

homosexual, bestial, or with children, 49–50

in Inquisition, 32

investigation and prosecution of, 46–47

John XXIII on, 47–48, 298

as spiritual incest, 42–43

Vatican secret directive on, 47–53

withholding absolution in, 40

as source of priest knowledge and sexual expertise, 208

structure of, 38–39

victim confidentiality in, 185

Confidentiality. *See* Communication, privileged.

Congregation for the Doctrine of the Faith (CDF)

abuse cases reserved to, 48

secrecy of, 51

Consecration, priest holding place of God in, 238

Conspiracy of silence. *See* Secrecy.

Continence, 334

canon law on, 129

Corporation Sole, church property held by, 253, 255

Corpus Iuris Canonici, 26, 297, 334

Council of Basle, 32, 297

Council of Elvira, 295–296

canons passed by, 13–14

Council of Trent, 298

on clerical celibacy, 10, 34–35, 62–63

on priests as angels and gods, 236–237

on sacrament of penance, 37

on visible and external priesthood, 234

Council of Treves, on soliciting sex in confessional, 43

Counseling, as source of priest knowledge and sexual expertise, 208

Court-awarded damages

dollar amounts in, xi, 103, 177–178

protecting church assets from, xi

Courtroom exposure

church avoidance of, 177

cover ups revealed in, 177

lying under oath in, 178–179

untrustworthiness of church in, 178

Cox, Craig

on canon violations in sexual impropriety allegations, 220

on relationships between priest and his bishop, 222–223

Cozzens, Donald, on church as society of unequals, 242

Credibility of bishops, lack of, 278

Credibility of church, ix

as reason for secrecy, 188

Credibility of victims, 118, 183, 189, 193, 198, 287

religious duress and, 230

Criminal defense, providing priest with, 120

Criminal law

in clerical abuse of minors, 110–111

in Doyle-Mouton-Peterson Report, 110–111, 119–122

Fifth Amendment rights in, 120–121

plea bargaining in, 121

priest superiors charged/sentenced in, 121–122

privileged communication and, 120

procedures in, from accusation to imprisonment, 119

providing criminal defense in, 120

reporting requirements in. *See* Reporting requirements, to civil authorities.

Criminal neglect, of superiors, 121–122, 189

Crisis Control Team

in Doyle-Mouton-Peterson Report, 95–96, 100–101, 166–171

members of, 166–167

scope of services, 168–171

Cum Sicut Nuper (Pius IV), 43

Damian, St. Peter, 20–22, 41–42, 63, 297, 332

De Modo Procedendi in Causis Solicitationis (John XXIII), 47–48, 298

Deacons
  bishop relationship to, 137, 143
  married, 141–142, 335
  permanent, 335
    bishop responsibility for, 141–142
    celibacy exception in, 9
Decree of Gratian, 24–26
Decree on the Pastoral Office of Bishops in the Church (Vatican Council II), 183
Decretals, 297, 335
Decretists, 25–26
Defrocking. *See* Laicization.
Degradation, definition of, 335
Delict, 335
Detection of Prepsychotics Who Apply for Admission to the Priesthood or Religious Communities, 70
Didache, 13, 296
Digest of Justinian, 16, 297
Diocesan priests. *See also* Incardinated clerics.
  celibacy violations among, differences from monks, 27–28
  classification of, 9–10, 333
  functions in order of importance, 279–280
Diocesan records
  canon law on, 134–135
  code-like language of, 190
  denying access to, 170, 193, 217. *See also* Forum, internal and external.
  denying existence of, 193
  in discovery process, 125
  in external forum, 219
  sanitizing/purging of, 125
  transferring to Apostolic Nunciature, 126
Diocesan synod, 341
Diocese
  in church organization, 335
  complicity in secrecy about abuse, 53–54
  creation of, 252
  hierarchy of, canon on, 145–146
  incorporation of, 256
  provinces and, 146
Directory on the Pastoral Office of Bishops (Vatican Council II), 183
Discastery, 335
Dogmatic Constitution on the Church (Vatican Council II), 183
Doms, Herbert, 7

Doyle, Thomas, 80. *See also Problem of Sexual Molestation by Roman Catholic Clergy: Meeting the Problem in a Comprehensive and Responsible Manner* (Doyle, Mouton, and Peterson).
  letter to Archbishop Pilarczyk after first VOCAL conference, 310–313
Drug abuse, as mitigating condition, 116, 153
Due process, for accused priest, 111
Duress, religious, 335
  and Catholic teachings about priests, 229–230
  fear and constrictions induced by, 289
  impact on sexual abuse victims, 242–250
  sacraments and, 232–234
  sin concept in, 234–242
Dutton, David, on trauma bond, 248
Dwyer, Robert J., Gerald Fitzgerald letter to, 301–302
Eastern rite, 9
Ecclesiae Sanctae (Vatican Council II), 183
Ecclesiastical property. *See* Church property/assets.
Enabling sex offender, in Doyle-Mouton-Peterson Report, 107
Encyclical, 336
Ephebophilia. *See also* Adolescents, sexual abuse of.
  definition of, 68, 336
  excommunication after, 14
  presumptive form of, 18
Episcopal, definition of, 336
Episcopal conference, 146–147
  reporting incidents to, 149
Episcopalian priest converts, celibacy exception in, 9
Eucharist
  Catechism on, 233
  priest power derived from, 233–234
  Excommunication, 336
  for absolution of sexual partner, 129–130
  for failure to report sex solicitation in confessional, 45
  for false denunciation about solicitation in confessional, 41
  in Gregorian Reform, 23
  in Medieval period, 30
  for sexual abuse of boys, 14
  for sodomy, 19
  for violating secret archives, 331

influence on canon law and church discipline, 24
on sodomy, 25
on soliciting sex in confessional, 42
Greek Stoic dualism, 6–7
Greeley, Andrew
on priest involvement with minors, incidence of, 212
on sex lives of Catholics, 208
Gregorian Reform, 22–23, 63
homosexual celibacy violation punishments in, 30
Gregory, Wilton, on sexual abuse as history, 259
Gregory the Great, St., 263
Gregory VII, on clerical celibacy abuse, 23
Gregory XV, 298
on soliciting sex in confessional, 43
Gregory XVI, on church need for renewal, 1
Grooming, of potential victim, 246, 337
Group of Four, in Doyle-Mouton-Peterson Report, 166, 171
Guardini, Romano, 276
Guilt feelings
of adolescents, about awakening sexuality, 230
of victims, 164, 243–244, 246, 259, 268–269
Gun control, passing laws on, 3
Haliczer, Stephen, 46
Harris, Michael, 281
Hartford Retreat in Connecticut, 71
Hayden, Jerome, Marselan Institute and, 70
Healing. See Forgiveness/healing.
Heckler, Victor, psychological investigations of priests by, 56, 58, 68, 299
Heresy, sodomy link with, 19
History, clerical abuse of minors in, openness of, ix
History of Celibacy (Abbott), 28
History of the Inquisition in Spain (Lea), 45–46
Holy Office, 337
Homosexual violations of celibacy
in Book of Gomorrah, 20–22
canon omission of, 180
condemnation of, 4
in early Christianity, 16, 18–20
effect on pre-Christian Roman attitude toward same-sex relationships, 15–17

gay lawyer/organization involvement in, 110
incidence of, 206, 210–211
in male environment, 210
in Medieval period. See Sodomy, in Medieval period.
particular friendships and, 210
Protestant Reformation and, 33
punishment for, 17
solicitation of, in confessional, 49–50. See also Confession, soliciting sex in.
Homosexuality
definition of, 337
pastoral care in, 299
pedophilia versus, 116, 180–181, 210
in victim moral confusion, 246
Horrendum (Pius V), 36–37, 298
House of Affirmation, 72
Hoye, Daniel, 94–96
Hughes, William, 178, 197–198
Hynes, Vincent J., Gerald Fitzgerald letter to, 303–304
Hypocrisy, sexual and financial, 275
Image of church
injury to, 101
as reason for secrecy, 188, 192
Image of priest, preservation of, 279–280
Imprisonment
incidence of, 217
sentencing requirements for, 119–120
sexual contact classification and, 110
Impure thoughts, 9
Incardinated clerics, 10, 337. See also Diocesan priests.
bishop communication with, confidentiality of, 220, 222–224
bishop liability for, in civil law, 122
bishop relationship to, in canon law, 137, 142–144, 181
Infamy of fact, 19–20
Infamy of law, 201
Inquisition, 337
church and secular collaboration in, 31–32
Institute of Living, 71
Insurance issues
bankruptcy filings and, 258
in Doyle-Mouton-Peterson Report, 111–112, 161–162
increased cost of liability, 162
liability in, 123–124
loss of diocesan coverage as, 161–162

Leave of absence, for priest perpetrator, 130–131, 198
Leo IX, on *Book of Gomorrah*, 21
Leo X, 298
Levada, William, 91
Lex Julia de Adulteriis (Caesar Augustus), 15
Liability
  of bishops
    in civil law, 122
    financial, apart from diocese, 112
    for incardinated priests, 122
    for seminarians, 124
    for visiting clergy, 124–125, 137–138
  of larger entities, 123–124
  of Vatican, 123–124
Liability insurance, increased cost of, 162
Life and Ministry of Priests (Vatican Council II), 180
Limbo, 235
Lothstein, Leslie, on soul murder, 243–244
Luther, Martin, on clerical celibacy, 33
Lutheran pastor converts, celibacy exception in, 9
Luxuria, 18
Lynch, Gerald, 98
Mahoney, Roger
  on Formation Privilege, 218
  lying under oath by, 179
  on relationships between priest and his bishop, 222–223
Maida, Adam, on control of church property, 254–255
Malone, James, 92
Malpractice, by clergy, 106–107
Manual. See Problem of Sexual Molestation by Roman Catholic Clergy: Meeting of the Problem in a Comprehensive and Responsible Manner (Mouton, Doyle, Peterson).
Marital sex
  as adultery, 6
  Council of Elvira on, 14
  narrow tolerance of, in Catholic teaching, 8
  as necessary evil, 5
  St. Augustine on, 6
Marriage, value of, x
Married priests
  avoiding sex with wives, 4, 62, 334
  Catholic laity acceptance of, 11
  clandestine, 59

Council of Elvira on, 14
Lateran Council on, 24
Marselan Institute, 70
Mauriac, François, on church in politics, 175
McCandish, Ted, 194
McGrath, John J., on ownership of church property, 254
Meaning of Marriage (Doms), 7
Media. *See also* Public relations.
  in breaching secret system, 203
  interest in abuse litigation, 102–105, 189
  restricting access to civil proceedings, 113
Medical/clinical issues. *See* Clinical/medical issues, in Doyle-Mouton-Peterson Report.
Medieval period, 297
  concubinage in, 24–25
    among monks, 28
    failure of, 29
    punishment for, 26–27
  degradation in, 335
  scholasticism and centralized papacy in, 23–24
  secular and church forces intermingled in, 29–30
  sexual fascination in, 6
  sodomy in, 18–20
    among monks, 28
    incidence of, 28–29
    punishment for, 30–32
Mental reservation, 338
Metropolitan archbishop
  authority of, 146
  definition of, 331
  reporting incidents to, 149
Military Vicariate
  definition of, 338
  endorsement of Fr. Peebles for active duty, 194
Minor, age of
  in canon law, 51, 180, 338
  and comprehension of abuse, 117
  in criminal law, 110
  as mitigating circumstance, 117
Misdemeanor, sexual contact classification as, 110
Modern era, clerical abuse of minors in, 53–61, 298–300
Money, John, 98
Monk, 338. *See also* Religious clerics.

Pius XII, on causes for clerics straying from celibacy, 57
Plea bargaining process, unavailability of, 121
Politics, church in, 175
Pontifical secret, 52, 339–340
Popes
  Alexander II, on *Book of Gomorrah,* 21–22
  Benedict XIV, on soliciting sex in confessional, 44–45, 298
  Gregory VII, on clerical celibacy abuse, 23
  Gregory XV, 298
    on soliciting sex in confessional, 43
  Gregory XVI, on Church need for renewal, 1
  John XXIII, on processing cases of solicitation, 47–48, 298
  John Paul II
    on celibacy, 11
    destruction of reform movement by, 65–66, 284–285
    on fear, 296
    on ordained ministry, 239–240
    on problem solving resources, 276
    Sacramentorum Sanctitatis Tutela, 300
    on sexually charged American culture, 61
  Leo IX, on *Book of Gomorrah,* 21
  Leo X, 298
  Paul VI, on celibacy, 11
  Pius IV, 298
    on soliciting sex in confessional, 43
  Pius V, St., 298
    on clerical sodomy, 36
  Pius IX, on centralization of church power, 284
  Pius X, St.
    on souls lost by miscreant priests, 277
    on stratification between clerics and laity, 240, 283–284
  Pius XII, on causes for clerics straying from celibacy, 57
Porter, James, 77–78, 178
Presybterorum Ordinis, 10
Priest(s), 340. *See also* Priest perpetrators; Sex lives of clergy, Violations of celibacy.
  on administrative leave, for sexual misconduct, 130–131
  as angels and gods, 236–237
  clinical/medical evaluation of. *See* Clinical/medical evaluation of cleric.
  as confidant for married women, 208
  desire for child to become, 229
  diocesan. *See* Diocesan priests; Incardinated clerics.
  diocesan versus religious
    celibacy violation types in, 27–28
    differences in, 9–10
  Jesus Christ represented by, 236
  laicization of. *See* Laicization.
  leaving to marry
    number of, 11, 59
    secrecy about, 11–12
  mystique surrounding, power and, 8–9, 235–236
  nonabusers, responsibilities of, 273
  psychological investigations of, 56–58
  psychosexual immaturity of, 57–58, 68, 73
  religious. *See* Religious clerics.
  religious duress and, 229–230
  sexual information and experience of, sources of, 208
  social contract with laity, 277–280
  speaking ill of, as sin, 229
  as special caste of people, 238, 240–242, 283–284
    sacrifice and, 232–234
    secrecy system and, 242
  as supernatural sexless men, 207
  suspension of. *See* Suspended clerics.
  visiting, bishop responsibility for, 124–125, 137–138
Priest candidates. *See also* Seminarians.
  barring from ordination
    for homosexuality or pederasty, 57
    indicators for, 200–201
    for insanity for psychological infirmity, 150
  inadequate preparation for lack of intimacy, 56–57
  psychological testing of, 70
  screening of, xi, 203
  selection and training of, 298
Priest-Penitent Privilege, 219
Priest perpetrators
  absolution for, steps in, 272–273
  administrative leave for, 130–131, 198
  canon law concerning, xi
  as childhood victims, 212–213
  civil law concerning, xi

defamation of character suits on behalf of, 311

failure to manage, ix

Fifth Amendment rights of, 120–121

financial support for, 115, 139–141

laicization of. *See* Laicization.

meeting with victims and families, 160

number of, 53, 214

other priests aware of, 203–204

recidivism of, 117, 189, 302–303

removal from office, 131–132

returning to diocesan functioning, 118, 159–160, 213–214, 303–304

secrecy about. *See* Secrecy, about priest perpetrators.

suspension of, 131–132
    bishop responsibility for, 139
    during clinical/medical evaluation, 156
    financial support during, 115
    rights to recourse, 115
    for sexual misconduct, 131–132

transfer of, 132, 186, 189–190, 193, 195, 198, 213, 288, 307–309

Problem of Sexual Molestation by Roman Catholic Clergy: Meeting the Problem in a Comprehensive and Responsible Manner (Doyle, Mouton, and Peterson), 60, 80, 99–174, 299

about authors of, 87

American Bar Association preparation for, 105

canon law in, 114–116, 127–151

case management suggestions in, 90

circumstances for writing, 88–90, 100–110

civil law issues in, 111–114, 122–127

clergy malpractice in, 106

clinical/medical questions in, 116–118, 151–161

confidentiality of, 102–103

criminal law issues in, 110–111, 119–122

enabling sex offender in, 107

financial consequences of, 101, 103–104, 107

history of proposal, 101–102

hypothetical bishop responses in, 108–110

insurance issues in, 161–162

media interest in abuse litigation, 102–105

original form of, 87–88

presumption of episcopal good will in, 88

project proposed by
    Committee in, 166
    components of, 166–168
    Crisis Control Team in, 95–96, 100–101, 166–171
    Group of Four in, 166, 171
    policy and planning group in, 167–168, 171
    scope of services, 168–171
    strategy of, 171–172

public awareness of abuse in, 108, 164–165

rejection of, 90–95

secret system breached by, 97

spiritual issues in, 162–164

as testimony to awareness of ongoing abuse, 98

variety of forms in, 108–110

victim trauma in, 107

Procreation
    Doms on, 7
    marriage only for, 7

Property of church. *See* Church property/assets.

Protestant Reformation, 32–34, 62–63
    and Catholic role in society, 32
    on clerical celibacy, 33–34
    secrecy pattern and, 62
    sexual and financial hypocrisy leading to, 275
    on visible and external priesthood, 234

Province, diocese and, 146, 331

Provincial, responsibility for religious clerics, 138

Psychiatric disorders, as mitigating condition, 116, 154

Psychiatry/psychology
    celibate/sexual system moving into, 67–68, 71–72
    church mistrust for, 188–189
    in clinical evaluation of accused cleric, 151–152, 157
        results as formation privilege, 224–225
    reporting laws and, 69
    reporting requirements in, 116
    in screening priest candidates, 70
    unholy alliance with religion, 78

Public relations. *See also* Media; Secrecy.
    church credibility in, 164

Sexual ethics
  Council of Elvira on, 13–14
  New Testament basis for, 12–13
Sexuality, awakening, adolescent guilt and
    shame about, 230
*Sexuality in the Confessional: A Sacrament
    Profaned* (Haliczer), 46
Shanley, Paul, 78, 178
Shaw, Russell, on clericalist mind-set, 241
Shengold, Leonard, on soul murder, 265
Silence. *See* Secrecy.
Sin
  mortal, 39, 341
    sexual expression as, 243
  original, 234–235
  religious duress and, 234–242
  sexual, 39
  venial, 39, 341
Sipe, A. W. Richard
  on closed celibate/sexual system, 55–56
  on homosexual orientation and activity
    of priests, 211
  on percent of clerics abusing minors, 69,
    212
  on percent of priests sexually active,
    58–59
Skylstad, William, 255
SNAP (Survivors Network of those
    Abused by Priests), 261, 290–291, 341
Societies of apostolic life, religious clerics
    in, 150
Society of Saint-Sulpice, 35
Sodomy, 341
  and dismissal from holy orders, 21
  Gratian on, 25
  Lateran Councils on, 27
  in Medieval period, 18–20
    among monks, 28
    incidence of, 28–29
    punishment for, 22, 30–31
  Pius V on, 36
  in Roman Empire, 16–18
Solicitation, 341
Soliciting sex, in confessional. *See*
  Confession, soliciting sex in.
Soul murder, 243–244, 265, 287
Southdown, 72
Spirit, in Stoic dualism, 6–7
Spiritual approach, to avoid reporting sex-
    ual abuse, 188
Spiritual directors
  as counselors of abusing priests, 203

  in maintaining confidentiality of sexual-
    ly abused victims, 185
  personal, 37–38
  psychological dimension of, 70
  sexual abuse by, in seminaries, 278
Spiritual incest, 42–43
Spiritual issues
  in abuse of minors, 162–164, 243–244
  in Doyle-Mouton-Peterson Report,
    160–164
  other losses similar to, 265–266
Statute of limitations, 217
  on clerical abuse of minors, 51
Stoic dualism, 6–8
Stuprum, 15–16, 341
  Gratian on, 25
Subpoena, of bishop files on priests, 111,
  170
Survivors Network of those Abused by
    Priests (SNAP), 261, 290–291, 341
Suspended clerics, 131–132, 341
  bishop responsibility for, 139
  canon law on, 184
  during clinical/medical evaluation,
    156
  financial support during, 115, 139–141
  indications for, 304
  rights to recourse, 115
  for sexual misconduct, 131–132
Synod, 341
Terruwe, Anna, 299
  on priest psychosexual immaturity,
    57–58
Theodore, St., 297
Theodosian Code, 438
  on same-sex behavior, 16
Thorne, Vance, 94
Transfer of perpetrator, 77, 132, 186,
    189–190, 193, 195, 198, 213, 288,
    307–309
Trauma bond, 247–249, 265
Treatment centers for priests and reli-
    gious, 69–72. *See also* Servants of the
    Paraclete.
  crisis team cataloguing of, 170
  history of, 69–72
  for psychosexual disorders involving
    abuse of minors, 73–74
  qualified to treat alcohol/drug depend-
    ence and sexual abuse of children,
    116–117
  referral to, by bishop, 83

results of, as formation privilege,
224–225
selection of, 118, 157–159
self-help groups in, 158–159
Trial court decisions, prior, 114
Tribunal, diocesan, 145–146
Tronson, Louis, on priests fulfilling obligations, 1
Vasa, Robert, 255
Vatican
directive against reporting requirement
to civil authority, 205–206
liability of, 123–124
naming in suit, 112
reporting abuse cases to, 51, 148–149
secret directive of, 47–53
on sexually charged American culture,
61
Vatican City, 342
Vatican Council II, 299
on episcopal duties, 1
on episcopal responsibility for Catholics
residing in his diocese, 183
on celibacy, 10, 180
clericalist mind-set after, 241–242
on definition of Catholic Church, xii, 65
on episcopal conference, 146–147
on incardination of cleric to diocese, 142
on laity rights, 186, 284
on marital love and procreation, 7–8
on permanent diaconate, 335
on priest as cooperator with bishop, 11
priest exodus after, 11
sexual crisis stimulated by, 278–279
Venial sin, 39, 235, 341
Vianney, St. John
John Paul II reiteration of, 239–240
on relative positions of priests and
angels, 238–239
Vicar, 144
shared responsibility for abuse, 183
Victims of abuse. *See also* Clerical abuse of
minors; Reporting requirements.
attitudes toward, 63, 79, 83, 286
bankruptcy filings and
delays in, 259
future compensation and, 260–261
portrayal in, 257
public relations aspects of, 258
bond with abuser, 247–249, 265
canonical/moral/pastoral obligations
toward, 115, 198

Catholic upbringing of, 244–245
confidentiality in confessional, 185
confronting abuser
emotional inability to, 56
other victims encouraged by, x, 77
credibility of, 118, 183, 189, 193, 198,
287
religious duress and, 230
denial by, 265
desire for revenge, 287–288
efforts to silence, 195, 197, 242
emotional and psychological turmoil
among, 243, 258–259
episcopal communication with, 286
failure to report, 247–248, 259, 271
grooming of, 246, 337
guilt feelings of, 164, 243–244, 259,
268–269
harmful effects to, 79–80, 107, 160–161,
182
loss of faith by, 265–266, 277
mistreatment of, by church authorities
and lawyers, 75–76, 186–187
moral confusion in, 246–247
need to overcome fear, 276
non-resistance of, 247
number of, xi, 60–61, 69, 212, 214, 217,
271
overwhelmed by power of priest, 230
perceived as seducers, 75
priest perpetrators as, in childhood,
212–213
public support for, 259
religious duress impact on, 242–250
spiritual effects of, 162–164, 243–244
Victims of Clergy Abuse Linkup
(VOCAL), 310–314
Violations of celibacy
by bishops, 61, 206, 271–272
concubinage as. *See* Concubinage.
Council of Elvira on, punishments for,
13–14
early church law and, 12–15, 209
expectations of, 63
homosexual. *See* Homosexual violations
of celibacy; Sodomy.
laity disappointment and disillusionment with, 270
Protestant Reformation and, 33–34
punishment for
in current era, 62–63
in Medieval period, 30–32

Acknowledgments

The authors are indebted to many people for two things in the production of this book—inspiration and toil. We pay tribute to the late Father Michael Peterson and attorney Ray Mouton, who were pioneers in calling the church's attention to the extent of abuse in the American church. The survivors of clergy abuse and their supporters lit in us an unquenchable flame. We have no choice but to let that fire burn in us with the hope of enlightening others.

This is a work of travail and tears. The distillation of nearly two thousand years of the record of clergy abusing minors is heartbreaking and overwhelming, intellectually and emotionally. Our gratitude goes beyond words to those who have sustained the pain to bring this labor to light. Denys Horgan's editing with his background in theology and journalism, and as director of editorial services at the University of California San Diego has made our text more readable. Jim Earnest has worked diligently at translating sources for us. Andrew Chan, Emily Quon, Marge Nelson, and Kourtney Murray have given our notes order and printability. The staff of Volt Press, Jeff Stern, Stephanie Adams, and Stephanie Penate, have encouraged the project from the beginning and been patient with us to its completion.

TPD/AWRS/PJW

Authors

Fr. Thomas P. Doyle, O.P.

Thomas Doyle is a Dominican priest with a doctorate in canon law and extensive experience with diocesan tribunals, the Catholic Church's court system where ecclesiastical issues are decided. From 1981 to 1986, he was a canon lawyer on the staff of the Vatican Embassy in Washington, D.C. At that time, a number of accusations of child abuse by priests, bishops, and members of religious orders were reported to the embassy and Fr. Doyle was responsible for preparing files, tracking correspondence, and preparing responses for the ambassador. He is a longtime advocate for victims of clerical sex abuse and has interviewed over two thousand survivors. He has contributed to several books and articles on the subject.

A.W. Richard Sipe

Richard Sipe has spent his life searching for the origins, meanings, and dynamics of religious celibacy. He spent eighteen years as a Benedictine monk and was trained to deal with the mental health problems of priests and religious. He has been married for the past thirty-four years and has one son. Both as a priest and a married man he has taught in Catholic major seminaries and lectured at medical schools. He has served as a consultant and expert witness in over two hundred cases of clergy sexual abuse of minors since 1992. Sipe has written four books on religious celibacy including his now-classic 1990 study *A Secret World: Sexuality and the Search for Celibacy.*

Patrick J. Wall

Patrick Wall, a former Benedictine priest, has pursued graduate studies in theology, political science, and canon law. His experiences as pastor, teacher, and member of a diocesan tribunal, have provided him with an insider's knowledge of the operations of Catholic parishes, schools, and legal system. He was also a member of a seminary sexual abuse response team. Now married, he is the father of one daughter. He is a member of the Canon Law Society of America, and for the past three years he has been a senior consultant at the law firm of Manly and McGuire in Costa Mesa, California, and given advice on over two hundred cases of clerical sexual abuse in the United States.